HOW THE SCOTS TOOK OVER LONDON

DAVID STENHOUSE

MAINSTREAM
PUBLISHING
EDINBURGH AND LONDON

This edition, 2005

First published in Great Britain in 2004 by
MAINSTREAM PUBLISHING COMPANY
(EDINBURGH) LTD
7 Albany Street
Edinburgh EH1 3UG

ISBN 1 84018 981 9

A catalogue record for this book is available from the British
Library

Typeset in Baskerville Book and Goudy Old Style

Printed in Great Britain by
Cox & Wyman Ltd

HOW THE SCOTS TOOK OVER LONDON

David Stenhouse is a writer and broadcaster, and the presenter of many programmes for Radio Scotland, Radio 3 and Radio 4. Formerly a columnist for *The Scotsman* and *The Herald*, he now writes an arts column for *The Times* and is a regular contributor to the *Sunday Times*. He is also an honorary research fellow at the University of Strathclyde. He lives in Edinburgh.

Contents

Acknowledgements 7

Introduction – A Tartan Takeover? 11

Part 1 – The Four Estates
1. Run by the Scotch 25
2. The Scottish Fourth Estate 58
3. Scottish Law 81
4. Scots at Prayer 95

Part 2 – A Home From Home
5. The *London Scotsman* 113
6. Paved with Gold? 133
7. Scots Wha Hae 147
8. The Scottish Version 160

Part 3 – As Others See Us
9. 'Traditional Sarcasms' – Scotophobia from Dr Johnson to
Boris Johnson 193
10. The State of England 219

Conclusion – Scots and 'Former' Scots 235
Select Bibliography 249
Index 257

Acknowledgements

Though this book argues that modern Scots have achieved their extraordinary dominance over London life without relying on the support of the Scottish societies and clubs which so entranced their Victorian ancestors, they share many of the same values, particularly their generosity towards new arrivals who have just got off the train from Scotland.

In researching this book I interviewed nearly 100 successful Scots from the worlds of politics, the media and commerce: without exception they were generous, supportive and insightful. Most are named in the text; a few politicians requested anonymity and I have respected their wishes. Not all of my interviewees will agree with the arguments which I advance here, but I am grateful to them all.

This book is a continuation in print of an argument which I have been having since the 1980s with many friends: Michael Gove, Rory MacMillan, Justin McKenzie Smith, Douglas Alexander MP, Professor Murray Pittock, Gordon Drummond, Matthew Fitt, Jane Sillars, Ian Docherty, Douglas Fraser, Tom Lynch, Eric Miller, Chris and Jan Prentice, my parents Lesley and Cameron Donaldson, and brothers Andrew and Gordon, will recognise some of what follows here.

I am grateful to my employers, BBC Scotland, for granting me a six-month sabbatical in 2003 to conduct much of my research, and I would also like to thank my editor at the Scottish edition of *The Times*, John Mair, for his enthusiasm and support.

Professor John Cairns of Edinburgh University and Alan MacLean offered valuable help on the subject of Scots in the

English Law, and Claire Sawers tracked down whole divisions of Scottish policemen who had worked in the Met. Roy Greenslade was generous and illuminating on the subject of Scots on Fleet Street.

I am a journalist not a historian, and the book follows journalistic practice throughout. I have avoided footnotes, though the provenance of quotations is clear from the text. Nonetheless, I have leant heavily on the recent flowering of historical research about Scotland. Anyone working in this area must also acknowledge the work of Professor Christopher Harvie, who first started exploring the relationship between the 'red' emigrant and the 'black' stay-at-home Scots more than 30 years ago. I am grateful to my colleague Dr Louise Yeoman of BBC Scotland for correcting my more appalling historical errors.

Bill Campbell, Ailsa Bathgate, Graeme Blaikie, Deborah Warner and others at Mainstream Publishing have offered expert advice on the text, and my agent Andrew Lownie, another successful London Scot, has been supportive and encouraging throughout.

My largest debt is to Claire Prentice who encouraged me to write *How the Scots Took Over London*, re-enthused me when I took time away from it and read and greatly improved the early drafts.

This book is dedicated to my grandfather, the Aberdeen publisher, William Cruickshank Brown.

This paperback edition of *How the Scots Took Over London* updates the story of Gordon Brown's struggles to become Prime Minister, corrects the odd error of emphasis and tidies up a few infelicitous phrases. Its central argument, that modern Scots have secured a remarkable double triumph, in securing a Scottish Parliament in Edinburgh whilst controlling some of the most important institutions of the English State becomes more politically explosive by the day.

'My lady, there are few more impressive sights in the world than a Scotsman on the make.'

Sir J.M. Barrie, *What Every Woman Knows*, 1908

'Like a gorged spider in the ghastly centre of the web
In which all human hopes like flies are caught,
London has flourished like a foul disease
In the wasting body of the British Isles
And drained all the world's wealth to its pirate's cave
By its callous and cowardly wiles.'

Hugh MacDiarmid, 'On the Imminent Destruction of
London, June 1940'

'I do not think it is an exaggeration to refer to England as a Scot-ridden country.'

T.W.H. Crosland, *The Unspeakable Scot*, 1902

Introduction – A Tartan Takeover?

Modern London is full of Scots: sentimental, sorry-they-ever-went-away Scots; glad-to-see-the-back-of-the-place Scots; assimilated Scots who only feel their blood surge when their home country faces England at Wembley or Murrayfield; city Scots from the Gorbals; country Scots from the Highlands; proudly working-class Scots; Sloaney Scots; and all kinds in between.

The Scots have been in the British capital since before Britain was a nation – as commoners and kings, engineers, scientists, doctors, actors, politicians and writers. For more than 400 years they have been feared and favoured, praised and condemned. Their ambition and drive has provoked envy and admiration, and their clannishness has aroused the suspicions of those around them. As one of the oldest immigrant groups in London, and the most successful, the Scots have made more of a mark on the city than any other.

The very streets of the British capital are paved, not with gold, but with a road surface invented in 1816 by John Loudon McAdam, who became the Scottish surveyor-general of metropolitan roads in England. Somerset House, the home of the Courtauld Institute and the Navy Board, was designed by Sir William Chambers. The world-famous Adam brothers designed Portland Place and the Adelphi buildings in the Strand.

The Scots are responsible for an almost full set of the bridges which span the Thames. Blackfriars was built by the Edinburgh architect Robert Mylne, who had walked all the way to London in search of opportunities that Scotland could not offer him.

Tower Bridge was constructed to the plan of Sir William Arrol, born in Paisley in 1839; St Paul's Bridge by the Scottish Sir George Washington Brown; and Waterloo, Southwark and New London bridges by John Rennie, born on an East Lothian farm in 1761.

And though the Scottish contribution to the physical environment of London is about more than just names, the names are there too: the long dusty drag of the Caledonian Road stretches from King's Cross to Holloway; Aberdeen Lane leads off Highbury Grove near the ground of Arsenal football club; and near West Ham Park, Glasgow Road joins Glebe Street, Gleneagles Close and roads called Glenesk, Glenelg and Glencoe as signs that in the poshest suburb or the darkest corner of the inner city, some town planner once had Scotland on his mind.

The Scots are present in less tangible ways, too: in a snatch of accent on the street, a kilt taken out for special occasions, the choice of sides in an international football match, or a taste for ale and whisky over bitter and claret. Today there are 11 closely printed pages of 'Macs' in the phone directory for central London alone.

Thomas Carlyle dubbed London a 'monstrous tuberosity', and twenty-first-century London, engorged beyond even Carlyle's imaginings, is a global city more than a British one; a place where men, women and children from every corner of the earth congregate. They come as refugees from pogroms, civil wars and ethnic unrest, as economic migrants, ambitious strivers and hopers after something better, searching for a new form of life in a 24-hour city where they work, play, eat, drink, dance and, sometimes, sleep.

But while London has been transformed by modern immigration, not all immigration is modern and not all immigrants are from overseas. Scottish immigration to London has been an important fact of life in the metropolis for more than 400 years.

The Scots came not in dribs and drabs following mercantile currents, or bobbing as human flotsam on the tide of the global economy, but in great waves, following dynastic upheavals and epoch-making political changes. They arrived in the wake of James VI and I, whose appearance on the London stage heralded a new Scottish dominance over English affairs, and later in huge numbers following the Act of Union with Scotland. And because the Scots arrived in London as the human evidence of political and economic disruption, they have always been viewed with wariness, and sometimes with outright hostility, by their English hosts.

In the seventeenth century, the Scots were barely-human savages, transformed by a stroke of cosmic luck into the countrymen of the King of England and taking full advantage of the opportunities for preferment that he offered. In the eighteenth century, after political union, they were locusts, swarming down from the barren countryside of Scotland to grab a share of London's riches. By the late nineteenth century, they were the ultimate insiders, so well established in London commerce, journalism, the army and medicine that they constituted a parallel London Establishment. Over 400 years, the status of the Scots has waxed and waned, from ungratefully received fellow Brits to established partners in the British Empire and, as the twentieth century ended, to something altogether more interesting.

In the last few years, driven by a modern political upheaval, uncertainty and hostility towards the Scots has reached a level unprecedented since the 1760s. Now, as then, the trigger has been a seismic shift in the constitution. The Union projected the Scots into the midst of a suspicious and resentful London; devolution has made London suspicious and resentful again.

But not just devolution: the affairs of Scotland are only ever of interest to a small number of Londoners, who have many other things to occupy their minds. The real trigger for the change in the role of the Scots was the election of a Government in 1997 which was dominated by them.

After 18 years of Conservative rule, the collapse of a Government which, in different incarnations, had directed British affairs for a generation was bound to usher in an entirely new era with its own distinct themes, unexpected events and characteristic tones. It came as a surprise to many in England just how Scottish that new era was destined to be. Overnight, men and women who had served their political apprenticeships in the Oxford and Cambridge Unions were swept out of power by politicians who had cut their political teeth in the debating

societies of Glasgow and Edinburgh universities. In the new
Government the Scots seized the highest offices of the British
state. In Tony Blair's first administration, the purse-strings of the
Exchequer were held by a son of the manse and Britain's foreign
affairs were controlled by a man who had once chaired the
housing committee of the Edinburgh Corporation.

And yet while the British Government was dominated by
Scots in London, the creation of the Scottish Parliament in
Edinburgh gave Scots at home an unprecedented amount of
power over their domestic affairs. As the English media reported
the creation of the parliament in Edinburgh, and Her Majesty's
secretaries of state defended the policies of the British
Government in brisk Scottish accents, many in England started
to realise that the Scots dominated British political and public
life as never before.

English commentators became confused, then restive. A
flurry of newspaper articles complained about the power of the
Scots and publishers rushed to print a genre of books which had
passed into desuetude since the 1720s: books which lamented
the death of England and the decline of its distinctive way of life.
Jeremy Paxman, the anchor of BBC television's *Newsnight*, wrote
The English, a whimsical guide to the traditions and history of the
inhabitants of the largest part of the United Kingdom, which
sold in unprecedented numbers in a country suddenly confused
about what being English actually meant. A battalion of other
books marched behind, in which England was lamented,
elegised and abolished, and Britain was portrayed as dead or
dying.

And while England was dying, interest in Scotland suddenly
soared. The Scottish historian Tom Devine saw his *The Scottish
Nation* shoot into the English bestseller lists. English journalists,
some of them with Scottish antecedents, were dispatched north
to find out 'just what was going on there', and arguments about
the Scots in England returned with a force not felt since the
union of the Parliaments.

Abroad, too, Scotland seemed of greater interest than ever
before. The Scots-American Duncan Bruce wrote *The Mark of the
Scots,* to argue that the Scots should be valued as 'hyphenated
Americans', as significant and distinctive a leaf in the American
salad bowl as their more visible Irish-American cousins. To

Bruce, the people from whom he descended are the single most important influences on American life, responsible for shaping the American Declaration of Independence and planting the genetic seed which took to the cosmos in the form of Neil Armstrong, the first Scotsman on the moon.

In Washington DC, the historian Arthur Herman was hard at work on his book *The Scottish Enlightenment: The Scots Invention of the Modern World*, though the American title, *How the Scots Invented the Modern World: The True Story of How Western Europe's Poorest Nation Created Our World and Everything in It*, gives a clearer indication of the chutzpah of its argument. The Scots Enlightenment, Herman argued, 'created the lens through how we see the final product' – modernity. Across the United States, from the south-east to the north, older notions of Scottishness started to exert a tug as Americans suddenly started going to 'Highland Games', in which they would dress up in tartan and celebrate the (sometimes invented) traditions of their ancestors.

And yet in Scotland, seedbed and heartland of much of this constitutional and cultural ferment, a curious silence descended on the opinion-forming classes. Whereas the 1980s and 1990s had seen much cultural *Sturm und Drang* on the subject of Scotland and Scottishness, in which many cherished ideas about the country were revised or overturned entirely, the post-devolution era saw a sudden drop in Scotland's intellectual barometer. Many of the leading intellectuals whose detailed historical work helped transform Scotland's view of itself have moved on to other projects, most noticeably pursuing a renewed interest in Scotland's role in the British Empire, and the newspapers which were, until recently, filled with a passionate debate about Scotland and Britishness are now preoccupied with adding up the costs of the thousands of pieces of differently shaped glass which make up the roof of the new Scottish Parliament building at Holyrood.

This book, written five years after the creation of the Scottish Parliament and seven years after the election of the Blair Government, asks two questions: how have the Scots come to exercise far more power in the United Kingdom than they or anyone else had expected, and why has the English reaction to the power of the Scots been almost entirely ignored in Scotland? It joins a growing shelf full of books about Scotland, and struggles to find space in the complete library devoted to London, but nonetheless it fills a surprising gap: those who are interested can find single-volume histories devoted to the experience of the Maltese in London, or the Huguenots, the Jamaicans, the Irish and the Jewish communities, but the story of the Scots in London has been curiously neglected by historians.

Anyone who argues that the Scots have gained unprecedented power in modern Britain has to be aware that the currency of such an argument has become seriously devalued. Scots have always taken what could be considered an exaggerated pride in the success of their fellow countrymen. Books about Scottish inventions, from those two staples of modern life, the telephone and the television, to penicillin and modern economics, still sell well and, until recently, every Scottish schoolchild would be forced to memorise a roll-call of successful Scots, from Rabbie Burns to David Livingstone. Nevertheless, though Scots at home and abroad have often taken excessive pride in the achievements of their countrymen, that is no reason to automatically discount them; the London Scots have plenty to be proud of.

In 1928, the Caledonian Society could boast, with some authority, that the army command was dominated by Scots.

Chief, Imperial General Staff	Gen. Sir George Milne
Chief, Indian General Staff	Maj. Gen. Sir Andrew Skeen
Aldershot Command	Lt. Gen. Sir David Campbell
Eastern Command	Gen. Sir Robert D. Whigman
Commanding First Division	Maj. Gen. Sir Robert Duncan
Commanding Second Division	Maj. Gen. Sir Edmund Ironside
Commanding Third Division	Maj. Gen. Sir J. Burnett-Stuart
Commanding Fourth Division	Maj. Gen. Sir A.R. Cameron

The Scottish domination of the upper echelons of the British armed forces was only rivalled by Scots control of the English medical profession: between 1750 and 1800, an astonishing 90 per cent of British doctors had graduated from Scottish universities and, in common with other professions where Scots dominated, like engineering, the popular British stereotype became Scottish; for that reason there is nothing more English than a Scottish doctor, engineer or bank manager.

And yet, while successful Scots became part of the British Establishment, sometimes mangling their accents to fit in more easily, the London Scots also formed their own clubs and societies, social networks and organisations in which they could meet apart from English company. Many of these are explored in depth in Chapter 5 of this book, but their very existence, and their conspicuous success, fuelled a persistent English suspicion about the Scots – that their clannishness overstepped the dividing line between cliquishness and nepotism. It is unarguable that many Scottish societies in London were firmly for Scots only; even if an Englishman had been tempted to join the London Banffshire Society, he would have found it hard unless he could produce a parent who had been born in Portknockie. Other societies, like the Scottish Masonic lodges, were even more exclusive, and an organisation which historically aroused suspicions was given another, national, reason to be distrusted.

Closed shops like this, and the memory of Scottish networks dedicated to supporting new arrivals from the north, fuelled English suspicions that Scots routinely advanced their own kind and that there existed a 'Scotia Nostra', a secret – or not-so-secret – cabal of Scots professionals who gave their own people a hand up and deliberately excluded outsiders: even though, in London, the outsiders were strictly the Scots.

But the London Scots also had their enemies at home. To some they had settled for an easy life in the soft south, or sold their birthright for English gold. To others they had forgotten about Scotland but still reserved their right to preach to those who had stayed at home.

'Just because they are doing all right for themselves doesn't mean they should tell the rest of us what to do,' was the view of one senior Scottish Nationalist politician whom I spoke to. He went on to label his fellow countrymen who choose to live in London as 'by and large, wankers'.

It's not hard to find stereotypes of what these 'wankers' do. They put on kilts at the drop of a tam o'shanter. They drink in the bar of the Caledonian Club, where their plaid trews strobe against the tartan carpets. They idolise the sentimental Rabbie of the Burns Suppers, though they don't know any of his poetry. They love to fly up to St Andrews or Gleneagles for a spot of golf, but they abandon their Scottishness when it suits them. They embrace a nationality which is ersatz rather than real, and they have 'gone native' as long as they can make a profit out of it.

It's perhaps not surprising then that the story of the Scots in London is so neglected, since it seems to generate such hard feeling on both sides. Yet even the critics of the London Scots admit that they are conspicuously successful, making their mark in commerce, the media, politics and the English Law. And contemporary Scots have achieved a prominence which rivals that of their Victorian counterparts.

The Victorian Scottish 'heids o' depairtment' have, in the twenty-first century, become the heads of international corporations, like Lord Blyth of Rowington, formerly chairman of Boots and now chairman of Diageo, the world's biggest spirits company, Sir Tom McKillop the chief executive of the pharmaceutical giant AstraZeneca, or Euan Baird the chairman of Rolls-Royce. The Victorian journalists who ensured that the sub-editors' desks of the weekly and daily press sounded with rolling 'R's and Scottish expletives have their counterparts in newspaper publisher Andrew Neil, or Michael Gove, until recently editor of the Saturday *Times*; the Victorian music hall of Sir Harry Lauder has disappeared but the careers of Robbie Coltrane, Ewan McGregor, Robert Carlyle, Sharleen Spiteri, Rhona Cameron and a thousand others prosper. And though the Victorians were too early to take advantage of the Scottish invention of television, Kirsty Wark, Lorraine Kelly and Gavin Esler dominate there as Eddie Mair, Jim Naughtie, Nicky Campbell and Edith Bowman do on the radio.

But the story of the Scots in London is not just the cumulative tale of a million James Boswells, carving out their glorious careers in the sunny pastures of the south. As this book's opening chapters show, Scots have made significant inroads into the three most powerful institutions of modern Britain: Parliament, the English legal system and the media. The extent of that influence raises the question of whether the London Scots should be seen less as a collection of talented individuals and more as a Scottish fifth column edging into the heart of the British state.

Debating Scotland's place in the United Kingdom has long been an anguished Scottish speciality, though one in which the power of Scots within their own borders has been of more interest than the power of the Scots in the British capital. Ironically, the conspicuous successes of today's Scottish politicians, journalists, performers and industrialists on the British stage is occurring at the very time when an increasing number of people in Scotland feel less British than ever before and want to sever links with England entirely.

But then London holds a curious place in contemporary Scottish thought. Whilst it is the location where many of Scotland's most successful sons and daughters forge their glittering careers, it is also viewed by many home-based Scots as the place responsible for draining their country of its lifeblood. The argument over whether Scotland is a subsidised financial drain on the coffers of the south or a generous benefactor dispensing its oil revenue still rages, but there is one precious natural resource which Scotland willingly shares with London: its people.

And Scotland's bounty continues to flow south. The latest census shows that the population north of the border is projected to fall 4.5 per cent from 5.06 million in 2001 to 4.83 million in 2026. Towns like Dundee are now smaller than they were in the 1830s. And whilst Scots traditionally emigrate to Australia, Canada and the US, the oldest and most popular destination for the Scot on the make is the capital of the United Kingdom. The 2001 census counted 7 million residents of London – 110,000 were born in Scotland. Take earlier Scottish emigrants and their children into the equation and the number of Scots living in Britain's capital is likely to be near 350,000.

And that, perhaps, is another root of Scotland's ambivalent attitude to London, for, while emigration is an accepted fact of life in Scotland, emigration to England is particularly hard to swallow. The Scots who left with James VI in 1603 were blamed for crushing Scottish court culture, virtually destroying the Scots language and ushering in an era in which Scottish political affairs were seen as parochial and uninteresting, suitable to be handed over to managers and political fixers. The argument has been raging, with different degrees of intensity, ever since.

And even while Scots who leave Scotland deprive their home

country of their labour and ingenuity, they also offer a rebuke to those who stay behind: if, as is generally observed about Scotland, all the best people go away, does that mean that the ones who stay can't be any good?

Is there a way to put the experience of Scots in London together with the experience of those who stay behind? Could the success of one group have important lessons for the other? There is no better time to ask the question.

Critics, and not only critics from the English Right, have started to claim that, far from being the underdogs of the United Kingdom, as many Scots believe themselves to be, we have carried off a remarkable sleight of hand: in modern times, we have utterly dominated the domestic governmental and civic structures of our own country and have now taken over the ones based in London.

To even suggest it sounds perverse, since it goes against the grain of more than a century of Scottish political argument and analysis. In the 1980s, Scottish culture, under pressure from a Thatcherism blue in tooth and claw, struggled to explain the collapse of Scottish political hopes. Writing in 1993 in the introduction to a wide-ranging *Companion to Scottish Culture,* the respected historian and cultural activist Paul H. Scott, who had made his career abroad in the British Diplomatic Service, argued that Scotland suffered from an 'internal colonialism', a deep-rooted self-disgust which stemmed from the political colonialism of the Union. Scott's description of the 'Scottish cringe', a profound embarrassment about the value of Scottishness in the face of a powerful and hostile neighbour, was a key idea of the 1980s and 1990s.

In another influential book of the late 1980s, Craig Beveridge and Ronald Turnbull wrote about 'inferiorism' in *The Eclipse of Scottish Culture*, applying to Scotland the ideas of sociologist Franz Fanon about the belittling effects of colonisation, where the peripheral culture was first found wanting by the values of the centre then had its differences 'reformed' away.

The journalist George Rosie gave these ideas a popular form in 1992 in his powerful investigation *The Englishing of Scotland*, which argued that Scottish institutions were being transformed according to an English model, and that more and more English people were seizing key Scottish positions. In response, the

Scotsman newspaper, which would itself soon be seized by its Scottish publisher Andrew Neil and transformed into an implacable opponent of devolution, ran headlines suggesting that English people were treating Scotland 'like the English Raj'.

Meanwhile, despite the political doom-saying, Scottish culture was blooming. A new generation of writers, some of them broken by Robin Robertson, a Scottish editor at Jonathan Cape, were coining new, unsettling images of Scotland which gained wide readerships north and south of the border. In the wake of the explosion in Scottish letters and the visual arts, some academics declared that Scotland was now 'culturally independent'.

The collapse of the Soviet Union and the re-emergence of once-proud nation states, which had long since been submerged within the Soviet Empire, gave new hope to Scottish Nationalists. But there were other voices too. Alongside the increasingly marginalised Unionists, like novelist and *Daily Mail* columnist Allan Massie, who tirelessly and, as it turned out, fruitlessly, pressed the case against devolution, other Scottish thinkers were turning their attention to exactly how much power had remained in Scottish hands after the Union. Lindsay Paterson's book *The Autonomy of Modern Scotland* argued that the distinctively Scottish institutions of the law, the education system and the Church retained a far greater degree of control over Scottish life than those who obsessed about Scotland's lack of a parliament gave credence to.

It was a fevered debate, and an exclusive one, conducted behind the wall of apparent English indifference to Scotland's obsession with its own identity. Belatedly, England has awoken to the changes which that debate has wrought in the structure of the United Kingdom. Like anyone aroused from a deep sleep, it seems confused, fractious and annoyed, but the Scots, who woke from their own sleep a generation ago, have treated the confusion of their bed partners for the last 300 years with indifference or contempt.

Modern Scots have been fixated by imaginary versions of what the English nation thinks about them or wants to do to them. This book listens more closely to what people in England really think about the Scots, both the ones in their midst and the ones in Scotland. It speaks to Scots who have ascended to the top of their professions, leaving English competitors in their wake, as well as those who, fuelled with a burning desire to change their lives, end up sleeping rough on London's streets. It looks back to the glory days of the Victorian Scots in London and forward to the future of the United Kingdom. It tells a story about the Scots in this unique historical moment which has never been told before.

Above all, it may come as a surprise to some Scots to learn that while they believe the story of Scotland and England is a tale of one-way oppression, at different times in their history many English people have also felt oppressed by the Scots – and a growing number are starting to feel that way again.

PART 1

The Four Estates

CHAPTER 1

Run by the Scotch

At the present moment England is virtually being run
by the Scotch. In the House of Commons, the Leader
of the Government, and practically the autocrat of the
Assembly, is the Right Honourable Arthur James
Balfour, a philosopher from Scotland who is so Scotch
that he plays golf. And the leader of the Opposition
(save the mark!) of an Opposition which in a
constitution like the British carries upon its shoulders
the heaviest responsibilities, is Sir Henry Campbell-
Bannerman, also a Scotch-man and, if the truth must be
told, a dullard. And in the way of a third party . . . we
have the Liberal Leaguers headed by that proud
chieftain of the pudding race, the Honourable Earl of
Rosebery. So that at the front of each of the three great
political forces of Britain, the forces which, when all is
said, mean everything to Britain as a nation, there
stands firm and erect some sort of a Caledonian. Such
a condition of things has never existed in England
before, and in the light of recent political happenings it
is devoutly to be hoped that it will never happen again.
        T.W.H. Crosland, *The Unspeakable Scot*, 1902

T.W.H. Crosland, the splenetic Scotophobe and anti-Semite,
whose book *The Unspeakable Scot* is a long, bilious attack on the
power of the Scots in English society, would have found much
to recognise and lament in the Britain of the early twenty-first
century.

At the beginning of the twentieth century, Crosland railed at the power of the three Scots who served as the leaders of Britain's major political parties; for him it was a high-water mark of horror. It was to get worse. Campbell-Bannerman won the 1905 general election to become the second Scottish Prime Minister of the century, and would lose to Herbert Asquith, who represented a Scottish seat. In the 1920s, Ramsay MacDonald, eventually disowned by his own party, became the first Labour Prime Minister. Forty years later Alec Douglas-Home, scion of an ancient Scottish family, replaced Harold Macmillan, the son of another, as Britain's Prime Minister. And, a century on from Crosland's warning, history seemed to be repeating itself.

For a little over two years, until November 2003 when, much to the relief of his party, Iain Duncan Smith was consigned to the Tory backbenches, Britain's three national political parties were once again led by Scots. Duncan Smith, with his pukka Guards accent, and Tony Blair, with his fluting metropolitan 'y'know's, might not have been walking linguistic advertisements for their nationality like Liberal leader Charles Kennedy, but the Tory and Labour leaders were Scottish too. Both Edinburgh boys, one was educated at Fettes, the Eton of the north, and the other quit his place of birth near Edinburgh's Turnhouse Airport for the army as soon as decency would allow. But then neither Bannerman nor Balfour had Scottish accents, and they were enough to set Crosland's antennae twitching.

Duncan Smith's leadership, despite his place of birth, never got off the ground, and his Welsh replacement, Michael Howard, has leant more heavily on his background as the son of immigrants from eastern Europe than on his Celtic birthplace. But though the brief alignment of three Scottish stars in the firmament of British politics had a symbolic value, the real Scottish dominance of Britain's political class comes from the hundreds of lesser planets, flaming meteors and dead asteroids orbiting around the Prime Minister.

Both of Tony Blair's administrations have been Scottish through and through: the Chancellor Gordon Brown seems to be the very embodiment of Scottish Presbyterianism, with his dour demeanour, financial prudence and punishing work ethic.

Blair's first Foreign Secretary, Robin Cook, who had made his name as the most terrifying parliamentary debater of his generation and quickly became enmeshed in the paradoxes of his own ethical foreign policy before quitting over the war in Iraq, is a Scot too. As if three Scots in the four senior government positions were not enough, Blair appointed another, his old friend Derry Irvine (later replaced by another old friend, and Scot, Lord Falconer) as Lord Chancellor, the senior figure in the English legal system. Taken along with the Chief Whip in the House of Commons, the Culture Secretary, Chris Smith, and a few more minor ministers, eight seats in the first Blair Cabinet were taken by Scots. All Cabinets are compromises, in which power blocks are bought off and old scores settled, but the Scots had become Labour's establishment and, besides, there were too many to outmanoeuvre; if the Cabinet had been composed in strict proportion to the British population, only two Scots would have sat around the most famous table in Whitehall.

Nor has the creation of the Scottish Parliament halted the careers of Blair's Scottish colleagues, as was widely predicted. After a quick realignment of his portfolio, Alistair Darling was given responsibility for Transport in May 2002, and John Reid, after a lightning-fast progress through some of the Government's most demanding jobs, was appointed Secretary of State for Health in June 2003. This was a position in which he became the inevitable focus of political controversy, since he seemed to be the very embodiment of Tam Dalyell's West Lothian Question: the minister who has responsibility for England's health, and yet is unaccountable to his own constituents, who have their health policy set by Holyrood.

The Blair Government also created Scottish enclaves in the Department of Trade and Industry, giving ministerial posts to veteran anti-devolution campaigner Brian Wilson and Edinburgh South MP Nigel Griffiths. The Cabinet Office became another Scottish outpost with Lord Gus MacDonald, the former shipworker turned journalist and television executive, and his deputy and eventual successor Douglas Alexander MP holding a steely grip on the very centre of government policy-making.

'I don't think that Tony Blair lies awake at night worrying

about the nationality of the people he is appointing to top jobs,' says Catherine McLeod, the veteran Westminster political editor of *The Herald*. 'I think he appoints people who are bright and who have talent. I think if there were a lot of [Scottish] dunderheads in government and English MPs were being excluded, then people could say there was favouritism, but nobody says that.'

But Blair's selection policy did raise comment, especially since the most Scottish-dominated British Government in modern political history coincided with the introduction of devolution for Scotland. In an article entitled 'The Insidious Rise of the McMafia', right-wing commentator Edward Heathcoat-Amory, the nephew of David, the Conservative MP for Wells, railed against the Scottish dominance of the New Labour Cabinet.

> Scotland is a small place, and all the significant and successful people there know each other. They belong to the same clubs, drink in the same bars, compete for the same jobs, and run off with each other's wives. Now they are in London, and are recreating this tiny incestuous world there.

Heathcoat-Amory's article was the first of many. 'Those of us who live in England were first hurt, then bemused and are now angered at the process of Scottish devolution,' wrote George Trefgarne in the *Daily Telegraph* at the beginning of 2002. 'It is a swindle, whereby the Scots receive better public services at English expense and then get to send their tartan army of MPs to Westminster, too.'

Devolution, one of the policies Labour had championed in Opposition and which Blair had retained, partly bemused some English commentators because they seemed to expect that it would automatically strip Tony Blair of some of his most significant Scottish allies. Before 1979, when a referendum in Scotland failed to achieve the 40 per cent majority required to establish its own Assembly, senior London-based Scottish politicians had signalled their intention to return home once their country had a devolved government. In 1999, though, Robin Cook toyed with the idea of returning to Scotland before rejecting it; Blair's Scottish Secretary Donald Dewar was alone in the senior ranks of New Labour in choosing to take the high road home again.

George Robertson, the Defence Secretary in Blair's first Cabinet, summed up the attitude of his Scottish Cabinet colleagues when he was asked whether he would consider taking up the post of Scotland's First Minister. Robertson mulled the offer over before rejecting it. 'No,' he said, 'why settle for Scotland when you can run the whole show?' For Robertson, the 'whole show' became NATO, after he was ennobled as Lord Robertson of Port Ellen, of Islay in Argyll and Bute, and took up the Secretary-Generalship of the Alliance. For Cook, the 'whole show' was the Foreign Office and for Gordon Brown it was the Treasury. Having spent much of their careers enduring the frustration of Opposition and having finally clambered to the top of the greasy pole of British politics, only one senior Scottish Labour figure was interested in going back to play his part in building the fledgling Parliament in Edinburgh.

'I've asked Gordon Brown twice why he doesn't go back home and become Scotland's prime minister,' the journalist Simon Heffer told me. 'He doesn't want to because he knows that his power and profile would be diminished.'

As a policy, devolution, the issue which had dominated Scottish political debate for almost 20 years, had barely registered in England before the 1997 election, and even afterwards it seemed to leave English opinion formers utterly bemused. Large articles appeared in English newspapers explaining how devolution would affect Wales and Scotland. Some confused devolution with Scottish independence, exactly the policy which Labour hoped it would stop in its tracks by introducing wide-ranging constitutional reform in Scotland. Others, realising that devolution would alter the relationship between Scotland and the rest of the United Kingdom for good, predicted the end of the line for Blair's Scottish colleagues: UK ministries would be barred to ambitious Scots. Many commentators went as far as prophesying the end of Britain itself. Other Jeremiahs declared that after it had its own Parliament, Scotland would become like Northern Ireland without the bombs – parochial and inward looking, and cut off from the mainstream of British life.

But though devolution hasn't denuded the Blair Government of its Scottish hard hitters, it has nonetheless thrown up a few constitutional road bumps to slow the forward progress of the New Labour machine. The vote in January 2004 over tuition fees in England, carried by the votes of Scottish MPs – though Scotland itself, under the authority of the Scottish Executive, does not have them – led to a mini constitutional crisis, fanned by the Opposition. Michael Howard, the new Conservative Party leader, announced that his Scottish representation would not vote on the measure, though since his representation in Scotland consisted of one man, Peter Duncan MP, the announcement had less force than it might otherwise have done.

But the Opposition parties have sensed that the restive residents of England can be riled, not so much on the constitutional niceties of their current position, but by its apparent unfairness. After foundation hospitals will come debates on toll roads and the reform of the railways in England. Other reforms which seem to crash against the prerogatives of devolution will inevitably follow. It's an issue which will become one of the major bones of contention in the approaching general election. And one man believes he predicted it all.

Tam Dalyell, the Father of the House of Commons, took me into a deserted Commons tearoom to explain how the current situation was 'not only predictable but predicted'. In the Eeyore-ish tones which have delighted his constituents and infuriated his parliamentary colleagues for 40 years, Dalyell argued that everything he foresaw in the 1970s has come to pass. 'I was called everything under the sun when I spoke about the West Lothian Question, but it is now an issue which confronts this Government. I don't believe that the people of England, and the Commons, will put up with it. It may not appear this way at the moment but I believe devolution will harm the careers of Scottish MPs. I believe that it will stop Gordon Brown becoming Prime Minister.'

Ian Lang, whom John Major rewarded for his long service in the Scottish Office and made Secretary of State in charge of the Department of Trade and Industry, also believes that devolution will damage the careers of Scottish MPs. Lang, who has said that in his opinion Scotland was better governed by the Scottish Office, believes that the long-term effect of devolution will be to make it politically unacceptable for a Scot representing a Scottish seat to become Prime Minister: 'I think Scotland is now cut off and has become a backwater. It isn't evident yet because all the top figures in government are Scots. But the supply of Scottish backbenchers will dry up and English resentment will rise, and is rising.'

It would be a chilling conclusion to Brown's career if, having spent much of his political life arguing for devolution, and all of it chasing his dream of becoming Prime Minister, one dream were to cancel out the other.

Dalyell will leave the Commons at the next election, but the question which he so famously and, for opponents, frustratingly framed may be around to haunt the Prime Minister and the current Chancellor long after he's gone – like a bad-mannered Caliban asking annoying questions long after Dalyell's Old Etonian Prospero has quit the stage.

How have the Scots managed to establish such a powerful grip on Britain's political class? In the past, Britain's rulers were drawn from shallow waters: a handful of public schools and a few old families. A degree from Oxford or Cambridge and a successful career in the army could pave the way to a career as a Conservative grandee, and Labour MPs would emerge from the aristocracy of the trade unions.

Conservative Cabinets were dominated by the products of Britain's elite educational establishments. Even Mr Attlee's 1945 Labour Government had 18 ex-public schoolboys around the table. A century of culture wars have disrupted the supply lines of those old traditions, and it is a measure of the revolution which occurred in Britain's political and cultural life in the last century that Mrs Thatcher's Cabinet was dominated by ex-grammar schoolboys, and a typical Blair Cabinet minister is more likely to have gone to a Scottish secondary school and a university north of the border than any other seat of higher learning.

Thatcher famously polarised Britain. Under her leadership, the country was said to be divided by a line at Watford. Below was the super-heating economy of the south-east; above, industrial decay and mass unemployment. But under Blair, Britain's political centre of gravity has lurched north. The men

31

and women who would take their places as Britain's ruling class of the twenty-first century were formed not in the balmy south of England but in the grimy Glasgow and inhospitable Edinburgh of the 1970s.

Edinburgh, the beautiful, chilly capital of Scotland, is now a thriving European city filled with designer clothes shops and style bars. George Street in the heart of the New Town has re-branded itself as the 'Bond Street of the north'. In Dundas Street, just down the hill, a handful of Scottish galleries grandly title themselves 'Scotland's Cork Street'. But in the 1970s, Edinburgh had more in common with Cork than with the capital of England. 'The question,' one cynic wrote of the city in the 1970s, 'is not whether there is life after death but whether there is life after dark.'

Edinburgh, famously, was the most under-catered city in Britain. Tourists would struggle to find a restaurant open after eight o'clock. The lucky ones would be served with ill-disguised bad grace. The unreformed licensing hours meant that it was hard to get a drink when you wanted one, and the annual gaiety of the Edinburgh Festival merely served to emphasise the lack of culture which reigned during the rest of the year.

In 1972, a visitor to the Abbotsford pub on Edinburgh's Rose Street might have seen an unusual couple propping up the bar. One was small, red-haired and animated, the other saturnine and brooding. Both were talking politics. During that year, Robin Cook, the future Foreign Secretary, had a regular drinking companion: a talented university student called Gordon Brown. Later they would become bitter enemies, but the two men were once close enough to meet for a drink, at Cook's estimation, 'once or twice a week'.

Then, Cook was the senior figure, a city councillor and Convenor of the Housing Committee, where he was responsible for disposing of much of Edinburgh's derelict housing stock. Brown was the precocious rector of Edinburgh University, a prodigy who had entered the university on a fast-track scheme at the age of 16 and already made a name for himself as a fiercely focused student activist by the time he turned 20. Brown, a son of the Scottish manse, as so many Scottish politicians have been, inherited a formidable work ethic and social conscience from his minister father. At an early age, he also showed signs of the strategic sense which would guide him throughout his career. Taking advantage of a recent rule change in the university's constitution, Brown had been elected as rector of the university while still a postgraduate student in the history department. The rectorial post, which had previously tended to go to showbusiness figures, carried with it the responsibility of chairing the university court, a dull job which celebrity rectors tended to pass on to their 'assessors' but which Brown embraced with relish. By mastering the court's arcane constitution, Brown delighted in outfoxing the conservative professors who otherwise dominated its proceedings.

Cook and Brown were not the only future Cabinet ministers to be found in Edinburgh at the time. Across the City Chambers from Cook sat a cerebral Edinburgh lawyer serving the ward of Newington called Malcolm Rifkind. Rifkind and Cook would be elected to Parliament on the same night and profiled together in the *Edinburgh Evening News*. In an article headlined 'Neck and neck in the race to the Commons', the paper pointed out that Cook and Rifkind had attended Edinburgh University together, where Rifkind had been president of the University's Conservative Society and Cook had led the Labour Club. The piece concluded, 'Like the Joneses you've got to hand it to the city's two new MPs in keeping up with one another.' It was a connection which would continue throughout their time in the Commons – they often shadowed one another, the unflappable QC locking horns with his preening, sarcastic opponent – and only end when Rifkind lost his seat in 1997. With Rifkind's selection in February 2004 as the Conservative candidate for Kensington and Chelsea, and Cook enjoying a new life on the Labour backbenches, the Edinburgh partnership looks certain to enter a new phase.

Earlier, on the outskirts of the city another future politician, Iain Duncan Smith, had quit his family home for a career in the Scots Guards, but, more importantly for the history of New Labour, the future Prime Minister was still studying at Fettes, entertaining himself with schoolboy acting and dreaming of Oxford, where he would study law and sing with the rock band Ugly Rumours.

At the other end of the M8, Glasgow University had been the forging ground for a band of MPs-in-waiting, including John

Smith, Donald Dewar, Menzies Campbell and John McKay, all of whom honed their forensic skills in the Glasgow University Union.

Two Glasgow institutions famously strike terror into the heart of visitors. The audience at the city's Empire Theatre is famous for booing Morecambe and Wise off the stage. The crowd in the Glasgow University Union is even harder to please. In an atmosphere famed for its merciless treatment of nervous speakers, Glasgow University debaters learn withering put-downs to subdue barracking opponents. In monthly 'parliaments', students take the roles of Prime Minister and Opposition spokesmen to debate the political issues of the day. As a training ground for Westminster, it cannot be bettered. John Smith and Donald Dewar came from the Glasgow University Labour Club and remained part of that reformist, convivial and cynical group for the reminder of their careers.

Nor was Glasgow's role in producing politicians exhausted after Dewar and Smith left. Less than a decade after Cook and Brown left university in Edinburgh, Glasgow would receive the latest political neophyte to benefit from its tough union training: Charles Kennedy, the red-haired son of a crofter, and the future leader of the Liberal Democrats.

For such a gilded generation to pass through Oxford or Cambridge would provoke little comment, but for such a combination of dominant political figures to find themselves in the environs of Scotland's two major cities at the same time is more than a remarkable coincidence; it is an indication of the shared roots, heritage and priorities which unite those at the top tier of British political life.

With the shared physical environment went an intellectual climate too. Scottish Labour in the early 1970s was a powerful monolith, but the cracks were starting to appear. The dominant figure in the Parliamentary Labour Party was Scottish Secretary Willie Ross, an old-style machine politician who objected to new thinking and prided himself on his capacity to deliver Scotland's Labour MPs in support of the leadership. Ross's attitude was that young Labour MPs had to prove themselves before they could be given the chance to exert any significant influence on party policy. Ambitious activists were to be encouraged up to a point, but only if they toed the party line.

This attitude, combined with the moribund state of many local branches, meant that Labour in Scotland was an ideas-free zone. The Wilson and Callaghan Cabinets were packed with assiduous diary writers, but anyone reading the diaries of Richard Crossman, Tony Crosland, Tony Benn or Barbara Castle can see how little of the intellectual input into the Labour Governments of the 1970s came from Scotland. In Harold Wilson's self-justifying autobiography, Scotland merits merely a footnote on one page.

Brown and Cook, whatever the political differences which would separate them later, were united in one belief: in order to transform life in Scotland, Labour needed to do more than repeat the traditions of the past. The party needed an infusion of new ideas. But coming up with those ideas would drive Cook and Brown into the path of Labour's Scottish establishment.

Gordon Brown was the first to feel the wrath of the party old guard. The year after the October 1974 election, Brown edited a book called *The Red Paper on Scotland,* a radical blueprint for the rejuvenation of Scotland's economy and civic culture. *The Red Paper,* which was to prove one of the most influential documents in the transformation of Labour in Scotland, could not have seemed less promising. Published by the university's Student Publication Board, it had a small print run of 5,000 and a tiny typeface which made it a strain to read – Brown wanted to cram as much into the book as possible. His own introduction ran to 10,000 words and his contributors included virtually every significant left-wing intellectual working in Scotland at the time. The playwright John McGrath, whose play *The Cheviot, the Stag and the Black, Black Oil* would transform the history of theatre in Scotland, wrote an article for *The Red Paper,* as did Tom Nairn, the leading political theorist of the day. There were articles on Scotland's oil, on local democracy, on the Scottish Development Agency. Robin Cook wrote on Scotland's housing crisis. Historian Owen Dudley Edwards wrote on 'Lessons from Ireland'. The book was a straining portmanteau of radical left-wing thought and it demanded nothing less than the wholesale reform of Scotland's political structures. Since most of those political structures were run by the Labour Party, it was guaranteed to rile the party grandees.

Nowadays, much of *The Red Paper* reads like the overly

theoretical proceedings of a conference of left-wing academics. In office, notwithstanding an unfortunate blip when he delivered a speech to economists about 'neo-classical endogenous growth theory', Gordon Brown restrains his use of incomprehensible jargon. As a young party activist, he was not so disciplined.

> Political power will become a synthesis of – not a substitute for – community and industrial life. This requires from the Labour Movement in Scotland today a positive commitment to creating a socialist society, a coherent strategy with rhythm and modality to each reform to cancel the logic of capitalism and a programme of immediate aims which leads out of one social order into another.

The influence behind all this was Gramsci, the Italian socialist thinker who would enjoy a vogue in the 1980s as the inspiration behind *Marxism Today*, the radical political magazine which in some respects prefigured New Labour thinking. Brown had first read Gramsci after his prison diaries were translated by the Scottish folklorist Hamish Henderson in 1974. Henderson, who founded the School of Scottish Studies at Edinburgh University, is also credited by some of Brown's friends with convincing the future Chancellor of the importance of devolution. Thus, the inbred nature of Scottish intellectual life introduced Italian communism into the heart of Edinburgh's Old Town.

The Red Paper was wholly behind devolution and, as such, it drove Ross and the other Labour grandees to apoplexy. Old-style Labour figures believed that devolution was merely a sop to Scottish Nationalism and Scottish Nationalism was inherently reactionary.

The year before *The Red Paper* was published, the Scottish Nationalists, or 'Tartan Tories' as Labour preferred to describe them, had broken through in Scotland and taken 11 parliamentary seats. Labour was convulsed with fear that the Nationalists would gain enough seats to ratchet up demands for Scottish independence, and the party was divided on how to deal with the challenge. The old guard believed that the Nationalists should be attacked as Conservatives in kilts, but radicals like Brown were starting to believe that recognition of the distinctive nature of Scottish society wasn't incompatible with socialism. The SNP would never again reach the same heights of electoral support, but the problem of how to deal with the Nationalist menace preoccupied Labour to the point of distraction.

In this febrile atmosphere, Brown proceeded to make himself thoroughly unpopular with his party. Most Labour grandees considered him too clever by half and even while still a student he became a figure of suspicion amongst Labour's upper echelons.

'I remember Gordon coming back from one meeting with Helen Liddell [then Secretary of the Labour Party in Scotland, briefly Scottish Secretary and now British High Commissioner to Australia] in tears,' says Owen Dudley Edwards, a contributor to *The Red Paper*. 'I don't understand people who say Gordon is a bully. The boy I knew was sweet and kind, and terribly shy.'

With no party office, but holding the chair of Labour's devolution campaign at the age of 29, the sweet-natured Brown set about trying to convince the Labour Party in Scotland of the need for devolution. Cook swithered on the issue, changing his mind twice, once before and once after his first election to Parliament, but in one respect he was able to identify with Brown's predicament – he was up against his senior Scottish colleagues too.

Elected to Parliament in February 1974, Cook set about noising up the Scottish Parliamentary party. He spoke out on foreign and defence issues, became a prominent campaigner on the need to control the security services and, as a member of CND from his teens, campaigned against nuclear weapons. 'Robin irritated a hell of a lot of the elderly in the parliamentary party,' explains a weary Scottish parliamentary colleague from that time. 'They felt threatened by him. Your face had to fit. Robin's fitted with none of them.'

Nonetheless, Cook and Brown plugged away at their careers, slowly forcing the party in Scotland to recognise that it needed to take on board new ways of thinking or it would die.

Brown and Cook's techniques differed. While Cook, the brilliant debater, believed that victory in public argument was enough to convince doubters, Brown recognised that people, not ideas, make politics. In his early 20s, Brown set about cultivating those who mattered and gathering a dedicated team of supporters around him. From university, he became friends with Colin Currie, a doctor and writer of light-hearted thrillers with a medical theme. Currie became a Brown speechwriter and later an adviser to Donald Dewar. Nigel Griffiths, another old Brown friend and ally, became a town councillor, an MP and a junior minister in the Blair Government. And Alistair Darling, a dashing advocate educated at the University of Aberdeen, became a Brown confidant, a key figure on the City of Edinburgh District Council and now Transport Secretary. Having formed a phalanx of loyal supporters, Brown ensured that it progressed as he did. Having fallen foul of Labour's Scottish network in his formative years, Brown was determined that it would never happen again and created his own. It would be the source of his power in years to come. Robin Cook, who preferred to walk alone, would discover in the future that he was being marginalised by men loyal to Brown.

While his two future Cabinet colleagues were setting their faces against the Labour Party in Scotland and taking their first steps on the road to power, Tony Blair was sitting his A levels. Blair went as an undergraduate to St John's College in Oxford, arriving in 1972. Avowedly apolitical, he avoided the Oxford Union and shunned the broad-left group of students who were attempting to take over the student union. A college contemporary recalls that one of Blair's catchphrases at Oxford was, 'He's too intense', normally used against any undergraduate who displayed an overwhelming interest in politics. If the young Blair and Brown had ever run into one another they would have quickly discovered that they had little in common. One was interested in playing with his band, the other in applying Gramscian ideas to the task of rejuvenating Scottish civil society. Blair believed that politicos should lighten up; Brown was the definition of intensity. The men who would become the dominant figures in New Labour had opposite temperaments from the beginning. So it would remain.

Though Blair had been brought up in Edinburgh, he moved in very different circles from his future ally and rival. His father,

Leo, had been a Conservative, so Blair had no grounding in the networks of the Labour Party in Scotland. Its internecine struggles passed him by, though, in his own way, Blair was assembling the group of supporters he needed to sustain him through the coming years. One key ally, Anji Hunter, who would go on to run Blair's private office, was a friend whom he had met at Fettes.

Nevertheless, even at Oxford, Blair was to be inspired by Scottish intellectual tradition. Previous Labour leaders might have read Marx. The current Prime Minister has spoken of his discovery of the work of John MacMurray as a significant intellectual turning point. MacMurray, a Scottish theologian, had studied at Oxford and produced a corpus of work that dwelled on the responsibilities of individuals and of society. MacMurray believed that there was a distinction between society and community. Community was based on pleasurable association, often embodied in faith groups. 'It surprises me,' Blair wrote in an introduction to MacMurray's writing in 1997, 'that John MacMurray is not the most famous philosopher in Britain.' The MacMurray enigma, for all that it has perplexed some commentators, might have less to it than it seems. It is hard to read his work and see how, if at all, his ideas influence New Labour; the Prime Minister's pet intellectual might be less a guru and more a good line to throw to those who claim he has no principles.

Blair, as an anti-ideological politician who would go on to lead an ideological party, always responded to practical assistance more than intellectual inspiration. After leaving Oxford, he was fortunate to fall into the sphere of influence of yet another Scottish Labour figure: Derry Irvine. Irvine employed Blair in his chambers after the young lawyer passed his Bar exams. The intellectually brilliant son of an Inverness roof tiler, Irvine had transformed himself into a millionaire QC through focus and sheer hard work. More importantly, Irvine, who had unsuccessfully stood as a Labour candidate in his youth, took pains to keep his Labour connections alive. He had been at Glasgow University with John Smith and was friends with Smith's circle, including Murray Elder, a Scottish political fixer who now sits in the House of Lords as Lord Elder of Kirkcaldy.

Irvine is a pivotal figure in Blair's story, responsible for arranging the two most fateful encounters in Tony Blair's life. He introduced Blair to his future wife, Cherie Booth, and he smoothed Blair's entry to the upper echelons of the Labour Party by introducing him to John Smith. Smith, who was entertainingly cynical about politics, particularly Labour politics of the left, enjoyed a convivial evening drinking with the young MP, and their personal relationship was warm for the remainder of Smith's life. Even though Blair had not grown up with the Labour Party in Scotland, he quickly became locked in its coils.

Brown's path took him to Westminster in 1983. In 1979, he had fought and narrowly lost Edinburgh South to the Conservative Michael Ancram, another Scot who would go on to occupy the centre stage of British politics. Friends report that Brown was devastated at his unexpected defeat, but, characteristically, he dedicated himself to gathering a new set of skills. He took a job as a political reporter at Scottish Television in Glasgow. There he became friends with Gus MacDonald, a senior producer who would go on to lead the company and reappear as a key ally in the Cabinet after being elevated to the House of Lords. Brown's brief career as a television reporter gave him some insight into how the media worked. As a backbench MP, he kept the press supplied with a steady stream of press releases, leaks from the Government and policy announcements. In pre-recorded interviews, he would repeat the same point over and over again, often using exactly the same words, so that he could dictate the form in which they appeared. (Labour's fascination with media control is often dated to the arrival of Peter Mandelson in September 1985, however Gordon Brown had been practising it for his own ends long before that.)

Because Brown sat out the 1979–83 Parliament, he was able to escape the ritual bloodletting which gripped Labour in its first term in Opposition. While the party in England grappled with the rise of Militant, the Bennite insurrection to seize control away from the parliamentary party and the breakaway of the SDP, north of the border the party struggled with the thorny issue of devolution, which had become tainted by its association with the dying days of the Callaghan Government. Brown's pro-devolution politics and awkward personal style meant that he struggled to find another seat and only managed very late in the day to gain the nomination for Dunfermline East. Blair was another late adoption, securing the nomination for Sedgefield at the last minute.

In 1983, the first Thatcher Government was in full cry. Labour limped back into Parliament with 27.6 per cent of the vote, its lowest in 60 years. Household names from the 1979 Labour Government lost their seats on election night. Brown and Blair entered Parliament that same day. As young MPs they shared an office.

The Scottish dominance of New Labour owes much to the electoral success of Thatcherism. As the Conservatives ate into Labour's English working-class base in 1983 and 1987, turning key seats from red to blue, they wiped out a whole generation of potential English Labour Cabinet ministers. In contrast, Labour in Scotland went from strength to strength, holding off the SNP and reversing the colour shift. By the beginning of the 1990s Scotland was as red as England was blue, and by the time Labour was returned to office, its senior posts were dominated by Scots who had worked their way up the party hierarchy, gained places on the National Executive Committee and grabbed the most powerful jobs for themselves. In successive elections, Brown's allies entered Parliament, filling the lower echelons of Labour with men and women loyal to the Chancellor. Brown set about headhunting talent which shared his own political outlook. He would go to extraordinary lengths to talent-spot younger Labour figures.

Douglas Alexander, now Labour MP for Paisley South and Minister for Trade, Investment and Foreign Affairs, was approached by Brown at a Scottish Labour Party Conference when he was about to sit his finals. Like Brown, he was a son of the manse and a history student at Edinburgh University. Like Brown, he was driven by a powerful Protestant work ethic. Within months he was working in Brown's private office, and returned to Edinburgh to qualify as a solicitor before fighting the Perth and Kinross by-election, standing again for Perth in 1997 and finally being elected member for Paisley South in one of the first by-elections of Blair's first term.

By the time New Labour took office, Brown had key allies at every level of Scottish politics. So complete is Brown's control of the party in Scotland that Labour insiders joke that when

Kirkcaldy District Council come to select a new head gardener there is a 'Brown candidate'.

Blair, despite his Scottish roots, has been happy to allow his Chancellor to have a free run in Scotland. Indeed, Blair's grasp of the mood and concerns of his Scottish party has never been as secure as his feeling for Middle England.

On a visit to Scotland to promote the wisdom of his devolution policy, Blair seemed to commit a serious gaffe which alienated some of his natural support. In an interview with *The Scotsman*, Blair appeared to compare the powers of the future Scottish Parliament with that of an English parish council. After his comments made the front page of the newspaper, Blair's aides first denied that the Prime Minister had said any such thing, and then, confronted with the tape, contrived to explain that the Prime Minister had been pointing out that *even* an English parish had elective power, so why then shouldn't a historic country like Scotland? The whole episode seemed to confirm Blair's feeling that Scotland was an incomprehensible fiefdom, as touchy as it was clannish. His bagpipe-playing press spokesman Alastair Campbell was even more direct. He blamed the Scottish press for stitching up his boss and declared that they were 'unreconstructed wankers'.

If Blair was wary of Scottish devolution before it was introduced, then the Scottish Executive has done little to endear itself to New Labour in London. Indeed, the whole project seems to have been something of a disappointment to Blair and his ministers. Whilst Blair has been in Downing Street, Scotland has seen three First Ministers. Donald Dewar, the first, died of a brain haemorrhage following complications caused by his triple heart-bypass and was replaced by Henry McLeish, a loyal junior player in Labour's ranks. McLeish was felt by many in the Labour Party in London to be a second-ranker but a safe pair of hands. In fact, McLeish was an uninspiring leader and was forced to resign after he bungled the office expenses in his Fife constituency. It seems to have been a careless error rather than an attempt at corruption, but Scotland's second First Minister left under a cloud.

Brown had sponsored McLeish's appointment, partly to block the progress of Jack McConnell, one of the few members of the Scottish Executive whose loyalty to Brown is questionable. Now that McLeish was gone, the job of finding a replacement allowed the Chancellor yet another chance to demonstrate his power in Scotland, but his favourite, Wendy Alexander, swithered for a weekend and then decided not to run, leaving the coast clear for McConnell to take over. He was the candidate that Brown least wanted to win and Brown's closest aides are scathing about a man whom they refer to as 'pompous and incompetent'. It was the only recent occasion on which the Chancellor had failed to get one of his allies a top job, and Brown is determined never to let it happen again.

But Scotland has embarrassed the London Government in other ways too. Blair's most telling accusation against the Major Government was 'sleaze'. Unfortunately for him, Labour's record, especially in the west of Scotland, is hardly clean. After the death of John Smith, the activities of Monklands District Council hit the headlines when it was accused of discriminating against employees on religious grounds. As the local MP, Smith allegedly knew about the allegations and had done nothing to clean up the council. Later, the spotlight fell on the activities of the council in Paisley, after its MP, Gordon McMaster, committed suicide. McMaster's death created the by-election that allowed Brown's ally Douglas Alexander to enter Westminster, but it was claimed that McMaster had been the victim of a vicious smear campaign. McMaster had suffered from chronic fatigue syndrome, which he blamed on the organophosphates he had worked with when he had been a council gardener. His enemies in local politics put around the false rumour that the bachelor MP had AIDS.

The creation of the Scottish Parliament has added a self-awareness to Englishness. Debates about English nationalism have sprung up, encouraged by opinion pieces in the national press. Simon Heffer has written a polemical book about English independence, Jeremy Paxman has written about the elusive nature of the English, and the St George's Cross, once the symbol of the anti-immigration Right, has begun to appear in the windows of taxis or in pub signs, and during the 2003 Rugby World Cup blanketed the terraces in swirling red and white.

There have been changes in the media too. Any change of

government often means a change of guard in Fleet Street. Analysts who may be experts in the secretive manoeuvres of the Conservative Party can be left guessing after Labour takes power. So it has proved in this case. Robin Oakley, the BBC's political editor and a man of stout right-wing views, was perfectly placed to commentate on the Thatcher and Major Governments. When New Labour took power, he was replaced by Andrew Marr, formerly of *The Economist* and *The Independent*, who was closer to Labour's high command and is married to Jackie Ashley, daughter of the veteran Labour MP Jack Ashley. Marr is a Scot, born just outside Dundee, who has written about the long struggle for a Scottish Parliament; it makes him an inside outsider, able to balance his intimate knowledge of the British political Establishment with a perspective on what has been happening 400 miles from Westminster.

Jim Naughtie, the presenter of the *Today* programme, who came to London as a successful graduate of the Aberdeen *Press and Journal* and *The Scotsman*, has impeccable Labour connections. He covered the devolution debate the first time around in the 1970s from the perspective of Scotland and has written a penetrating book, *The Rivals,* about the intense relationship between Blair and Brown.

But all these Scots brought their problems too, and one was the very perception that Labour was a UK party dominated by Scots. It was a problem that predated Blair. When John Smith led the party, it was often observed that his closest aides were all Scots. One Scottish aide, currently a senior Labour figure in the Lords, says, 'Every so often, one of the papers would get hold of the idea that John's office was dominated by Scots and we would scramble around trying to find the English boy in the office so he could go out and make a statement.'

Smith himself didn't share the sensitivities of his aides. 'I remember being at a party with John Smith,' the editor of the *Financial Times* magazine, John Lloyd, told me, 'and he said, "Why don't they [the English] realise we're just *better* than them?"'

After Smith's death, one of the factors which hampered Brown's campaign to become Labour leader was known as the 'two Scots' problem. If one Scottish Labour leader was immediately succeeded by another, would it convey the impression that Labour was no longer a truly national party?

Neil Kinnock was of the opinion that John Smith's Scottishness had been a handicap to him. For Brown to replace Smith would draw even greater attention to the issue. The anglified Blair, representing an English seat, proved a less controversial choice.

But the dominance of a cadre of sophisticated Scottish politicians wasn't just a shock to Westminster and Whitehall, or a potential political flashpoint; it was the result of a step change in the Labour Party in Scotland. The Scottish Labour MPs of the 1970s may have been party loyalists, but their input into the Wilson and Callaghan Governments was negligible. While Cabinet posts were dominated by sophisticated English Labour politicians, the stereotyped Scottish Labour MP was a 'Jimmy', a Neanderthal politician of firm and unremarkable opinions, used to keeping his local party onside, probably a graduate from its ranks and unused to raising his eyes to the national horizon.

Scottish Labour produced the lobby fodder for the Labour governments of the 1970s, reliable Scottish foot soldiers who would dutifully vote the way their government wanted them to before some of them re-entered one of the many bars in the House of Commons. The fact that all Scottish MPs obeyed the same timetable, leaving Westminster on a Thursday night to travel back to Scotland, often staying up drinking on the Glasgow or Edinburgh sleeper, bound them together and forged close relationships across the party divide. It was a tough, masculine world, and its members were scathing about those who got above themselves.

In the twenty-first century, though, the flight from Heathrow has replaced the sleeper and the Jimmys are in the minority; the Scottish party is now home to Labour's officer class. The reasons for that transformation lie in the closed world of Scottish politics in the 1980s and '90s, a time when Scotland and England seemed to become two entirely different political cultures. As Scotland's politics became, to outsiders, an incomprehensible discussion about nationality, devolution and culture, they left Scotland to its own concerns. And while English commentators focused on their own backyards, the seeds of Britain's future began to be sown in Scotland.

New Labour is routinely thought of as a metropolitan plot, a virus which spread out from an Islington wine bar to the far corners of the kingdom, where it overcame the weakened resistance of politicians too demoralised by years of defeat to mount a decent defence of their real values. In fact, many of New Labour's most successful strategies were being worked out in Scotland in the 1980s, where Labour, while careful to keep up its working-class rhetoric, made extraordinary inroads into the Scottish middle classes.

The election of the consultant surgeon Sam Galbraith for the posh Glasgow seat of Strathkelvin and Bearsden in 1987 showed that middle-class Scots were willing to vote for successful professionals who stood under Labour's banner. In 1983, the seat had been a Tory one, held by the Scottish Conservative Chairman Michael Hirst, and after Galbraith retired the Labour vote fell by 7,000 in the 2001 election, indicating that much of the vote was a personal one.

The councils, too, proved that they could be an important breeding ground for New Labour talent. The Lothian Regional Council of the late 1980s and early 1990s proved particularly fertile. Alistair Darling, now Secretary of State for Transport, and Professor David Begg, now the Government's top transport adviser, were colleagues at the council. Whilst the image of Labour councils in England was being tarnished by the antics of the 'loony left', London councillors with their lesbian crèches and the rest, Edinburgh was a model New Labour council before the term was coined, skilfully cooperating with the city's old-fashioned business community and introducing a radical transport policy for the city which kept bus fares pegged to a flat rate for much of the late 1980s. In their willingness to work within the financial guidelines set by the Tory Scottish Office, they prefigured the first Blair Government, which famously pledged to work within Tory spending plans for its first term.

But the real reason why Scots have succeeded in entering the higher echelons of British politics with such conspicuous success is devolution. Whilst Labour at a national level had its revolution during the Kinnock era, in which the process of party reform and the disposal of the party's outdated ideological assets grew apace, Scottish Labour's internal revolution had come more than a decade earlier. The fight for Labour in

Scotland to adopt the policy of devolution had been as bloody and stressful as the battles over Clause Four, compulsory reselection by constituency parties and all the rest would prove in England. It pitted Labour MPs against each other, forging lasting alliances and eternal enmities. Carried on far from the attention of the political commentators of Fleet Street (who probably wouldn't have been interested in following its arcane twists and turns even if they had been able to), it engaged a whole generation of Scottish journalists who joined the fray as combatants. It was a cultural as well as a political battle, and those who survived the culture war emerged battle-hardened and with a degree of political sophistication which their English colleagues could only envy.

When Labour in Scotland committed to devolution in the days following the 1979 election victory of Mrs Thatcher, the policy allowed the party to position itself as a defender of Scotland's interests against a Conservative Party elected across the UK but with a strong south-of-England bias. The policy shored up a bulwark against Scottish Nationalism which allowed Labour to entrench its position in Scotland, and it meant that Scottish Labour politicians were working in a cultural, political zone quite different from their colleagues in the south. That identification between the aims of the party and the 'ethos' of Scotland, increasingly portrayed in centre-left terms of egalitarianism, equality and social integration, meant that Labour in Scotland prefigured Blair's attempts to forge the same kind of consensus in England. All the Blair rhetoric about New Labour being the 'political wing of the British people' was already a standing argument in Scotland, where Labour had positioned itself as uniquely connected to the hidden drivers of Scottish society and in a natural position to represent their values in government.

It is a profound irony: the forging of a policy that would partially separate Scotland from the Government of the United Kingdom was the very process which would eventually give Scottish politicians the skills to assume positions at the very top of the British Government.

Nor were these skills purely practical or strategic. Since the rise of the SNP as a serious electoral force in the late 1960s, every Scottish election has been a four-cornered fight, in which arguments about Scottish culture have been as important as pure policy. In more than 35 years of antagonism with the SNP, successful Scottish Labour politicians developed a highly sophisticated range of references. They could negotiate the difference between a nation and a state with ease, argue the case for Scotland's position within the British state with an almost continental degree of political sophistication; Antonio Gramsci's name was heard more often in Scottish Labour debates of the late 1980s and 1990s than that of Keir Hardie.

For years these seemed to be arcane skills, useful for a political scientist but unnecessary for a practising politician. But the introduction of political devolution in the United Kingdom has meant that these once abstruse ideas are becoming the intellectual fibre of politics. As British politicians try to untangle the practical impact of devolution on the workings of the House of Commons, and argue about the rights and wrongs of Scottish MPs voting on measures which will not affect their own constituents, many are clearly grappling with the new reality with some difficulty. Scots are at an advantage: it is as though the speakers of an obscure language once confined to a chilly northern kingdom have imposed it as the lingua franca of the south. No wonder they speak it with more authority and plausibility than anyone else.

The Scottish dominance of English politics is not just a matter of senior politicians elected from Scotland holding top English jobs. The 1997 election showed the amazing ability of Scots to penetrate into English seats. The 1997 and 2001 elections placed an unprecedented number of Scots in the House of Commons as members for English constituencies:

SCOTTISH-BORN MPS REPRESENTING ENGLISH SEATS AFTER THE 1997 GENERAL ELECTION

Michael Ancram – Conservative MP for Devizes since 1992, former MP for Edinburgh South and junior minister in the Scottish Office during the 1980s. London-born but from a Scottish family, he gained his law degree at Edinburgh University.

James Arbuthnot – Conservative MP for North East Hampshire since 1997, previously MP for Wanstead and Woodford

1987–97, who, though born in Deal, claims descent from James VI.

Norman Baker – Liberal Democrat MP for Lewes since 1997, born in Aberdeen.

Jackie Ballard – Liberal Democrat MP for Taunton since 1997, born in Dunoon.

Tony Blair – Labour MP for Sedgefield since 1983, born in Edinburgh.

Virginia Bottomley – Conservative MP for South West Surrey since 1984, born in Dunoon to English family.

David Clark – Labour MP for South Shields since 1979 (retired in 2001), born in Castle Douglas.

Ann Coffey – Labour MP for Stockport since 1992, born in Inverness.

Yvette Cooper – Labour MP for Pontefract and Castleford since 1997, born in Inverness. Wife of Gordon Brown's key adviser Ed Balls.

James Cran – Eurosceptic Conservative MP for Beverley and Holderness since 1997, previously MP for Beverley 1987–97, born in Kintore, Aberdeenshire.

Jim Cunningham – Labour MP for Coventry South since 1997, born in Coatbridge.

Jim Dobbin – Labour MP for Heywood and Middleton since 1997, born in Kincardine, Fife.

Iain Duncan Smith – former Conservative Party leader and MP for Chingford from 1992 and redrawn Chingford and Woodford since 1997, born in Edinburgh.

Michael Fallon – Conservative MP for Sevenoaks since 1997, previously MP for Darlington 1983–92, born in Perth. A member of the St Andrews mafia which included Michael Forsyth.

Jim Fitzpatrick – Labour MP for Poplar and Canning Town since 1997, born in Glasgow.

Eric Forth – Conservative MP for Bromley and Chislehurst since 1997, previously MP for Mid-Worcestershire 1983–97, born in Glasgow.

Liam Fox – Conservative MP for Woodspring since 1992, born in Lanarkshire.

Barry Gardiner – Labour MP for Brent North since 1997, born in Glasgow.

Ian Gibson – Labour MP for Norwich North since 1997, born in Dumfries.

Linda Gilroy – Labour MP for Plymouth Sutton since 1997, born in Moffat.

James Gray – Conservative MP for Wiltshire South since 1997, born in Glasgow. Alumnus of Glasgow University Tory Association, describes himself as '100 per cent Scot'. His father was the Very Revd Dr John R. Gray of Dunblane Cathedral and a Moderator of the General Assembly of the Church of Scotland.

Doug Henderson – Labour MP for Newcastle-upon-Tyne North since 1987, born in Edinburgh.

Bernard Jenkin – Conservative MP for North Essex since 1997, born in London but proud to declare himself 'three-quarters Scottish'. The son of Patrick Jenkin, the Edinburgh-born MP for Wanstead and Woodford 1964–87.

Tessa Jowell – Labour MP for Dulwich since 1992 and redrawn Dulwich and West Norwood since 1997, born in Aberdeen. Secretary of State for Media, Culture and Sport since 2001.

Andy King – Labour MP for Rugby and Kennilworth since 1997, born in Bellshill, Lanarkshire.

Tom King – Conservative MP for Bridgwater since 1970 (retired in 2001), born in Glasgow.

Eleanor Laing – Conservative MP for Epping Forest since 1997, born in Glasgow.

Jacqui Lait – Conservative MP for Beckenham since November 1997, born in Giffnock.

Andrew Love – Labour MP for Edmonton since 1997, born in Greenock.

Stephen McCabe – Labour MP for Birmingham Hall Green since 1997, born in Johnstone.

Ian McCartney – Labour MP for Makerfield since 1987, born in Lennoxtown.

Anne McIntosh – Conservative MP for Vale of York since 1997, born in Edinburgh.

Shona McIsaac – Labour MP for Cleethorpes since 1997, born in Dunfermline.

David Maclean – Conservative MP for Penrith and the Borders, since 1983, born on the Black Isle.

Denis MacShane – Labour MP for Rotherham since 1994, born in Glasgow.

Fiona MacTaggart – Labour MP for Slough since 1997, born in London but daughter of the Glasgow multi-millionaire Sir Ian Auld MacTaggart.

John McWilliam – Labour MP for Blaydon since 1979, born in Grangemouth.

George Mudie – Labour MP for Leeds East since 1992, born in Dundee.

Doug Naysmith – Labour and Co-operative Party MP for Bristol North West since 1997, born in Musselburgh.

Bridget Prentice – Labour MP for Lewisham East since 1992, born in Glasgow.

Gordon Prentice – Labour MP for Pendle since 1992, born in Edinburgh.

Richard Shepherd – Conservative MP for Aldridge Brownhills since 1979, born in Aberdeen.

Geoffrey Johnson Smith – Conservative MP for Wealden since 1983, born in Glasgow.

Ian Stewart – Labour MP for Eccles since 1997, born in Blantyre.

Ann Taylor – Labour MP for Dewsbury since 1987, former Leader of the House, born in Motherwell.

Teddy Taylor – Conservative MP for Rochford and Southend East since 1997, born in Glasgow.

George Turner – Labour MP for Norfolk North West since 1997, born in Corby but 'the son of Scots parents who had migrated in the 1930s in search of work'.

It's an impressive list, and even more so when compared to its opposite: the list of Scottish constituencies represented by English-born MPs. In Scotland during the same period, only seven MPs were born outside the country: Malcolm Bruce, Liberal Democrat MP for Gordon, born in Birkenhead; Malcolm Savidge, Labour MP for Aberdeen North, born in Surrey; Norman Goodman, Labour MP for Greenock and Inverclyde, a Scot born in Hull (retired in 2001); Alistair Darling, Labour MP for Edinburgh Central, born in London; George Foulkes, Labour/Co-operative MP for Carrick, Cumnock and Doon Valley, born in Oswestry; Tony

Worthington, MP for Clydebank and Milngavie, born in Herefordshire; and Donald Gorrie, Liberal Democrat MP for Edinburgh West (now a member of the Scottish Parliament), born in Dehra Dun, India.

There are clearly anomalies in both lists: the fact that Virginia Bottomley was born in Dunoon does not make her Scottish any more than the fact Donald Gorrie was born in Dehra Dun makes him Indian. Nevertheless, even after removing names which it is clearly silly to think of as Scottish (Yvette Cooper or Tom King, for example) from the first list, it is clear that 1997 marked a sea change in British politics in the sheer number of Scots holding elected seats at Westminster.

Nor, as the above list shows, do the Scots who hold English seats come exclusively from one party. Though Labour's dominance in Scotland during the 1980s seemed to some observers to make 'Scottish' synonymous with 'socialist', every party in England seems willing to open its candidates' list to Scottish applicants. In the 2005 election, the Conservatives, the party most closely identified with English interests, nonetheless fielded more Scottish candidates for English seats than ever before. Some, like Sir Malcolm Rifkind, who re-entered the commons as the MP for Kensington and Chelsea after a failed attempt to retake his Edinburgh Pentlands seat, had shown themselves unable to hold a Scottish constituency. Others, like the journalist Michael Gove, selected on his first attempt for the plum Conservative constituency of Surrey Heath, had never sought selection in Scotland. Scots stood as candidates for every party fighting for English votes in 2005; by and large English nationalism remains sufficiently diffuse as to offer no barrier to one of the most fascinating political phenomena of our time.

There is nothing new about Scots holding English seats – one of the most pronounced effects of the Act of Union was the speed with which the Scots who came to England started to take English parliamentary seats in the House of Commons. Linda Colley points out that between 1754 and 1790, 60 Scots fell into this category. But those 60, over a 36-year period in the eighteenth century, are a mere trickle compared to more than 30 sitting in one parliament today. Today's Scots have made far greater inroads into English political life in the early twenty-first century than their ancestors did in the eighteenth, and far greater than English politicians have made into Scotland.

Because that final statement flies in the face of what many Scottish people feel about their own country, it is worth examining for a moment. It is certainly the case that Scotland has had its fair share of English or Anglo-Scottish MPs: before the Second World War large swathes of the Scottish countryside were held by London-based English or Scottish QCs. Winston Churchill famously represented Dundee before the First World War, and William Wedgwood Benn, the father of Tony Benn, held Edinburgh Leith. But that number has been in steady decline, a decline which has coincided with the rise of political nationalism in Scotland.

It may be that Nationalism has realigned domestic Scottish politics to such a degree that politicians from outside the country find it much harder to engage in the Scottish debate. It may be, too, that Nationalism has pressurised those parties standing against the SNP to select candidates who cannot be accused of being unsympathetic to Scotland, or who, once they open their mouths, do not seem to be outsiders. Or it may be a sign of the closed, almost tribal, nature of Scottish politics in the late twentieth and early twenty-first century. Either way, despite the fact that Scotland is now home to some 400,000 English people, since the late 1960s English candidates have found it increasingly difficult to be selected for Scottish seats, and once selected, find it much harder to win.

But the opposite is clearly not the case. Bridget Prentice is the able, likeable Glasgow-born Labour MP for Lewisham East, a seat which she has held since 1992. I went to see her in her impressive corner office in Portcullis House, with a commanding view over the Thames to the former headquarters of the Greater London Council (GLC), a site now occupied by the Saatchi Gallery, where the nearby London Eye revolves once every 20 minutes.

'I remember when I was first elected in 1992 and London of course had done particularly badly in 1987 because of the mad, lunatic, far-left policies that your man across the road [then GLC leader Ken Livingstone] was advocating.

'I remember coming into the tearoom and there was a group of Scottish MPs and they recognised that I was a London member, though I hadn't spoken to them, and I was a woman.

And they said, "Hmph, it's all your fault we lost the election because of the way you London folk behave." And I said in my Glasgow accent, "Yes, and we had a bigger swing in London last time than you had in Scotland last time."'

Prentice, who joined the Labour Party in London, is following in the footsteps of Labour leader Keir Hardie, who stood successfully as the Labour candidate for South West Ham in 1892. Then, Hardie's working-class background ensured an easy identification with his constituents. Now, Prentice says that she would find it hard to represent a seat which did not have a sense of community like the one she remembers from Glasgow.

Prentice and many of her Labour colleagues representing English seats are proud to stress their connections to Scotland, but other prominent Scots in British politics have always had a looser connection to Scotland and seem to have made far greater concessions to English society. It would take the linguistic detective work of a Professor Higgins to uncover the Shetland accent under Norman Lamont's anglicised purr, but Lamont, the Conservative Chancellor of the Exchequer in John Major's Government, was proud to take the title 'Lord Lamont of Lerwick' when he entered the House of Lords after the Conservatives' defeat in 1997.

Born in Lerwick, but educated at Loretto, one of Scotland's more highly regarded private schools, he was part of a Cambridge mafia of future Conservative Cabinet ministers. As a contemporary of Kenneth Clarke, John Selwyn Gummer and Norman Fowler, Lamont has always seemed to be a model of self-assuredness and metropolitan sophistication. When he took his family on a tour of the Shetlands, one of his children asked their mother, 'Was Daddy really brought up here?'

I met him in his offices just off Park Lane, where he explained the British and Shetland aspects of his identity were to the fore. 'In terms of nationality, I've always thought of myself as British then Scottish. I've always thought of myself as from Shetland. Shetland's obviously not a nationality, but in some ways Shetland does not always have wonderful relations with Edinburgh or view the rest of Scotland altogether benignly. One can exaggerate this, but I think there is a kind of slightly self-conscious quality. I find it very easy to be British first, Scottish second, but because I don't have the obvious trace of a Scottish accent, though I'm sure if I was talking to my mother on the telephone it would come out, people say, "You don't sound Scottish", but I think of myself as Scottish, of course.'

Though Lamont says that he toyed with the idea of seeking selection for a Scottish seat after Kingston-upon-Thames, which he represented for more than 20 years, had its boundaries redrawn, he accepts that his political and business life in England has separated him from the political debates which have been raging in Scotland over the last 30 years.

'I feel quite divorced from Scottish politics. I can't understand what's going on. I am a unionist. I think of myself as British and Scottish. Some of the things that Scottish nationalists say some of the time I find deeply offensive – the hostility to the English. I think [SNP leader] Alex Salmond is a charming man, but I don't like that at all. I think there is a chippiness in Scotland, there is a feeling that the English are responsible for everything. I thought *Braveheart* was an absurd film, an absolutely absurd film, and I didn't enjoy it at all but I think a lot of Scots identify with that attitude of mind.'

When I pose a version of Norman Tebbit's 'Cricket Test' to Norman Lamont, he is quick to say that he would support Scotland against England every time, but Lamont (whose habit of pronouncing his name with the emphasis on the second syllable occasions some derision in Scotland) is clearly anglicised, partly because, historically, the Conservative Party expected its leaders to speak in a certain way. Because of his Anglophilia, he strongly dislikes the rising tide of English nationalism, viewing England's traditional reticence on the subject of its own nationality as a sign of its confidence. He also doubts whether there is any mileage in one of the arguments currently being aired in response to the power of the Scots: English votes for English members in the House of Commons. 'Devolution is very higgledy-piggledy and there is something to be said for the argument that you should have symmetry between England and Wales, that English MPs should only vote on English legislation, but how you would do this in the House of Lords I can't imagine. Am I Scottish or am I English?'

Lamont's confusion is typical of a generation of Scots who achieved their political and business ambitions south of the border, but their day may be ending. The number of Scots representing English seats has so far afforded little comment in England, though the increased awareness of nationality which has followed Scottish devolution may start to change that, creating a situation where nationalist sentiment and unconscious cultural prejudices could endanger cross-border political careers.

In the meantime, recognition of the increased political power of the Scots has started to galvanise the English political Establishment. In January 2004, Lord Barnett, who devised the 25-year-old formula which sets government spending levels in the different countries of the United Kingdom, was roused from a long political slumber to declare that he considered his formula to be outdated and unfair and that it was only retained because of the power of the 'Scottish mafia'.

Barnett's formula, which pegs expenditure to a series of indicators, including population levels, was always a piece of political sleight of hand dressed up in the mock authority of economics, and the growing antagonism towards it across the political spectrum suggests that within a decade it will be substantially readdressed, or dismantled entirely.

More pressing is the issue of whether the apparent iniquity of Scots voting on purely English measures in the House of Commons can be turned into the focus of a serious political argument about the power of the Scots. The Conservatives have turned the action of the Scottish MPs who supported the Government over tuition fees in January 2004 into a test case on the unfairness of devolution, and have argued that English MPs are discriminated against because they cannot vote on legislation in Scotland whilst their Scottish colleagues can vote on purely English matters: Tam Dalyell's West Lothian Question. One response is that English MPs alone should be permitted to vote on English affairs. (Though, ironically, many of those 'English MPs' are in fact Scots.) But the logic of this argument – that Westminster should, at least some of the time, stop being the United Kingdom Parliament and stand in as the Parliament for England – worries others in the Conservative Party because it would be a dilution of the party's traditional unionism. Others note quietly that the issue didn't seem to worry the Conservatives when English MPs voted for the poll tax to be introduced in Scotland in 1989, prior to its introduction south of the border.

Another Scot representing an English seat, David Maclean, the Conservative MP for Penrith and the Borders who was born on the Black Isle, believes that sooner or later the Conservatives' stance will have to change.

'We believe in the UK Parliament but the UK Parliament is now unbalanced. I am a second-class citizen in the UK Parliament because I go in there and I have no right to vote on devolved issues, but, similarly, I don't want Scottish MPs voting on English issues. That causes English nationalism – that causes resentment, and it is unfair. It's a dangerous argument to make, but I think we should look again at purely English votes for English matters.'

It is a political dilemma which the Conservative Party has never had to face before. But then this is an unprecedented situation, as even T.W.H. Crosland might have recognised.

In the past, Scots have held high government office, led their parties and their country. In the past, Scots have represented English seats in the House of Commons. But the Scots have never done such things at the same time as a Scottish Parliament sits in Edinburgh, or at a time when Scottish political life has become almost hermetically sealed against outsiders. That fact makes the Scottish takeover of English political life even more remarkable.

Indeed, there are signs that some English opinion formers now accept the current situation as inevitable. In May 2004, *The Independent* commissioned a poll of experts to look forward to the general election of 2008. Its political scientists, journalists and observers gazed into their crystal balls and came up with a striking prediction; Sir Malcolm Rifkind would lead the Tories, Gordon Brown would lead Labour and Sir Menzies Campbell would have replaced Charles Kennedy as leader of the Lib Dems. The shared nationality of the three men predicted to lead Britain's main political parties passed without comment: if English society so meekly accepts that its political future will be determined by clashes between powerful Scots then the eternal battle between Scotland and England has entered a fascinating new phase.

The English have always had a set of handy stereotypes available for the Scots. But next to the engineer, the doctor and the bank manager, those trusty images of the Scot as a reliable second-in-command, they now need to find another: the Scot as boss.

CHAPTER 2

The Scottish Fourth Estate

In the late 1920s, the English journalist H.V. Morton got in his car and drove around Scotland. By trade, Morton was a newspaperman, but his books *In Search of England* and *In Search of Ireland* had become a highly profitable sideline, establishing him as one of the great travel writers, a whimsical visitor with a reporter's eye for a telling incident.

His book on Scotland came close to completing a full set; *In Search of Wales* would come out the following year. But whereas his books on England and Ireland were loving portraits of countries he knew well, he came to Scotland for the first time knowing next to nothing about it. After a leisurely journey through the Borders by motor car and visits to Edinburgh, Glasgow and Dundee, which he packed with historical anecdotes and vivid pen portraits, he reached Aberdeen. Though he had never been to the city before, he had met some of its citizens:

> English Journalism is red with the hair of Aberdonians. Newspaper proprietors feel better when these hard-heads are about, because they reduce to the lowest minimum the risk of libel actions. The dreadful blue pencils of the Aberdonians travel cautiously over the world's news, cutting out the cackle and getting down to the bare bones of reality. A pencil in such hands ceases to be a pencil: it becomes a surgical implement . . . I hit up against the Aberdeen mentality when, as a young journalist from the provinces, I took

the post of junior sub-editor on one of the big London dailies. One night a reporter wrote a short article stating that the fig-tree in St Paul's Churchyard had given birth to seven figs. In the course of a long night's work I sub-edited this and put a headline on it and forgot it. Three days later I was carpeted by an Aberdonian night editor.

'Did you do this?' he asked, flinging a clipping at me.

'I did.'

'Don't you know,' he cried, hitting his desk at every word, 'that the fir-r-st-requirement-in-your-profession-is-accuracy? . . . St Paul's is five minutes' walk from this office! Did ye not think of running down to count the figs?'

Morton was exaggerating, but only just. The Scots had established their dominance in London's weekly, fortnightly and periodical press as early as the 1820s, when John Gibson Lockhart, Sir Walter Scott's son-in-law, was tempted to move to London to edit the *Quarterly Review*. Thomas Carlyle would leave Scotland in 1834 and others, like the Ibsen expert William Archer, who was considered to be the most important theatre critic in London before the First World War, would follow him as the century went on, leaving contemporaries lamenting that the brain drain had reduced Edinburgh to the status of a provincial town when it had once been a capital city with its own distinctive and high-minded culture.

Edinburgh's loss was felt in London, where the Scots soon made their mark: the first editors of *The Spectator* and *The Economist* were Scots, dedicated to scrutinising British life from the centre, and they were soon joined by others who helped shape Britain's print culture in a profoundly Scottish mode.

The Scottish writers, editors and sub-editors who left their homes in the middle years of the nineteenth century were driven by the temporary stagnation of the newspaper industry in Scotland, and also by the realisation that their backgrounds were peculiarly suited for life in a newspaper office.

The Scottish education system, which is often described as one of the roots of Scots success in London, played its part: literacy levels were unusually high in Scotland, the presentation of rhetorical arguments was encouraged and, crucially, Scots were urged to be generalists who could devote their attention to a wide range of subjects, from literature and science to religion and current affairs. Dr Johnson had observed that Scottish education was so widely spread about that no one man could get a decent meal from it, but it was the perfect preparation for life as a newspaperman, where a wide and thin base of knowledge was a greater asset than a deep specialism.

The heroic figure of Robert Mudie is illustrative of the trend. Born near Forfar, he travelled to London in 1820 and eventually became editor of the *Sunday Times*. He supplemented his journalist's salary with hack bookwork and by the time he died in a debtors' prison had written 90 volumes on scientific, philosophical and cultural subjects.

Most of this work was badly paid until the early 1920s, and many Scots scrabbled around writing odd pieces or submitting work under a raft of pseudonyms. By the 1860s, London newspapers were starting to benefit from a steady stream of Scottish journalists coming south as graduates of Scotland's city dailies.

In 1896, Charles Cooper, the editor of *The Scotsman*, looked back on his life as a Scottish newspaperman in London in his autobiography *An Editor's Retrospect*. He had been sent to the capital as *The Scotsman*'s first correspondent in London and was instrumental in breaking the monopoly which the London daily newspapers had over the press gallery at Westminster. He introduced other innovations too, including new printing presses, and pushed for the introduction of a cheap and reliable telegraph service which could send accurate copy from London to Scotland almost instantaneously. It had an effect as important as the introduction of the Internet today, but Cooper complained about the cost.

In the twentieth century, the Scots domination of Fleet Street was almost entirely due to the influence of one man, Max Aitken, Lord Beaverbrook. Beaverbrook was a Canadian Scot, like Roy Thomson, the newspaper magnate and founder of Scottish Television, and like Thomson had an idiosyncratic sense of his national identity and a desire to employ Scots in key positions. The *Scottish Daily Express*, founded by Beaverbrook to be a 'word for Scotland', soon started serving as a feeder of talented and ambitious Scottish journalists to London. But

Beaverbrook's interest in Scotland didn't stop there; he also rated Scots as editors and appointed many of them to head his titles. The *Daily Express* had a run of three Scottish editors in the early 1970s, but the real Scottish journalist's home from home was the *Sunday Express*, which for almost 60 years was edited by Scots. The most remarkable, in every sense of the word, was John Junor.

John Junor was editor of the *Sunday Express* for an astonishing 32 years at a time when it was one of the most popular Sundays in Britain. Mercurial, irascible, fiercely loyal and scathingly critical, he ran his empire with an iron will. In her book *Home Truths*, his daughter, the journalist and Royal biographer Penny Junor, describes how her father's prodigious energy and attention to detail were marshalled by his love of routine. He would rise every morning at the same time, eat the same breakfast each day, catch the same train to work and return at the same time in the evening. But while Junor's life was organised with military precision, he was renowned for his wilful, almost random, prejudices. The Royal family, British tradition and Selina Scott were good, so good, in fact, that he would hear nothing said against them; black people and Irish people were doubtful; homosexuals, criminals, the IRA and 'do-gooders' were beyond the pale. Junor also had unprintable opinions about men who wore hats, men who smoked pipes and men who drank white wine.

But there was much more to Junor than this eccentric mixture of prejudices. He was the first newspaper editor to sense the changing mood of the country and started to publish pieces hostile to the Royal family in the mid-1980s. After a run-in with a couple of young policemen, he became increasingly critical of the police, and his slavish adoration of some members of the Establishment didn't stop him from thinking that many were bloody fools.

But Junor preserved many of his strongest prejudices for his native Scotland. Once he spiked a piece by a journalist who had stayed at a hotel in Scotland and reported that he had cereal for breakfast, not porridge. When he was told that there had been no porridge on the menu, Junor declared, 'Nonsense, of course there was porridge, there's always porridge in Scotland.'

And if Scotland was a land running with milk and porridge,

it was also a place which was immune to the passing fads and fancies of metropolitan London. Along with 'pass the sickbag, Alice', one of Sir John's most famous coinages was his valorisation of Auchtermuchty, the Fife town most famous for siring the great Scottish accordionist Jimmy Shand. In Junor's prose, Auchtermuchty became a pre-lapsarian Eden of settled morals and down-to-earth attitudes. Black people? Not in Auchtermuchty. Trade unions? Definitely not. And no homosexual was ever to be found in Fife. But Junor's adoption of Auchtermuchty was a calculated, not an instinctive, decision. Penny Junor told me, 'It was his Brigadoon, a sample of real honest life. He found the name because he was a member of the Royal and Ancient Golf Club and when I was at St Andrews University he used to come up to play golf and visit me, and he would go and visit the Glasgow offices of the *Sunday Express*, hire a car there and drive through Auchtermuchty, and the name took his fancy. In fact, he couldn't decide whether to use Auchtermuchty or Ecclefechan but decided Auchtermuchty had the better ring.

'He was very proud of his roots. He would not in a month of Sundays have wanted to go back to Scotland, but he was always fiercely proud of being Scottish and being working-class Scottish. The great thing about coming from Scotland with a Scottish accent was that he became classless, and he was able to move in the most elevated circles without feeling that he had to change his accent at all.'

And Junor's sense of community was a vital weapon in the battle for readers. He had a keen awareness of the interests, preoccupations and anxieties of Middle England, and they found their way into the *Sunday Express* and the column which he wrote after he retired. But as well as sensing the wider community of *Sunday Express* readers, he also ran his newspaper as an organic entity and, like many Scots, retained a keen sense of the importance of kinship. When he succeeded in luring Peter McKay, now the *Daily Mail*'s Diary columnist, to London from Aberdeen, he took a fatherly interest in the affairs of the young man. Who, he demanded, would do his laundry? Would he send it home to his mother? The thing to do was to buy nylon shirts. They could be rinsed in a sink at the end of a day and by the morning they would be dry. So keen was Junor on the idea of these shirts that he advanced the reporter £10 from his first wage packet to go and buy them. It was a bizarre incident, but Junor was exhibiting much the same sense of his responsibilities to new arrivals from Scotland as Victorian Scots in the capital had.

Despite his ambivalence about establishing a permanent base in Scotland, Junor was tempted back in the 1980s to appear on a BBC Scotland television programme called *Two of a Kind*, which aimed to introduce two successful Scots whose careers had mirrored each other. Junor was paired with Andrew Neil, the then editor of the *Sunday Times* and later the publisher of the *Scotsman* titles. The researcher on the programme was Allan Little, now the BBC correspondent in Paris, who expressed surprise that these two towering Scottish figures of London journalism had never met each other before. On paper they had a lot in common: both were newspaper editors and both were proud of their Scottish roots, but on the screen there was little chemistry – the two were very different characters. Junor, the pugnacious old-style newspaperman, had made a successful career out of using his version of traditional Scottish values as a stick to beat the excesses of London society. Neil, on the New Right, preferred to confront British, and eventually Scottish, society with a view of the world and the importance of the market gathered in the United States.

If many of Junor's views about his native Scotland seem to come from the Kailyard, that is hardly surprising. Scottish sentimental writing, with its valediction of hometown values, was a strong influence on the careers of many Scottish journalists throughout the twentieth century and can be seen even in those whose careers seemed to shrug it off.

In one of the few setbacks of Junor's early career, he lost out on the chance to write a current affairs column in the *Express* to James Cameron, then a rising star and later the hero of many Fleet Street newspapermen for his pioneering foreign affairs coverage, buccaneering personal style and prodigious capacity for drink.

Cameron's father, William Ernest Cameron, was a son of the manse who practised as an English barrister at the Inner Temple. He found the life tough and seemed to be a singularly ineffective lawyer, so he sought to supplement his income by writing for the papers. For some time he contributed a weekly column to the *Glasgow Evening Citizen*, but his real salvation was producing sentimental adventures for journals like *Strand Magazine, Answers* and *Titbits*. In adulthood, Cameron junior kept his father's books lined up on his shelf, titles like *Such and Such Things, The Devil's Due, A Maid and her Money* and others. As writing such stuff was seen to be incompatible with a life at the Bar, Cameron senior wrote under a pen name, Mark Allerton.

James Cameron's father ended his days in a hotel room in Dundee, writing stories and slowly drinking himself to death. This isolation portended his son's, when he travelled the world as a foreign correspondent, holed up in hotels with just a typewriter and a drink for company. When James Cameron quit the *Express* in protest at its proprietor Lord Beaverbrook's habit of sniping at the post-war Labour Government, he took a job writing for the *Picture Post*, where he was attracted by the chance to write extended pieces. One of his first assignments, alongside the photographer Bert Hardy, was to cover the Korean War.

What Cameron and Hardy found horrified them. The UN-backed South Korean forces of Dr Syngman Rhee were oppressing the North Koreans who opposed him, despoiling whole villages and brutalising the men they found there. Cameron said later that the starving huddled men he encountered in the custody of the South Korean forces reminded him of the detainees at Belsen, they were so malnourished.

Cameron's piece for the *Picture Post,* neutrally entitled 'An Appeal to the United Nations' and accompanied by Hardy's bleak photographs, caused a political furore. Edward Hulton, the *Post*'s proprietor wanted the piece removed. Cameron and the *Post*'s editor, Tom Hopkinson, refused. Hopkinson was sacked and Cameron resigned, again in protest at the interference of a proprietor. But the resignations had shaken Hulton and damaged his reputation, which until then had been high. Eventually the magazine folded.

Cameron's career soared. He covered the atomic bomb tests at Bikini Atoll, reported on the escape of the Dalai Lama as the Chinese occupied Tibet, and spent as much time as possible in India, the country which he loved most of all. A half-century before, Scots in the service of the British Empire had administered its affairs in far-off provinces around the world. In the 1950s and '60s, with the British Empire disintegrating and the new superpowers of America, China and Russia assuming many of its old imperatives, James Cameron became a globetrotting journalist, often first on the scene in a crisis, who would secure a hotel room, a telephone and a convenient bar, and fire off tersely worded and beautifully crafted copy for the *News Chronicle* at home.

Cameron's politics were broadly left wing, but his real instincts were anti-authoritarian. His scathing portrait of Albert Schweitzer, the philosopher and theologian whose hospital in French Equatorial Africa Cameron found to be squalid and inefficient, was as shocking in its way as Christopher Hitchens' demolition of Mother Teresa of Calcutta decades later. Schweitzer was revered as a living saint. Cameron found him a sanctimonious humbug whose hospital was a failure and a monument to his own hubris; even benign authoritarianism made his hackles rise.

In marching against the atomic bomb and serving as one of the founders of CND, many of his contemporaries believed that Cameron had crossed the line between being a reporter and being an activist, but his insights and the sheer brilliance of his writing spoke for themselves.

A later career in television, fronting documentaries where he had the rare ability to deliver pieces to camera which were fluent, self-deprecating and entirely off-the-cuff, provided further exposure for his talents, but his demons were catching up with him. Like his father, he had become dependent on alcohol and years of chain smoking had taken a toll on his health. A car accident while travelling in a jeep to cover the Bangladesh Emergency led to a string of heart attacks, and he never fully recovered.

Aside from the journalist's vices of booze and cigarettes, Junor and Cameron seem to have had little in common. But both were towering figures in their profession, men who were not so much Scottish journalists – though in their different ways they were both profoundly shaped by Scotland – as leading British journalists who happened to be Scots.

The era of Cameron and Junor is long gone in Fleet Street, and many of its characteristic vices and virtues have faded to be replaced by a culture of longer hours and professional presenteeism, in which journalists are more likely to be found sitting in a cubbyhole accessing the world through the telephone and the Internet than actually out in the world nursing contacts through an afternoon of drinking intended to secure a particular insight. But the Scottish presence on Fleet Street is undiminished.

Charles Wilson, once the husband of Anne Robinson and a man whom Junor tipped for a job as his deputy, edited *The Times* for seven years from 1983 to 1990. Andrew Neil served as the controversial editor of the *Sunday Times* during its dispute with the print unions over the move to Wapping and saw the paper enlarge and spread into separate sections.

Scottish journalists were also highly politicised, and not just like Harry Conroy, the Scottish General Secretary of the NUJ, or Bobby Campbell, the Communist Party stalwart who struck up an unlikely rapprochement with Andrew Neil when they worked together on the *Sunday Times* and came to Edinburgh when Neil became publisher of *The Scotsman* to set up the paper's online coverage. Scottish journalists were also becoming increasingly politicised on the issue of Scotland itself.

Neal Ascherson became something of a sage for those in Scotland who were looking to combine their commitment to Scottish independence with a European world-view. Writing in *The Observer* and in the *Independent on Sunday,* his allusive and erudite columns, combining learned references to Polish history and elaborate geological analogies to the shifting of tectonic plates under the surface of British politics, made him a home-grown, engagé intellectual anxious to usher in Scotland's own Velvet Revolution. In the run-up to Scotland's abortive devolution referendum in 1979, Ascherson returned to Scotland as the political editor of *The Scotsman*, a move which was heralded on that newspaper's front page and taken, in itself, as a sign that Scotland was moving to the centre stage of British politics.

In common with many journalists of the time, Ascherson didn't confine himself to reporting on the subject of Scottish politics; he was also a founder member of the short-lived breakaway Scottish Labour Party. The SLP was founded by the former Labour MP Jim Sillars and his protégé Alex Neil with

the twin aims of establishing socialism and independence for
Scotland. The party enjoyed a fantastic press at first, partly
because it was led by Sillars, one of the most inspiring political
thinkers and speakers of his generation, and partly because it
contained so many journalists. But the honeymoon was short
lived – the SLP collapsed after being infiltrated by the
International Marxist Group, a precursor of the 'entryism'
which bedevilled the British Labour Party in the 1980s. Then,
British Labour staggered, but recovered, and was able to
reassert itself. The tiny SLP, despite its support from Scotland's
intellectual left, did not.

In the aftermath of 1979, Ascherson moved back to London,
where, now devoted to writing books, he also teaches at the
University of London about 'social archaeology', a process by
which states use archaeology to uncover significant myths about
their own foundations.

His recent book *Stone Voices* is a learned meditation on
Scotland's political and social history, part autobiography, part
archaeological monograph. Ascherson has a profound
commitment to un-puzzling Scotland, to getting to grips with its
apparently maddening politics and to relating it to developments
in Europe, particularly eastern Europe. From his position as a
seasoned observer of the Scottish political scene, he confesses
that he finds much of the current political environment
something of a puzzle: 'Is there a Scottish ingredient in current
politics? You could interpret a lot of what New Labour stands
for in terms of Scottish Enlightenment attitudes, I think; but it
would be quite impossible to interpret it in terms of the Scottish
socialist movement of the late eighteenth and nineteenth
centuries – it's alien to that. What would the ILP think of what
Tony Blair is doing now? They'd be horrified. Keir Hardie
would go bananas, but there is something about [New Labour's
commitment to] hard work, contribution, competing hard and
yet not being entirely individualistic – cohesion in the sense of
being a collective, a community.'

For much of his life, Ascherson has lived in London, and
though he confesses that the life of the London Scots has never
concerned him too deeply, he does see them as conforming to a
model which has been identical wherever the Scots have settled.

'Something which has always interested me is the patterns of

Scottish colonialism, Scottish settlement outside Scotland, one of which, of course, is [settlement in] England. There are certain patterns which are deeply, deeply persistent, whether it is in Singapore, Poland or London. These patterns suggest to me that the Scots are naturally oligarchic and authoritarian, and they create these oligarchic structures to which people belong and then they recruit younger people into them, from the home country, and within those structures they are extremely communitarian – they put the collective structure first as long as you do what you're told. They are authoritarian but they look after their own with often quite touching care and effort to find out what is going on with people.'

The failure of the 1979 devolution referendum prevented Ascherson's permanent return to Edinburgh, but when devolution was eventually passed in Scotland in 1997, Scottish journalists were in the forefront again, covering the story: some, like John Lloyd of the *New Statesman* and the *Financial Times,* as gently sceptical supporters, others, like Kevin Toolis of *The Guardian*, as implacable critics.

For many London-based Scottish journalists, coverage of Scotland's debates on devolution seemed to serve as an unpleasant reminder of just why they left Scotland in the first place.

Toolis's piece, 'Scotland the Vainglorious', in *The Guardian* of 24 April 1999, is a detailed attack on Scottish myth-making about national identity. Born near Edinburgh's South Clerk Street, Toolis left Edinburgh at the age of 21.

> We were working class and proud. We loathed the Scottish middle class, who constantly betrayed Scotland by sucking up to the English, changing their accents, moving south, and generally joining in with those Sassenach bastards . . . What is Scottishness? No one, as yet, has the answer. I hope, as a Scot, that it is something more than the bundle of myths and hatred that I grew up with. I wish we had no need for it at all.

This article, and many others, showed the flipside of Scottish fears that emigrants will forget about their home country: many London-based Scottish journalists and writers seem more preoccupied with Scotland than those who stay at home. Writing in the *London Review of Books* on 31 October 2002, Andrew O'Hagan reviewed Ascherson's *Stone Voices*. As a Hallowe'en gift it was more trick than treat. 'Scotland's Self-pity', O'Hagan's lengthy article, fingers Scots for being touchy, spoiled and 'addled with punitive needs and false memory syndrome'. 'A half-hearted nation will want to hold fast to its grievances,' O'Hagan writes. 'In that sense Scotland has done well.'

For all Scotland became a bigger feature of Fleet Street's news coverage in the run-up to devolution, the 1997 result did not provoke the flood of journalists to the north which had been gearing up in 1979. But unlike then, Scots in what remains of Fleet Street are not purely backroom boys and sub-editors. The number of Scottish columnists in today's daily newspapers reflects not just the quality of individual Scottish journalists but the range of Scottish routes to the centre of British journalism.

Euan Ferguson of *The Observer* came to the paper in the wake of Andrew Jaspan, then the editor of *Scotland on Sunday*. Jaspan's career at *The Observer* was short-lived but Ferguson hung on. Ferguson and the right-wing commentator and editor of *The Times* on Saturday, Michael Gove, had served together as trainees on the Aberdeen *Press and Journal* and left the paper over the strike which dented its reputation in the early 1990s. Andrew McKee, now obituaries editor of the *Daily Telegraph,* and Deborah Orr, the wife of Will Self and one-time editor of the *Guardian* magazine, came to the paper directly from university in Glasgow, as did Kate Muir, who has served as a *Times* foreign correspondent in New York and Paris. Her new column in the *Times* Saturday magazine allows her to go on 'dates' with people she wants to meet and then write about them. 'But I realise,' she says 'just how disproportionately Scottish my list is. I guess that just shows how much my mental list of celebrities is determined by a Scottish mindset.'

'I was always quite determined not to live in London permanently,' explains Kirsty Wark, the Scottish interrogatrix on BBC television's *Newsnight.* 'I've turned down work which would keep me down there, but I'm astonished that people are astonished when I tell them that I get the sleeper home after presenting *Newsnight.* In America, people commute huge distances to work. Why shouldn't I work in one world and live in another? I feel equally at home in London, I just choose to sleep in Glasgow.'

When Kirsty Wark sits down to present *Newsnight*, or Andrew Marr prepares to deliver a piece to camera about the Blair Government's latest upheavals, they, and the countless other Scots working for the BBC, can thank the fact that in 1922 John Reith posted a letter.

The young Scottish engineer, a 33-year-old bachelor, was living at the Cavendish Club in Piccadilly and applying, with a mounting sense of doom, for jobs which he hoped would stretch him. The advertisement in the *Morning Post* was authoritative but vague: the British Broadcasting Company hoped to fill several key posts, among them general manager, chief engineer, director of programmes and secretary.

Typically, Reith, who had lamented in his diary a few months before of being 'conscious of abilities which almost overwhelm me', applied to be the boss. He had no idea what broadcasting was, but he had some sense of the way to get a job.

After belatedly looking up *Who's Who* to check the entry for Sir William Noble, the chairman of the Broadcasting Committee and the man who would lead his interview panel, Reith realised that he had omitted a crucial qualification. He retrieved the letter and added a line to it: 'I am an Aberdonian and it is probable that you knew my family.'

Reith, who was in fact a Glaswegian, though one born in Stonehaven, had found the key which would unlock the rest of his life. His days of applying for jobs as Director of Housing for the City of Glasgow or at the Ministry of Munitions were behind him. On 13 December, Reith was interviewed and Noble greeted him 'with all the cordiality of an old friend'. He was offered the job the next day.

Reith's rewritten letter might seem to be an odd act for a man who became famous for his sense of moral propriety, but, in fact, it was in keeping with his keen sense of a Scottish network. One of his first acts as general manager was to insist that the company should 'keep the Sabbath', and he arranged for the minister of St Columba's Church of Scotland in Pont Street to come and lead prayers the night before the new venture opened its doors for the first time.

The fact that Reith knew nothing about the area in which he was going to work wasn't a hindrance; in fact, nobody knew anything about broadcasting and the company, which would become the Corporation in 1927, started from scratch.

It was, at least in the early days, the creature of the radio manufacturers, intended to provide the content for the domestic radio receivers which were coming on the market. As Ian McIntyre, Lord Reith's biographer, noted, 'the origins of British broadcasting . . . were almost entirely commercial'. Reith soon found himself deep in the world of copyright and patents, negotiating with wireless manufacturers and securing licences. It was all uncharted waters, but Reith had an extraordinary natural authority and an unwavering sense of where his new organisation should be heading.

The company which Reith took over, of course, is now the most respected broadcasting organisation in the world, with 12 radio and television networks, foreign correspondents around the globe and a worldwide audience of up to 150 million. Ironically, given the empire which has arisen on the foundations he laid, John Reith would probably not get his job if he applied for it at today's BBC. His lack of experience would undoubtedly count against him, and it's easy to imagine the personality profile which would pick up his drive, determination and vision but mark down his dogmatism. Flexibility, the one word which the BBC now values as highly as creativity, was one characteristic that its founder utterly lacked.

His peculiar character was spotted even by his contemporaries. In the army, he had been noted for not being clubbable and was excluded from social events. He would go to absurd lengths to prove a point, once walking along the lip of a trench in full view of the enemy whilst a rival crawled along in the mud, hidden from view. Above all, he had to be *right*, a characteristic which brought him considerable pain in his personal relationships and which he had inherited from the certainties of his childhood in the Church of Scotland manse.

Ian McIntyre, a Scot, was controller of Radio 4 and Radio 3. His biography of Lord Reith, *The Expense of Glory,* published in 1993, drew heavily on Lord Reith's diary, which he had kept up to date with daily entries from 1910 until his death in 1971. Reith had allowed Asa Briggs partial access to it when the official historian of the BBC had been writing his history of the Corporation, but McIntyre got to see the lot. He had expected, perhaps, to get a sense of Reith's daily life at the BBC and an insight into his personality. What he discovered was an extraordinary document full of righteous fury, simmering resentment and heartbreaking loneliness. Reith, the man whose fierce moral intensity had shaped one of Britain's most important national institutions, was, it seemed, of a romantic disposition, easily hurt by real or imaginary rejection. His later life was taken up with a series of friendships with attractive younger women, and his earlier life had been occupied by a passionate love for a young man called Charlie Bowser. The reaction to McIntyre's book was phenomenal, but Reith's character had always preoccupied and perplexed those who worked for him. For years after he left, BBC staff told stories about him. His famous intolerance of divorce was real, and staff knew that their career could be over if they were named as a co-respondent in a divorce action. (The company's chief engineer Peter Eckersley left for exactly that reason in 1929.) He also disliked smutty references and jokes about drunkenness and mothers-in-law and would strike them from any script that came his way. Clever staff soon began to do it for him, and his writ ran the length and breadth of the Corporation.

When Richard Dimbleby retired, he made a speech about how, after his first broadcast, the Director General had phoned the news editor and said that he never wanted to hear Dimbleby's voice on the airwaves again. Typically, Reith got wind of the joke and took huge offence, writing to Dimbleby to deny that it had ever happened. It took several letters to smooth over the imagined feud.

Reith's character is of more than just anecdotal interest, though: with its curious combination of piety, authority and quirky personal morality, it was the BBC's guiding light for many years. His famous dictum that the Corporation existed to 'educate, inform and entertain' was to inspire the BBC for years, and nothing which followed has come close to its pithiness and force.

Reith also stands as a major Scottish figure directing a British institution with a shamelessly Scottish ethos. His drive was part and parcel of that, a sterling example of the famed Calvinist work ethic in action, but Reith's Scottishness went beyond mere personal dynamism. His aim for the company was 'uninterrupted service', a radio network which blanketed the country, and his vision of the BBC's reach was more than purely technical: he had a vision, perhaps a sentimental one, of his imagined audience.

In the *BBC Handbook* of 1928, Reith described the BBC's mission:

> The shepherd on the downs, the lonely crofter in the farthest Hebrides and what is more important the labourer in his squalid tenement, equally the lonely invalid on her monotonous couch, may all in spirit sit side by side with the patrons of the stalls and hear some of the best performances in the world.

The crofter, the exhausted tenement worker: Reith's BBC would be a truly national organisation but one cast in a particularly Scottish style. Reith was greatly preoccupied with invalids on their couches: when an old lady wrote to him from her sickbed describing the pleasure which a BBC broadcast had brought her, he had the note copied and distributed to all staff. But Reith's vision for the BBC went beyond parish work. He also wanted it to be a centre of excellence: artists should not just appear because they were popular, but because they were working at the highest levels in their fields.

As an employer, Reith was paternalistic and judgemental. In the first debate on charter renewal, Sir Stafford Cripps slammed Reith in the Commons for his dictatorial management style and his interference in the private lives of staff, complaining that he discouraged association, trade union activity and any systematic pay grades. The record was mixed: the BBC was one of the first employers to introduce PAYE, women and men were on the same pay scales and its pension provision was generous; however, Reith's management style was undeniably autocratic, interfering and ungovernable.

In other respects, Reith was an inspiring leader. Above all, he had a respect for the power of words and for their danger. BBC broadcasts were scripted and honed, formal statements of authority and impartiality. One of the first radio studios in Broadcasting House was decked out as a sitting room complete with sofa and fire, but the presenter was faced by a large portrait of George Washington, presumably as a warning not to speak anything but the truth. Some BBC announcers thought the portrait had been placed there as a joke; all obeyed its implicit message.

Above all, the BBC should not take sides on controversial political issues, though some complained that Reith's support of the Government during the General Strike was what had secured its Royal Charter. The criticism of the BBC's conduct over the General Strike shook Reith, and he seems to have made something of a personal undertaking not to become involved in anything like it again, preferring to see the BBC as the 'voice of the nation', the natural port of call in the event of national disasters, deaths or state occasions. (The viewing figures of the BBC's coverage of the funeral of Diana, Princess of Wales shows that it retains much of this moral monopoly, despite the presence of the respected ITN network.) It was as well that Reith did not seek to become involved in political controversy, as throughout his life he had a very poor grasp of political complexities. The framing of the BBC mission in terms of universals like 'fairness' or 'impartiality', which were generally accepted and understood, avoided the point-by-point analyses of political issues which would have led to disaster.

But though the BBC was being driven by a particularly Scottish dynamo, it was also responsible for enforcing the hegemony of 'BBC English', that peculiarly patrician sound which bore more relation to the voice of the Establishment in the south-east of England than to the way British people spoke across the country.

In October 1979, the BBC published the result of a fascinating consultation exercise. A letter to the *Listener* magazine on 5 April 1979 from Alvar Liddell, a retired BBC announcer, had complained about the standards of spoken English on the airwaves. Entitled 'Newsweeding', Liddell's letter complained that the news was subject to 'widespread distortion, an endemic disease arising from insinuation and implication'. Liddell's ideal newsreader would be one:

> . . . speaking educated southern English without
> affectations or mannerisms or defects, and reading

accurately and impersonally . . . before the war we had
the benefit of individual coaching by Professor Lloyd
James, whose chair at London University was in
phonetics . . . Sir John Reith had him appointed to look
after the speech of the London announcers/
newsreaders. This he did on a weekly tutorial basis for
each of us, reviewing and criticising recorded samples of
our previous week's work and teaching us semantics
and pronunciation during the session.

The BBC response to the letter was magisterial. Rather than
respond directly, it secured the services of three experts,
commissioning Denis Donoghue, the Professor of Modern
English and American Literature at University College Dublin,
Robert Burchill, chief editor of the Oxford English Dictionary,
and Andrew Timothy, a former BBC Assistant Head of
Presentation, to examine the issue.

The three listened across the BBC's national and regional
output, interviewed newsreaders and announcers and called
up LPs of the BBC's broadcasting from the 1930s and '40s.
Their report, written at the time when Thatcherism had
begun to dismantle many of the sacred institutions of the
British Establishment, makes fascinating reading. Burchill
pointed out that many of the letters sent to the BBC
complaining about pronunciation and grammar were
themselves full of spelling mistakes. He took evident pleasure
in the fact that several of Alvar Liddell's old recordings
contained syntactical errors or mispronounced words, and he
discovered from Robin Day that when he emphasised the
word 'and' in a sentence it was often because he didn't know
what on earth to say next.

But Donoghue's contribution came closest to understanding
the cultural importance of the BBC's presentation style. In his
conclusion, he argued that BBC English had such a hold on the
public imagination because London 'is the centre of Great
Britain', because the BBC was free from commercial pressure
and because its tradition of excellence led listeners to expect the
highest standards from it.

Donoghue was also the only member of the distinguished
triumvirate to deal with the issue of regional accents, saying, 'I

think the real problem is that broadcasters do not know what the relationship between the BBC and the country as a whole should be.'

It was an issue which had bedevilled the BBC from its beginnings. When the BBC's news bulletins were proposed, Reith had shown considerable sensitivities to the commercial interests of regional newspapers by bowing to their request that news should not be read before 7 p.m.; if the BBC had given the headlines, newspaper proprietors in Glasgow, Manchester and Liverpool were concerned that they wouldn't be able to sell their evening editions. As the BBC began to introduce regional programmes, these too caused controversy. Some regions felt that they were being deprived of national broadcasts. Others questioned the need for national broadcasts at all.

In 1957, the Scottish National Party published a report called *Broadcasting in Scotland – an Examination of BBC Policies*, which had been compiled by a special committee of the party. It articulated a Scottish dissatisfaction with the way the BBC portrayed Scotland and covered its news.

> It is evidently the opinion of the BBC that important topics can be discussed only by speakers from London or from studios in London. The corresponding tendency on the part of the staff in Scotland is to concentrate on programmes which can be given a 'tartan twist' and many programmes are embarrassing in their parochialism. This is accentuated whenever a variety programme is arranged in Glasgow, and is taken (though this is seldom) by an English region. Immediately the script writers bring whisky, haggis and bagpipes into the act.

> News Bulletins:
> We repeat the proposal put forward by the SNP in their evidence to the Royal Commission that news bulletins should be prepared by the BBC staff in Scotland in the same way the news is presented by *The Scotsman* and the *Glasgow Herald*... The criticism [of the proposal] stated that this would be an extension of the BBC's news services, whereas, in fact, it should replace the present London-based bulletins.

The Scottish bulletins followed, but were placed after the national news, which still came from London. The discussion about how Scottish and British national news should sit together still causes controversy, as witnessed by the row over the BBC's plans for a Scottish *Newsnight*, or the introduction of a Scottish evening news bulletin, 'The Scottish Six'.

In other respects, however, the SNP's complaint of the 1950s was curious. The BBC both in Glasgow and London was recruiting an increasing number of Scots as broadcasters and producers. Reith himself had always been keen on employing Scots, especially those who came from a similar background to himself. One of the first to benefit was W.C. Smith, a Scottish journalist and a former missionary, hired by Reith as his 'press man' in the early weeks of 1923. Others were to follow, either directly recruited by Reith himself or brought into the Corporation's London centre after periods in its Scottish offices.

Scottish artists, too, benefited from the BBC's exposure. The first radio appeal in Britain was given by Ian Hay, the Scottish author who would later write regularly for the BBC and had earlier written *The Oppressed English,* an ironic book about how the Scots had taken over the Empire. The programmes with a 'tartan twist' which the SNP had complained of brought in Scottish traditional musicians. Some like Moira Anderson and Kenneth McKellar went on to national careers.

Reith, of course, was not the only Scottish Director General. In the 1980s, Alasdair Milne led the Corporation through a series of battles with the Government. He had been born in India, the son of an Aberdonian father and an Edinburgh mother. Milne had been trying to get back to Scotland from London, mounting a bid for the franchise of STV in an attempt to take that 'licence to print money' away from Lord Thomson in the mid-1960s. The bid failed. So too did an attempt to become Director of Programmes for BBC Scotland when he was interviewed by a panel which included Stuart Hood, the great Scottish Controller of Programmes for Television and the man ultimately responsible for all of the BBC's output during much of the 1960s. Milne eventually made it as Controller of BBC Scotland at the age of 38, after undergoing a crash course in Gaelic to cement his Scottish credentials.

His bid to take over STV, though, says much about the

smallness of the Scottish media establishment and the speed with which it could move when it chose to. After first discussing the idea with Alastair Burnett, the editor of *The Economist* and later one of Britain's most loved newsreaders, Milne raised the issue at a party given by Ludovic Kennedy and his wife, the ballet dancer Moira Shearer. Since Jo Grimond was due to retire that night, Kennedy, who had stood as a Liberal Party candidate before coming to television, exactly as Robin Day had, telephoned him. He agreed to come on board as chairman of the consortium. It was the work of a few hours, and the wheels had been greased by personal connections.

Since the 1960s, and not least as a result of the pressure of independent television and radio, the style of BBC broadcasting has changed, becoming less formal, more reactive to events and also harder hitting. The BBC voice, which had previously been a model of restraint and authority, began to soften and become more accessible. Scottish accents, once kept down or Anglified at the Reithite broadcasting corporation, began to appear on air with greater regularity in the late 1960s and '70s. Some, like the eccentric Fyffe Robertson, seemed to have been brought on as a comic turn. Others, like the hugely respected Donnie B. MacLeod, were the Eamon Holmes of their days, sitting on comfy sofas at BBC *Pebble Mill* for much of the 1970s and hosting hours of live television a day.

In the 1980s, the Glasgow-born Jeremy Isaacs was appointed as the Controller of Channel 4. Earlier he had been responsible for *The World at War,* one of the greatest historical television series ever made; later he would move to another world at war, the Royal Opera House. But though he hadn't expected to be given the job, judging himself 'too Scottish and too Jewish', Isaacs used his position to introduce new talent. Scots in particular seemed to be able to take full advantage of the opportunities which the new television station offered: Mike Bolland, the Glasgow-born director of seminal programmes like *After Dark* and *The Tube,* cast presenters like Muriel Gray and the lawyer Helena Kennedy, and actors like Robbie Coltrane.

In February 2004, Sir Peter Burt was appointed chairman of ITV; with Charles Allen serving as the company's chief executive, two Scots held the most powerful positions in British commercial television. Peter Burt, like John Reith 82 years earlier, came to his job with no broadcasting experience. Insiders explained that his most important role was to decide the fate of Allen, whose performance had been criticised by some shareholders.

But the recent domination of Scottish voices in broadcasting is closely related to developments in the world of British politics. Much as Scots dominate the political world, they are also dominating the world of news and current affairs on British television and radio. Nicky Campbell, whose career began on Northsound Radio in Aberdeen and was tipped as the replacement for Jimmy Young, remains a fixture on Radio 5 Live and is BBC Television's replacement for *Kilroy*. Eddie Mair, a graduate of Radio Tay and BBC Radio Scotland, is the anchor of *PM*, Radio 4's drivetime programme. Kirsty Wark presents *Newsnight*, after starting her career on BBC Scotland presenting political programmes like *Left, Right and Centre*. Meanwhile, Kirsty Young, who entered the world of network television through STV after a brief spell at BBC Radio Scotland, presents the news on Five.

The Young route is not untypical. The Scottish media, with its own institutions and local versions of national bodies, is often seen by ambitious broadcasters as a stepping stone to bigger things. The television presenter Sheena Macdonald, who was almost killed in 1997 by a speeding police car, believes that the structure of the Scottish media allowed her a degree of experience before she hit London, which prepared her for her later success.

'When you are presenting a programme in Scotland, there are lots of writers or artists who might be doing a British tour, and who, because they are interested in Scotland, come and do interviews with you. It means that you get a real exposure to prominent people. It also means that if you are starting off, you get a real crack of the whip, and early.

'I remember when I was still working in Glasgow being told by a well-known Scottish journalist that my career wouldn't go anywhere because I was a dolly bird. Well, I am still here because I took the chance to go off and have a career in London. I don't know what happened to the guy who told me that I had a limited shelf-life, but I bet he stayed in Scotland.'

But journalists go to London not only because they have

banged their heads against the tartan ceiling which limits their ambitions. For news and current affairs presenters, of course, London has always had an irresistible appeal because London was where politics was. Jim Naughtie says ruefully that, 'You can't present the *Today* programme from Edinburgh. If you were a political reporter, you came to Westminster to ply your trade. And that was a simple fact.'

But while political journalists have been drawn to the centre of Britain, other Scots have been attracted to foreign postings, perhaps responding to the ancestral Scottish tug of Empire. In the wake of James Cameron came Scots like Angus Roxburgh, covering the Soviet Union in its dying years, Gavin Esler covering Washington at the same time, and Allan Little, the BBC's correspondent in Paris. The voice of Britishness abroad often broadcasts home with a Scottish accent; Lord Reith, who coined the phrase 'Nation shall speak peace unto nation', would be gratified.

CHAPTER 3

Scottish Law

The inquiry into the death of Dr David Kelly was a very English affair, conducted in an atmosphere of restraint and intensity. Witnesses were addressed as 'Mr' and 'Mrs'. The principals whose disputed actions had brought the lonely suicide of a harassed government civil servant to the top of the news agenda seemed subdued by the quiet manner of Lord Hutton and the forensic ability of his legal team. But despite the calm and orderly way in which the inquiry proceeded, the stakes could not have been higher. The reputation of three great British institutions – the BBC, the Government and the Civil Service – were at stake. Careers were on the line. Some predicted that the Prime Minister himself could be forced to resign if Lord Hutton's verdict cast doubt on his integrity.

The man in the eye of the storm, Alastair Campbell, had more to fear than most. His methods of news management had been criticised for years; now it seemed possible that he would be found at least partly responsible for a man's death. In such a situation, the choice of an unflappable lawyer was essential. To represent him at this most English of inquisitions, Campbell chose a Scot.

Alan McLean was educated at Lenzie Academy and Oxford. He was a Kennedy Scholar and came first in his year when he trained for the Bar. He is renowned as one of the finest barristers of his generation, and he was not the first Scot to respond to a crisis call from the English Establishment.

When the case against the young men accused of the murder of the black London teenager Stephen Lawrence collapsed, Sir

William Macpherson of Cluny chaired the investigation. Macpherson admitted that before the inquiry he had no knowledge of London's black street life. As the head of the Clan Macpherson and a founder of the territorial SAS, it would have been surprising if he had. Nonetheless, Macpherson's inquiry was praised as a model of insight and precision. When it concluded that the Metropolitan Police were guilty of institutional racism, the accusation gained much of its force from the fact that the man making it was a dry Scot and not a fashionable left-wing London barrister.

There are other Scots at the English Bar, of course, most famously Lord Irvine, Tony Blair's old master, appointed Lord Chancellor in the first Blair Government and replaced on his retirement by Lord Falconer, another Scot, another London barrister and another friend of Blair's. Falconer and Irvine followed Lord Mackay of Clashfern, the dry, highly respected Scottish lawyer whom Mrs Thatcher appointed as Lord Chancellor after the retirement of Lord Hailsham.

But while the Labour leader's appointments drew accusations of cronyism, Thatcher wanted Mackay because he *wasn't* a crony. She intended Mackay's appointment to send a message to the English legal Establishment that they would be reformed without fear or favour by a man who came from outside their ranks. When Mackay was expelled from the Free Presbyterian Church for attending the Catholic funeral of his friend Lord Wheatley, the affair briefly sent a frisson through liberal London. The idea of a flinty Scottish lawyer who still clung to the beliefs of a hardline Calvinist splinter group seemed to be an astonishing indication that Scotland was another country entirely.

But even this run of three Scottish Lord Chancellors isn't remarkable; there have been eight since 1793, with two, Earl Campbell and Lord Cairns, serving within a decade in the 1860s. Given the formal ease with which lawyers could enter the English Bar, the list is perhaps less surprising than it might at first seem.

Qualification for the English Bar is in one sense negligible, requiring little more than the formality of attending a certain number of compulsory dinners. In Scotland, practice at the Bar is more clearly formalised, requiring a law degree from a

Scottish university, two years as a solicitor and a further year working unpaid as a 'devil', a pupil serving under his 'devil master', an experienced advocate. In the seventeenth century, the English requirement was as lax but the Scottish even tighter: the Faculty of Advocates insisted that applicants should have studied a full philosophy course in addition to the law before seeking to become an advocate.

The faculty's insistence on a philosophy degree was, in part, a recognition of the different bases on which legal decisions were made in Scotland and England. Scottish law was based on principle and drawn from Roman law, whereas English 'common law' was based on precedent.

Historical accounts of Scottish lawyers working in the English Law have tended to emphasise the number who transferred jurisdictions after 1707. Though the Union preserved the integrity of the Scottish Law and Scottish institutions, it increased the influence of English domestic politics over Scottish affairs and opened the doors of English institutions to Scottish lawyers who were willing to undergo the formalities required to enter them.

But though the 1730s showed a huge growth in the number of Scottish lawyers practising in England and scholarly attempts to systematise the distinctions between the two legal traditions, with James Innes publishing a book in 1733 called *Idea Juris Scotia,* a summary of the laws of Scotland intended for English readers, Scots were working in the English Law before 1707.

The records of the Middle Temple, one of the four Inns of Court to which English barristers belong, show that as early as October 1604 James Fowlis of Colinton was admitted as a Templer. A few months later, in February 1605, Sir Robert Stewart, brother of the Earl of Orkney, and Sir John Skene, the Clerk Register, were admitted as honorary members. In 1608, the Middle Temple came under a patent issued by James VI and a number of his advisers joined, including the Duke of Lennox, Sir James Kennedy and Sir James Hamilton.

These early Scottish admissions to one of the Inns of Court are a clear sign of Scots being drawn into the study of the English Law as a result of regime change. James's retinue were encouraged to take such positions as part of the King's strategy of placing his own men in key English institutions. Those individuals who followed were drawn by the increased proximity to power, promise of wealth and greater influence.

That pattern, of Scots entering English institutions to cement the power of their patrons or increase their own prospects, is of course a familiar one, but the presence of Scots in the English Law is particularly interesting because of the significance of the distinct legal system in Scotland and its continuing independence even under the Union.

Indeed the Scottish Law, preserved by the Act of Union along with the education and religious systems, has a strong case for being considered not just a distinctive part of what makes Scotland Scotland but also a bulwark which protected the country from insensitive outside interference.

The fact that Scotland's relationship with England was enshrined in a set of legal documents made appeals on the legality of English legislation possible. The most famous modern example of such an appeal came in 1953, coronation year, when one of the fathers of modern Scottish nationalism went to court. At the highpoint of celebrations of the new Elizabethan age, 'King John' MacCormick along with Ian Hamilton, one of the band who had repatriated the Stone of Destiny after stealing it on Christmas Day 1950, challenged the Lord Advocate, Lord Clyde, over the right of the newly crowned Queen to call herself 'Elizabeth II' in Scotland.

Despite passionate argument over exactly which title should be embossed on Scotland's pillar boxes, the two lost their case, but in an appeal in front of Lord Cooper, the Lord President upheld one of MacCormick's arguments and made an important declaration of the constitutional distinctions between and English and Scottish practice.

> The principle of the unlimited sovereignty of Parliament is a distinctively English principle which has no counterpart in Scottish constitutional law . . . Considering that the Union legislation extinguished the Parliaments of Scotland and England and replaced them by a new Parliament, I have difficulty in seeing why it should have been supposed that the new Parliament of Great Britain must inherit all the peculiar characteristics of the English Parliament but none of the

Scottish Parliament, as if all that happened in 1707 was
that Scottish representatives were admitted to the
Parliament of England. That is not what was done.

MacCormick and Hamilton were lawyers, and Hamilton went
on to a distinguished career as a Scottish QC. The judge, Lord
Cooper, was a Conservative, who was sufficiently conservative
in matters relating to the Scottish legal system that he defended
its integrity, even in a case which related to the honour of the
sovereign. But there was something very Scottish about this
scene. In Ireland and across Europe, nationalist movements
were setting bombs and reverting to direct action in pursuit of
their claims. In Scotland, notwithstanding that a small number
of Nationalist agitators took matters into their own hands and
blew up a few pillar boxes, distinguished lawyers were locked in
debate about whether the insignia on a few bright-red mail
boxes contravened the Treaty of Union. The IRA might have
favoured the armalite over the ballot box, but the ballot box and
the post box were the SNP's weapons of choice.

Writing exactly 40 years after the case of MacCormick vs the
Lord Advocate, John MacCormick's son, Neil MacCormick, the
Regius Chair of Nations and Nature at Edinburgh University,
argued in an article on the importance of the law in Scotland
that it is the pre-eminent institution which 'makes Scotland
Scotland'. He continued, 'Without the independence of the legal
system, who can say what would have become of Scotland these
last 300 years?'

MacCormick was quoting Walter Scott, another lawyer who,
in response to proposed changes in the Faculty of Advocates in
1807, had turned to a friend with tears in his eyes and declared
that, 'Little by little, whatever your wishes may be, you will
destroy and undermine until nothing of what makes Scotland
Scotland will remain.'

In keeping with its role as the safeguard of Scottish national
integrity, from the time of the Union of the Parliaments
onwards, the Scottish legal system has been remarkably
resistant to efforts to transform or 'reform' its distinctiveness
away. Indeed, from Scott's impassioned plea of 1807 onwards,
attempts to clean up and rationalise the Scottish Law, which in
practice would have meant the end of Scottish distinctiveness,

have fallen foul of the concerted efforts of one of the most powerful and well briefed of institutional lobbies: Scottish lawyers themselves.

Yet despite the persistence of its distinctive ways of doing business, the Scottish Law is clearly a minority jurisdiction in the United Kingdom, and the jurists who attempted to codify Scottish law, from even before the Treaty of Union, were aware of the distinct approaches of English law. James Viscount Stair's magisterial *Institutions of the Law of Scotland of 1681* contained references to and comparisons with English law, but Scottish law, with its basis in Roman law, also looked to similar legal systems in Europe, and Scottish lawyers were more likely to have trained in Utrecht, Paris or other parts of the continent than in London.

The legal system in Scotland doesn't just preserve its own integrity; it has also been conspicuously successful at upholding its social status. The law is still one of the professions which ambitious middle-class Scottish parents dream that their children will enter. The Scottish lawyer is, at least in his public image, decorous and hard working, the very model of professional achievement.

But the Scottish Law is, of course, merely the law which has authority over the territory of Scotland and, by chance, a few offshoots of the former British Empire who adopted it as the basis for their penal code. And like all Scottish institutions it has often not been big enough for Scottish lawyers. One of the first Scots to assume high status in the English Law was William Murray, Lord Mansfield, who became Lord Chief Justice in 1756 and presided over the trial of John Wilkes, the anti-Scottish agitator, as well as making a landmark anti-slavery ruling in the 1780s.

Murray's story is a remarkable indication of the way in which even those Scots who seemed to come from the wrong social and political background could clamber to the top of key British institutions in the eighteenth century.

Murray came from the wrong side in the battle for dynastic supremacy in Britain. His father was a prominent Jacobite, and the Old Pretender had stayed in the family house when the young Murray was ten years old. After education in Scotland, Murray was enrolled in Westminster School then at Christchurch College, Oxford.

Murray's first legal case was concerned with the fall-out from the South Sea Bubble, a case which came to the Lords on appeal from the Court of Session in Edinburgh. A Scottish merchant who had bought South Seas stock at the height of its value from a London broker and then seen the price plummet sued for the purchase money plus interest. The sympathetic Scottish courts had awarded for the plaintiff. The House of Lords reversed the decision, with Murray as junior counsel for his unsuccessful countryman. This case from north of the border was followed by another, but then Murray was able to move away from Scottish cases altogether.

When Wilkes was tried by Murray, he took it as a sign that the Scots had succeeded in burrowing their way into the heart of the English Establishment; he was right, but it would have been more remarkable for an Englishman to reach a position of similar eminence in Scotland. For while the English Law has been singularly porous to Scottish outsiders who wanted to come in and practise it, the Scottish legal Establishment has been much less accommodating to English-trained lawyers. The Faculty of Advocates, a smaller body than the Inns, and with an annual turnover smaller than some wealthy London chambers, has been much less attractive to English outsiders. It may be that the Scottish Bar is less attractive because the potential rewards are much smaller (though, of course, it has afforded a handful of Scottish lawyers extremely good livelihoods) or it may be that the pupilage system of 'devils' supported by established advocates is itself conservative and likely to support newcomers in the image of the old, or there may be another reason entirely.

'I have many good friends at the Scottish Bar,' says Ian Macdonald QC, the Glasgow-born expert on immigration law who has practised at the English Bar since the early 1970s. 'But it's a very different world. The English Bar can be a very middle-class place, but the Scottish Bar is socially very small and peer opinion is very important.'

Macdonald's area of expertise, immigration, is clearly most usefully pursued from England, the same jurisdiction in which the Home Office makes its judgements, but his position at the Bar in London has also afforded him the opportunity to act in fascinating international cases which would have been denied him had he stayed in Scotland. After serving as a member of the international commission of inquiry into the disappearance of the Portuguese General Delgado, he was awarded a Portuguese knighthood; not an honour which often comes the way of members of the Scottish Bar.

It is certainly true that the English Bar has shown itself more willing to entertain mavericks. The Scottish Bar has not thrown up radical figures of the left like Michael Mansfield in England. Radicalism in the Scottish Bar is often no more than flamboyance, like that displayed by the late Sir Nicky Fairbairn or Donald Findlay: technical brilliance with a bit of top spin.

It's also debateable whether lawyers like the Gorbals-born Helena Kennedy, who named her son Keir after the founder of the Labour Party, or Derry Irvine, whose pompous public manner belies his ordinary origins, would have been able to succeed at the Scottish Bar. Could the fact that these two, from conspicuously humble beginnings, have managed to scale the top of the legal Establishment outside their native Scotland be a sign that the middle-class Scottish Bar is less attractive to working-class outsiders, and less receptive to their talents when they get in?

* * *

On 16 November 1967, a Scottish solicitor took her place in the Palace of Westminster as the newly elected MP for Hamilton. Winifred Ewing was only the second Scottish Nationalist ever to be elected as an MP. The first, Dr Robert McIntyre, who had entered the Commons in April 1945, only lasted six weeks before losing his seat in the general election. His successor would enjoy a career as long as his was short, pressing her case for Scottish independence not just at Westminster but also in the European Parliament in Brussels as 'Madame Ecosse' and finally in the Scottish Parliament, the only British politician to carry off such a hat-trick.

The day Winnie went to Westminster was a gala day for Nationalists; she disembarked at King's Cross station from the Glasgow train while a piper played 'Scotland the Brave' to bemused commuters. After unpacking at a Kensington hotel, she processed to the gates of Westminster itself, surrounded by a cheering crowd. The first person to meet her was a Scottish policeman called Manus 'Jock' Boyle, one of the regular House of Commons police. Boyle retained close links to Scotland; he had a brother who played for Celtic Football Club, and he had a quote handy for the *Daily Record* reporter sent down to cover the event: 'She's rather sweet, isn't she? She's bound to cause quite a stir.'

It was a small symbolic moment: the Glasgow solicitor dedicated to the dismantling of the British State greeted at the gates of Westminster by a Scottish bobby on duty defending the Mother of Parliaments.

For despite the stellar contributions which Scottish lawyers have made to the London law, arguably the most important English legal institution that Scots have made their own is the Metropolitan Police. Since before the Met was founded, Scots have been as essential to its work as the Irish have been to the New York Police Department of the nineteenth and twentieth centuries.

Indeed, one of the men who first identified the need for a police force in London at all, Patrick Colquhoun, was a former Lord Provost of Glasgow, a man who had made a fortune trading on the east coast of Virginia before the age of 21 and returned to Scotland to found Glasgow's Chamber of Commerce, create its first coffee house next to the Stock Exchange and become chairman of the Forth–Clyde Canal.

Colquhoun's justification for a police force in London, *A Treatise on the Police of the Metropolis* of 1797, was enormously influential and went through seven editions in ten years. Appropriately for a man who was essentially a merchant, albeit one with wide-ranging philosophical interests, Colquhoun's argument was that the police would defend private property against the criminals who delighted in stripping traders of their goods. But Colquhoun's influential argument for a police service also dealt head-on with one of the most forceful historic objections to it: that the police would be a branch of the State, which would undermine the liberty of free men. In a rhetorical flourish which would lay the course for the creation of the first professional police force in the metropolis, Colquhoun turned the argument on its head: far from undermining the British constitution, the police would secure it.

> Next to the blessings which a Nation derives from an
> excellent Constitution and System of general Laws, are
> those advantages which result from a well-regulated and
> energetic plan of Police, conducted and enforced with
> purity, activity, vigilance and discretion.

Those ideals, of regulation, activity, discretion and the rest, became the founding principles of policing in Britain. Colquhoun's vision of the police, which also involved a wide-ranging reform of the magistrates system and the criminal law, was based on the French model, which placed a priority on the prevention of crime rather than on the simple capture of criminals. Given that one of the objections to the police in Britain had been the fear of French-style 'spies', who would take an undue interest in the affairs of private citizens, Colquhoun's admiration for police work across the Channel was potentially dangerous, but his indefatigable defence of a British-style police force, backed up with a skilful use of early crime statistics, began to convince politicians.

Prior to Colquhoun's proposals, policing in Britain had been undertaken by a patchwork system of watchmen and parish constables. In 1750, Henry Fielding had established a police office at Bow Street and employed 'runners' who were popularly known as the 'Raw Lobsters' because their uniform contained a red vest. It was a valiant experiment but the embryonic police force lost much of its moral authority when an investigation revealed that many of the runners were corrupt, taking back-handers from the very criminals they were supposed to be arresting. Colquhoun proposed systemising the patchy coverage under a police board of five 'indefatigable' police commissioners, under the control of the Home Secretary. Every parish should have its own professional police force and to help the local police do their job, there should be a central system disseminating information about known criminals. Colquhoun appeared before a Select Committee of Parliament to argue his case, which was supported by important sections of the press, but, temporarily, the project seemed to falter.

Undaunted, and as befitted a man with a keen knowledge of the mercantile importance of shipping, Colquhoun followed his first influential treatise with another in 1800 on the *Police of the*

River Thames, devoted to the subject of how ships on the river could be protected against thieves. At low tide, when ships were left dry on the mudflats of the Thames, they were easy prey for thieves called mudlarks, who boarded them and carried off whatever they could find. For the first time, Colquhoun put a figure to what had until then been dismissed as an occupational hazard of the river trade: there were 10,000 thieves working the profitable scam, alongside pickpockets, prostitutes and ruffians who made the quays of the Thames unfit for decent Londoners after dark. But it was the fact that Colquhoun could put a cash value – half a million pounds – to their annual loss which spurred the shipping merchants into action.

In response to Colquhoun's investigation, the shipping companies pressed for the introduction of the Thames River Policing Act, establishing what was effectively a private police force for London's waterway. It proved to be conspicuously successful: where public debate and political will had failed the landlocked citizens of London, commercial interests secured shipping on the Thames.

The political will necessary to create a police force for the whole city – which had faltered after the Gordon Riots of 1780 – hardened again after a series of high-profile murders in 1811. There had always been murders in London, of course, with one modern commentator suggesting that more than half the homicides in Britain have occurred within the city's sprawling limits. Under the watch of James Munro, the first Scottish Commissioner of the Metropolitan Police, public fear about violent, apparently random crime would peak again in 1888, provoked by the activities of 'Jack the Ripper'. As with the Ripper murders, panic at the apparently motiveless slaughter of the Marr family was fuelled by the press, which poured over the grisly details of the disembowelled corpses. When the murderer was caught, he evaded justice by killing himself, but his body, and the banal murder weapon – a ripping chisel – were paraded through London on a cart.

Underlying the arguments about the need for a police force, and the occasional outbursts of violent crime which fired them into a white heat, was the simple demographic fact of London's exploding population: the city grew from 677,000 in 1750 to 960,000 in 1801. Such a growth compressed humanity into stinking streets and overcrowded tenements, collapsed the distinctions between the lawful and lawless poor (the middle classes could always escape to the west, and had begun that movement by the beginning of the nineteenth century) and increased social tension.

Peel's Metropolitan Police Act of 1829, responding to these pressures and a growing political awareness of the need to regulate the exploding metropolis, enshrined many of the ideas which Colquhoun had espoused a quarter century before. Though the new police force would be uniformed, it was not to be a quasi-military organisation. Though it was to be in ranks, recruitment avoided former army officers; pay rates were kept low to make the job appeal to ordinary men and women who, it was argued, would be closer, socially, to the people they policed. Its ethos was embodied in the two men who were appointed as the first police commissioners: Colonel Charles Rowan, who had fought at Waterloo, and Richard Mayne, an Irish barrister then aged 33. In the space between the army officer and the Irish lawyer, the Metropolitan Police thrived, taking from one a sense of discipline and order, and from the other, concern with the due process of law.

But Colquhoun's idea that the police should also display 'purity' and 'discretion' was there too: the instructions issued to the first London officers specified that the police officer 'will be civil and obliging to all people of every rank and class. He must be particularly cautious not to interfere idly or unnecessarily in order to make a display of his authority.'

Judging by the turnover in the first months of the new operation, few of the new recruits came up to the standard required. Drunkenness was a major reason for being dismissed from the force; heavy handedness was another. But by 1840 London was policed in a 15-mile radius of Charing Cross.

From 1830 to 1940, recruitment for the force mostly drew police officers from London itself and from the English counties. The discussion about where policemen should come from waxed and waned during this time. One argument was that the policeman should be drawn from the community he served; another, equally strong, was that this form of 'community policing' undermined the authority of the officer and left him open to moral or financial pressure from those he might have known before he entered the force.

The Scottish influence on the Met was negligible during that period, though in the 1890s the man responsible for checking the health of new recruits as chief surgeon to the Metropolitan Police, a Scot named Alexander MacKellar, favoured the recruitment of current or former agricultural labourers, acting as another London centrifugal force pulling rural men into the city.

It was as part of this ongoing debate about where to source the capital's policemen that in the 1950s and '60s the Met deliberately followed a policy of recruiting from Scotland. The argument was an old one: policemen from outside London were less likely to be corrupted by their relationship with the populace, and the London police even went so far as to open a recruitment office in Glasgow in the early 1960s, working on the assumption that Scottish city life would be the perfect preparation for London policing. Because the Met was considered to be a job for life, and the pension was secure, Scots routinely recommended their friends in the Scottish forces for transfers, or encouraged those who had not joined the police in Scotland to apply straight to the Met.

When Don Ratcliffe, the Inverness-born General Secretary of the Metropolitan Police Federation, sought to join the force in 1967 as a cadet, his uncle, Chief Inspector of the Outer Hebrides Police, advised him that, 'the Metro was second only to the Glasgow City Police'. When he joined the Bow Street Station in 1970, he was astonished at how many of his colleagues were from Scotland. 'And not just that. Once I arrested a particularly rowdy football supporter from a West Ham match, and when I put my hand on his shoulder, he turned around and it was one of my old school pals from Ayrshire.'

Gordon Cowie joined the force in 1965 and found that his nationality was a significant asset. Employed as a CID officer out of the King's Cross station, his job was to hang around the bars in the area looking for criminals who were trying to sell the goods they had stolen from local firms earlier in the day. 'There was always some kind of threat, so we all had to look out for one another, whether it was fear of entrapment, being photographed, having to appear in court, talk to newspapers or stand accused of taking bribes, we all knew we could rely on each other for support all the time. It was real cops and robbers stuff every day. Scotland just seemed like Mickey Mouse stuff in comparison.'

The deliberate policy of targeting Scots as Met recruits ended in the 1980s, ironically at the very time when Sir David McNee, another Scottish Police Commissioner, was in office. It remains to be seen whether Sir Ian Blair, a career officer whose parents are from Edinburgh, appointed Metropolitan Police Commissioner in 2005, will consider renewing the policy. Either way, the Scottish policeman serves as an important stereotype of the London Scot, and with good reason: the Scots always seem to have had a knack for police work, contributing a disproportionate number of officers to the Indian police and founding the Hong Kong police force. The police were also heavily connected with Freemasonry, which provided yet another network by which Scottish recruits could be advanced through the ranks.

Such close connections have been given a bad name as a result of a series of inquiries into police cover-ups or incidents where members of the police force have supported their colleagues in the face of complaints from the public; but for many years the bond between police officers was considered to be an important part of the job. The Scots, who needed little encouragement to look after one another, took full advantage, ensuring that the police headquarters at Scotland Yard more than earned their name, and that the London policeman on the beat, charged with the responsibility of keeping order in the metropolis, was always disproportionately likely to be a Scot.

CHAPTER 4

Scots at Prayer

In January 1902, the newly appointed minister of St Columba's Parish Church in Knightsbridge stood for the first time to address his flock. Archibald Fleming was a son and grandson of the manse, rooted in the ways of the Church of Scotland; he had been the minister at the Tron Church in Edinburgh and had preached before Queen Victoria at Balmoral. His message for his London congregation was unequivocal:

> Here in London there is a Scottish population equal to that of a great city. And our chief business is with them. We are not a Presbyterian Mission to Englishmen, we are at peace and in sympathy with the great National Church of this southern kingdom . . . we are neither Non Conformists nor Dissenters. We are exiled Scots. Here, then, we are waiting to receive into open and brotherly arms the regiments of our fellow-countrymen who are poured into this capital year by year; we are saying to them that if they wish to worship God as their father worshipped, if they wish the friendship and warmth of a Scottish welcome, here they will find what they look for. We cannot estimate what relief it will give to many an anxious parent's heart at home to know that we are here, to receive their sons and daughters – those who will offer them friendships that are honest and kind, so that the love and care of the old Church of Scotland will still be over them and the familiar services will recall the tender and sacred association of the home and religion of their youth.

Comfort, community, communion and the promise of an activity which reassured the parents; all attractive Scottish themes, and 1902 was the high point of the Scottish churches in London. The Great War, which would cut at the roots of London's traditional Scottish societies, was more than a decade away, but the nineteenth century boom in Scottish churches which saw the creation of 19 new congregations from Southwark to Watford had passed. The year before, a bazaar held at St Columba's had raised £800, which finally cleared the debt incurred in building St James's Scotch Church in Goose Green, Dulwich; it had been dedicated in 1896 and would be the last Scottish church built in the capital. By 1966, the congregation at Goose Green had fallen to 170, and the building was levelled.

In Scotland too, church worship was to suffer a steady decline in the coming century though as an institution the Kirk remained symbolic, and central. By the end of the twentieth century, no Church of Scotland minister could share Fleming's confident declaration that the aim of his church was to minister solely to the Scots; declining church numbers meant that parishioners were welcome from wherever, and from whatever denomination, they came. Nonetheless, even as their congregations declined, the Scottish churches in London would remain an important part of the traditional network of Scottish life there, serving as embassies for the Church of Scotland, retaining their own core congregations and also welcoming Scots who were part of a transient population, brought to the city by the demands of their work.

The building in which Fleming preached was destroyed during the Blitz on the night of 10 May 1941. In the interregnum, the congregation worshipped in Imperial College, but in 1955 the new church, designed by Edward Maufe, the architect who created Guildford Cathedral, was open for worship.

Today, St Columba's in Pont Street dominates its corner of Knightsbridge. The Scotch House opposite Harrods might sell classy Scottish knitwear to Japanese tourists, but tucked a block behind Harrods, Maufe's white, organic design dominates its own Scottish corner. Inside, The Reverend Barry Dunsmore explained that his reasons for accepting the charge were closely bound up with Fleming's. Like him, he was wrestling with the Scots sense of community.

'We are by no means a ghetto. I wouldn't have been interested in a charge which was country dancing at prayer and nothing could be further from the truth. Fifteen to twenty per cent of the congregation are not Scots. We have a big number of Americans, Canadians and Africans who are Presbyterian in background and so find this kind of worship amenable. And because we are so central, we are easy to find and that gives an international flavour to the congregation, and that enriches the congregation.'

St Columba's, alongside the Church of Scotland at Crown Court, across the road from the Drury Lane Theatre, makes up the Kirk's full complement in the capital in the twenty-first century. Whilst Crown Court (where broadcaster Jim Naughtie and former Culture Secretary Chris Smith are elders) is a thriving congregation, Pont Street has always had a reputation as the posher of the two.

'I think it is also correct to say that the nature of the congregation has changed dramatically,' the Revd Dunsmore says. 'It's true that at some stages in the late nineteenth and early twentieth century the kirk session here might have looked like a photocopy out of *Who's Who*. A lot of Scots made good at that time and that was the nature of our congregation. The Church of Scotland here has a very high profile – all my predecessors have held the position of Moderator of the General Assembly. We hosted Radio 4's *Any Questions* and [BBC broadcaster] Hugh Pym and his wife are elders here.'

It's not just socially that Pont Street finds itself on the map; it's such a well-known landmark that the church is part of 'the knowledge' for London taxi drivers. In Scotland, most churches are arranged on the parish system, but in London the gathered congregation is drawn from across the city, and the church can no longer afford to restrict itself to Scots. 'It's a much more mobile, slightly more fragmented, community and this church is not immune to the condition of the Church in Scotland. People don't go to church in the same way as they used to, therefore when Scots come to London the Church is not particularly high on their list of priorities in the same way as it would have been in the 1930s and '40s. If you couple that with the logistics of travelling around London, gathered congregations suffer. It's not so bad on Sunday morning, but by Sunday lunchtime Putney Bridge is like it is on Monday morning. If you have children then it is a real commitment for the congregation to come here – we're glad that we are so centrally located. But we get 300 on a good Sunday, and 50 per cent will have travelled more than an hour to get here.'

In recent years, in recognition of the changing face of modern worship, the Church of Scotland has been scaling down its operations outside Scotland, even closing the Scots Kirk in Paris, which, through its minister, Donald Caskie, 'the Tartan Pimpernell', was such an important symbol of the Auld Alliance in the time of the Second World War. But despite the contraction of the Kirk's work in London, Pont Street is a secure charge, sending elders to the General Assembly every second year. Dunsmore, a vigorous and driven minister, is adamant that it won't be his final charge, and that, in the course of time, he will return to Scotland and take up another before he retires.

That international and cross-border aspect to the Kirk's work is sometimes missed by those who worship in Scottish pews each Sunday, but it has been an important element of the Church's history since its beginning.

The first Scottish churches in England were created by Scots who had taken their learning and inspiration from the teaching of Calvin. Together in 1566 they founded a thatched 'Meeting House' in the Wiltshire village of Horningsham, where they worshipped using the Scots psalter of 1564. The meeting place is still in use, and proudly bears the name of 'The Oldest Free Church Building in England'.

By 1584, there was a sizeable Scots community of worshippers living in London and the arrival of James VI and his court established Scots congregations in the environs of Westminster. By 1662, Scots Presbyterians were meeting in Founders Hall in Lothbury, and within a few years the congregation was so large that the building became known as the Scotch Church.

The explosion of Scottish piety in the capital which gathered pace during the nineteenth century was due not just to the continuation of these congregations and the founding of new ones, but to a process of ecclesiastical colonisation; Scots congregations would gradually take over churches, and the style of worship would be transformed according to the Scottish model.

The common thread was a dedication to St Andrew, Scotland's national saint, who gave his name to many churches, most notably St Andrew's National Church, Stepney, which was the place of worship for the many Scottish sailors and their families who lived around Wapping.

The Church of Scotland in London may now seem settled, decent and douce, but the Kirk's ministry in London has not always been so uncontroversial. In the 1830s, it became the focus of a theological scandal as the unlikely home for a nineteenth-century version of the Nine O'Clock Service. In the process, the most charismatic young minister in the Scottish Church in London found himself in the centre of a theological maelstrom.

Edward Irving had taken the charge of the former Gaelic Chapel in Cross Street in 1822. He was well connected. The writers Thomas and Jane Carlyle were close friends and he had a powerful mentor in the Church of Scotland, having served as an assistant to Thomas Chalmers, who was then leading an innovative 'home mission', evangelising in some of Glasgow's most deprived areas. Twenty years later, Chalmers would split the Church of Scotland by leading the Disruption in Edinburgh. His protégé was also destined to leave the Church which he served in controversial circumstances.

In the 1820s, though, Irving's inspiring ministry and oratorical gifts marked him out as a rising star in the world of the Scottish Church in London. His services proved so popular that within two years of taking up his charge, the Cross Street Chapel was too small to hold the throngs of people attracted by his powerful brand of evangelical fervour.

In 1827, Irving was given a newly dedicated church, the Regent's Square National Scottish Church, which was perfectly located to draw a congregation of MPs, wealthy bankers, insurance men and writers.

But if Irving's well-heeled parishioners expected an Establishment version of the gospel, they were to be disappointed. Irving had a strong Millennialist streak and preached a gospel which emphasised Jesus's humanity, teaching that even Christ had 'sinful flesh'. Tensions in the congregation started to grow as the Establishment figures in the pews began to resent the evangelicals attracted from across London by Irving's message. Irving's ministry was about to implode, driven by spiritual forces emanating from his native Scotland.

In March 1830, a woman in Port Glasgow started to speak in tongues. Mary Campbell was an ordinary parishioner of a minister called John McLeod Campbell. Like Irving, Mr Campbell was on the evangelical wing of the Kirk. During one of his sermons she began to ululate and speak wildly in an unknown language. News of this outbreak of religious enthusiasm was widely reported in Scotland. Thomas Chalmers, Irving's old mentor, wrote to the woman's minister asking for more information. The minister replied:

> Mary does not understand the languages which she speaks. When praying in them she feels much nearness to God and sensible communion with him – but not distinct intelligent association of ideas with the several words. She described to me the first reception of the gift as if something were just poured into her and made to pass through her lips without volition. Two other individuals, two brothers, McDonalds, shipbuilders or carpenters in Port Glasgow, have also received the same gift. They speak freely and . . . nothing could be more striking than the contrast of the animated and apparently eloquent manner of their utterance and gesture as contrasted with the soberness and awkwardness I may say of their natural manner.

The very ordinariness of the parishioners added to the significance of their outbursts; Mary Campbell and the McDonalds were practical, working people. Spiritualism and talking in tongues would later attract intellectuals and members of the upper classes, who would form groups in which the voices of the dead could be heard around their suburban dinner tables and spiritual forces gripped their hands to produce screeds of 'automatic writing'. *The Kabbalah Unveiled,* an English translation of the Hebrew interpretation of the Old Testament by a Scot, MacGregor Mathers, would become the foundation text of the occult group the Golden Dawn in the late 1880s, after its source was discovered in a bookseller's pile in 1884 on the Farringdon Road. But in the 1830s, such fringe beliefs were confined to a handful of cranks, and the residents of Port Glasgow had, until now, been immune to spiritual visitation.

Chalmers reported the news to Irving, who took it as a sign that the gift of prophesy, a significant source of revelation in the New Testament, was being restored to ordinary Christians in preparation for the Second Coming. Right on cue, his own parishioners began to speak in tongues.

In November, one of Irving's sermons was interrupted by a Miss Hall, who had to rush out of the church when overcome with the desire to spout glossolalia, and was heard speaking loudly to herself in the vestry. The Scottish press had been sceptical about the events in Port Glasgow, though they had got sporadic coverage. When outbreaks of spiritual babbling occurred in one of the most established churches in London, Fleet Street began to take an interest. The following week the pews were filled with journalists from the London newspapers, their shorthand notebooks at the ready, waiting to transcribe any otherworldly voices. The voices duly came.

The sensational events at Regent's Square were widely reported, and the church attracted more and more people on a Sunday morning, desperate to take part in the ecstatic experiences going on inside, or to gawp at the women who cried out, screamed, babbled to themselves and fell catatonic into the aisles. Irving, who had created the febrile atmosphere which allowed these spiritual outbursts to flourish, was at a loss to know how to deal with them. He instinctively believed that they were inspired by the Holy Spirit, which would have allowed him no alternative but to admit them as a part of his worship, but he had enough political sense to realise that his unorthodox services would be viewed with horror by the church authorities. As he swithered, the speaking in tongues continued and spread out from his church into Bristol and the West Country. One of the phrases which occurred again and again was 'Behold the Bridegroom cometh. Go ye out to meet him', taken by believers as a sign that Christ was on the verge of a reappearance.

The Presbytery of London was faced with a theological and public relations nightmare. One of their most successful young ministers was presiding over a church in which women swooned, babbled nonsense and gave every sign of being under demonic possession. In April 1832, Irving was tried before the Presbytery of London. Within a week, they had made their decision. On 2 May, it was decided that Irving was unfit to remain minister of the National Scottish Church. He left the church, taking with him many of those who had been attracted by his preaching in the 1820s.

But Irving wasn't finished, and he found a new home amongst those who shared his conviction that the Second Coming was at hand. As charismatic teaching took root in the English south, many of its practitioners were expelled from mainstream churches, and in 1833 they banded together to form the Catholic Apostolic Church, a Millennialist grouping with a strong Scottish contingent. The Catholic Apostolics believed that talking in tongues was spiritual prophesy and that the days of the fallen world were numbered.

From their ranks, they appointed 12 'apostles'. Three of the apostles who would greet the risen Lord were taken from the Church of Scotland, eight from the Church of England and one from an independent Church. The apostles were all men of upstanding Christian character and they were all noticeably successful; three were leading barristers, two were Members of Parliament and one was Keeper of the Tower of London.

In 1833, Irving was ordained as an apostolic 'angel' or bishop and served the new Church until his death at the end of 1834. His belief in the sanctity of the body and the power of the Holy Spirit led him to distrust conventional medicine. Three of his children died – one almost certainly unnecessarily – because of his reluctance to engage medical help. His own death was unattended by doctors, though Mr Campbell, in whose church the first outburst of talking in tongues had occurred, was a frequent visitor.

The Church which Irving had joined prospered in the years after his death. Pentecostal in style and evangelical in approach, the Catholic Apostolics were on a mission to convert. They devised beautiful services from a hotchpotch of other traditions, drawing on influences from the Orthodox Church with elements of the Catholic Mass and Anglican Communion. The Church was heavily hierarchical, with angels, elders, seven prophets and seven deacons to each church. Like many fringe groups, the movement was prone to schism, and split in the late 1830s before order was restored. But the post-schism Church had sown the seeds of its own downfall. To quell disagreement within the rank and file, the apostles took responsibility for authorising all acts of prophesy. Since the Second Coming was nigh, they didn't expect to exercise this prerogative for long.

As the next decade followed, the Church honed its rituals, abandoning many of the liturgical practices it had borrowed from the Church of Scotland and the Anglicans. In 1847, it authorised the use of 'extreme unction', in which the faithful were slathered in oil. This was followed by another innovation: 'sealing', in which those who were to be saved had to be literally stopped up against the 'great tribulation' to come.

The Church was never more than a fringe religious belief, though its expectation of the Second Coming prefigured many of the tenets of American Pentecostalism and spurred those US movements which believe in the forthcoming 'gathering' of the faithful before Armageddon.

Throughout the 1840s and 1850s, the whole Church waited for the Apocalypse. And waited. Like all Millennialist creeds, the Church was weakened by the non-appearance of the Second Coming. Denied eternal life, the all-powerful, but all-too-human apostles began to die. After the first death, the debate on whether to replace him split the worldwide Church and led to the creation of the 'New Apostolic Church' of Germany. This church has been active in North and South America and boasts having 'sealed' 15,000 converts in Java. The last apostle died in 1901 and the final angel died in 1960. Since the hierarchy preserved the power to administer all the symbolic functions of the Church, the movement effectively died with him. Appropriately for such a colourful and visionary sect, the Catholic Apostolics left an interesting artistic legacy. In Edinburgh, the Catholic Apostolic's Mansfield Place Church was decorated with murals by the celebrated late Victorian artist Phoebe Anna Traquair. Coincidentally, the Catholic Apostolic Church sired two important Scottish writers: the poet James Thomson, who wrote the apocalyptic *The City of Dreadful Night* about London, and was brought up by parents who had been part of the original Port Glasgow revelations; and Nigel Tranter, the prolific writer who devoted his life to chronicling the most colourful moments in Scottish history, and who attended the Mansfield Place Church. When his church closed its doors in the 1960s, he became an Episcopalian.

Speaking in 1902, the new minister of St Columba's was careful to portray the national Churches of Scotland and England as complementary bodies, ministering to separate national congregations, both anxious to avoid conflict. But there are profound cultural and institutional differences between Scotland's national Church and the established Church in England – differences which go to the heart of English and Scottish identity. The most obvious, of course, is that the Church of Scotland doesn't have the formal connections to the State enjoyed by the Church of England. But even this can be overstated; the Moderator of the Church of Scotland may not sit in the House of Lords, but the formal and informal connections between the Church of Scotland and Scottish civic society are as strong, perhaps even stronger, than their equivalent in England. It's no mistake that the Scottish Parliament sits, while its new home is prepared for it, in the Assembly Hall in Edinburgh normally occupied by the Church of Scotland's General Assembly.

These are structural concerns, of little interest to ordinary church-goers, but the real differences between the two churches are embodied in the popular image of the man, or now woman, in the pulpit. English culture is obsessed with its well-meaning, slightly wet vicars, portrayed on television and film by comic actors like Derek Nimmo, Rowan Atkinson or Dawn French. The vicar in his white surplice is the perfect comic foil, ideal for sending up in a million *Two Ronnies* sketches or in Rowan Atkinson's comic turn in Richard Curtis's *Four Weddings and A Funeral*. These clergymen from central casting are gentle, ineffectual characters who typically minister to rural communities. Essentially unthreatening and benign, no one could be expected to take them too seriously.

The stereotype contains more than a grain of truth; it is easy to portray Anglicanism as slightly wet. From the Vicar of Bray onwards, the Church of England's watchwords, whether on women priests or gay clergy, are flexibility, debate, discussion and compromise.

This willingness to consider extreme opinion and take the middle way is utterly alien to the religious tradition in Scotland, which has cleaved to hardline positions and gloried in dividing the saved from the damned, a process in which condemnation has seemed to afford as much pleasure as salvation. The post-Knox reformed Scottish Church was as much an instrument of social control as an agency of grace, an ever vigilant moral police force which would haul up sinners, adulterers, drinkers and the rest, and shame them in the eyes of the community.

Unsurprisingly, ministers loom large in the Scottish imagination. From the unforgiving hardliner John Knox onwards, a collection of foul-tempered, mean-spirited and restrictive Scottish ministers march across the landscape of Scotland, like black thunderclouds about to spoil a picnic. Filled with Calvinist fervour, judging and controlling, they represent the harsh, unforgiving side of the Scottish character – at least they do in half the novels in Scottish literature. The other half (discussed at greater length in Chapter 9) were written by ministers themselves. In the novels of the Kailyard, the minister is the centre of Scottish life, the still point which observes the travails of a small Scottish village, recounting the weakness of parishioners, soon to be resolved.

If they aren't being cloying and couthy, ministers are controlling and cruel: either way, they are seen as central to Scottish life and identity in a way which the Church of England, for all its establishment, is not. Famously, the Scottish political theorist Tom Nairn declared that Scotland would only be free when 'the last minister had been strangled with the last copy of the *Sunday Post*'. No one could suggest that throttling a vicar would transform the state of England.

In England the very word 'Calvinist' is regularly used as shorthand for 'Scottish', used to label Scots as unforgiving, austere and judgemental. For much of the last century, Calvinism has been a focus for the rage of artists from Edwin Muir to Andrew O'Hagan and James MacMillan, who blame it for Scotland's harsh attitude to creativity. Though no one seems willing to admit to being a Calvinist any more, from beyond the grave the ideology has been made to carry the can for Scotland's joylessness, its loathing of pleasure, its miserablism.

But Calvinism isn't just the tap-root of everything which is harsh and austere in Scottish life; many Scots, regardless of their church affiliation, if indeed they have one, are labelled with the idea of the Calvinist work ethic. Scots Presbyterianism isn't just a religious belief, it's a social stereotype in which hard work and a sense of mission sits with intense self-control, a slightly humourless exterior and a mild priggishness. The ultimate Presbyterian stereotype is the son of the manse, driven by a home-installed sense of duty and turbo-charged with Calvinist seriousness.

Eric Liddell, of *Chariots of Fire* fame – the man who placed the sanctity of the Sabbath in front of his desire for worldly sporting success – was a son of the manse, as was the writer and politician John Buchan, while in modern politics David Steel and Douglas Alexander MP exemplify slightly different aspects of the breed. But the ultimate son of the manse, driven by a concentrated social gospel in which 'help thy neighbour' and tax banding all sit on the continuum, is, of course, Gordon Brown, the brooding überCalvinist who combines the dark demeanour of the vengeful Old Testament God with a Nietzschean will to power, and who genuinely sees Labour as a continuation of a moral crusade. It used to be said that the Labour Party owed more to Methodism than to Marx. For Scottish Labour, John Knox is a vital part of the mix, too.

But the roots of the differences between the two traditions go deeper than just social stereotypes. Anglicanism has always been a top- down religion, created as an ingenious political compromise by Henry VIII to ease his troublesome marital situation, whereas the roots of Scottish religious beliefs are essentially revolutionary – a grass roots movement of committed ideologues who saw it as their duty to defy State power, and even to overthrown the Scottish State itself.

But though the Church of Scotland bills itself as the Church for the nation, it is by no means the only faith which boasts Scottish nationals among its ranks. At Kingston the large Orthodox Jewish synagogue is run by Edinburgh-born Rabbi David Mason, and a short walk from the Church of Scotland at Crown Court another Scottish clergyman runs one of the more unusual chapels of the Church of England. Tucked down the side of the Savoy Hotel, the Queen's Chapel of the Savoy is an attractive church set back from the road, surrounded by its own cemetery. The priest in charge of this 'Crown Peculiar' is a Scot, Father Bill Scott, who was born in Dundee and educated in Edinburgh and Glasgow. In the vestry, he explained the complex connections between Scotland and the Church of England.

'My first proper charge was in Bridgewater, which was quite a contrast after working in the Gorbals. The bishop there, Jock Henderson, had Scottish connections, his father had been bishop of St Mary's Edinburgh. I stayed there and went to four villages, and to four after that. Then I was asked to do a strange job, to be chaplain to an Anglican community of sisters called the Community of All Hallows [who] ran a school and a hospital community in Norwich where they did work with the homeless and retreat work. I stayed there for eight years, then I was asked to come to London. I had a parish behind Sloane Square called St Mary's Bourne Street which was very exotic, very high, and I stayed there for 12 years.

'In my day, the culture in the Episcopal Church was just like the Church of England, except with a Scottish accent. It had its own history, of course, and its own liturgy that was couched in its own terms but close to the Book of Common Prayer, and so moving from Scotland to England was nothing which concerned me in any way.'

Father Scott's chapel has its own links with Scotland; the father of a Jacobite rebel is buried under the altar, but the Scottish tradition of involvement in Anglicanism is very much on the surface. For though the Church of England is often described as 'the nation at prayer', at crucial times in its history it has been led by a Scot.

The playwright J.M. Barrie lamented in 1928 that it had been a lean year for the Scots; they only had one archbishop in England, not two. Cosmo Gordon Lang had left the Bishopric of York to assume the role of Archbishop of Canterbury, where he succeeded Thomas Davidson, another Scot. But even this lineage of Scottish bishops (Lang's predecessor at York had been William Dalrymple MacLagan) had begun 60 years earlier.

In 1868, Archibald Campbell Tait was appointed the first Scottish Archbishop of Canterbury. He had been brought up as a Presbyterian in Edinburgh but the trajectory of his career brought him into the very centre of English life. Transformed by his experiences at Oxford, where Tractarianism changed his religious beliefs for good, he was appointed the headmaster of Rugby School after the sudden death of Dr Arnold in June 1842.

From the Deanery of Carlisle, Tait moved to the Bishopric of London, where he marked himself out as an energetic evangelist, spreading the gospel in omnibus yards and the wards of hospitals. He created the Bishop of London's Fund which, in the first 5 years of its existence raised £350,000 for the erection of churches, schools and parsonages in the poorer suburbs of the metropolis. In 1868, Disraeli appointed him Archbishop of Canterbury, the first Scot to hold the role.

Tait's unusual position didn't seem to trouble him unnecessarily. Even when he oversaw the disestablishment of the Irish Church, he continued to see his position not as an interesting quirk of church history but as a personal honour. When he returned to Edinburgh on a ceremonial visit, *The Scotsman* reported that, 'The first Scottish-born Archbishop of Canterbury received a hearty welcome.'

There was, of course, no reason why Tait, as a Scot, should not have become the head of the Church of England; even while at Oxford, he had dreamed about being Archbishop of Canterbury, and his friends had often written to him jokily referring to him by that title. As a young man, Cosmo Gordon Lang, the third Scot to become Archbishop, had even loftier ambitions. As a small Scottish schoolboy, he wrote an imaginary entry for himself in *Who's Who*. In it, as Earl of Norham, he became Prime Minister in 1912 and fathered eight children, one of whom married the Duke of Richmond and Gordon.

There was more to Lang than just Scottish drive, though. He may have been a repressed homosexual and certainly appeared to be a classic Scottish buttoned-up personality. At Leeds, one of his earliest charges, he was described by a woman parishioner as 'one of those Scotsmen who never allow you to see their minds in undress'.

Reticent and repressed or not, Lang became an effective leader of his church, steady and influential during the abdication of Edward VIII. But then he had known such a steady religious influence at home, as a son of the manse in Scotland. Nor did his elevation exhaust the family's religiosity: his brother would go on to be Moderator of the Church of Scotland, a double triumph which was a first for any Scottish family, and a record unbroken today.

The Church of England's unique constitutional position can

lead to such apparent anomalies, but the successful penetration of the Church of England by Scots (Lord Runcie, the former Archbishop of Canterbury, was born in Kilmarnock, where his father, James, had a draper's shop, and the current Archbishop of Liverpool, the Right Reverend James Jones, is a Scot too) exemplifies one reason why the Scots have been so conspicuously successful in English society; no formal or informal barrier exists to their advancement. In Scotland, the Church of Scotland welcomes Americans, Canadians, Africans and all other Presbyterians to join its worship, and some become ministers, but the Kirk remains by tradition and ritual a profoundly Scottish organisation, far more than the Church of England is purely English.

Today, of course, the appointment of a Scottish Archbishop of Canterbury would provoke a fierce debate about the role of the Scots in English society. When the distinguished Welsh theologian Rowan Williams was appointed to the role in 2002, one commentator sniffed that he had only got the job 'because New Labour couldn't find a suitable Scotsman'.

The Church of England is unlikely to split over the role of the Scots; it has more pressing issues to attend to. Nonetheless, the peculiarly English fudge of Anglicanism continues to throw up some telling paradoxes. Father Bill Scott, the Dundee-born high Anglican who ministers to the Queen's Chapel of the Savoy, is an appointee of the Duchy of Lancaster, which means that his ultimate boss is the Chancellor of the Duchy.

When we spoke, the Chancellor of the Duchy was Douglas Alexander MP, a son of the Church of Scotland manse. It's an interesting anomaly; the Scottish priest, in the Church of England vicarage, appointed by the son of the Church of Scotland manse. An appropriate image for the way Scots have penetrated the porous mass of the English Establishment. Even if anybody wanted to, there is no moving them now.

PART 2

A Home From Home

CHAPTER 5

The *London Scotsman*

Tourists or decanted Scots who are desperate to uncover London's secret Scottish cultural activities can always avail themselves of the services of the office of the Scottish Tourist Board based next to a Thai restaurant near Trafalgar Square. Though most of the leaflets on offer in the tartan-bedecked visitor centre are designed to lure London's foreign visitors on to Scotland, offering cut-price tours of Scottish castles or Nessie hunts in the Highlands, tucked away in a folder is a checklist of London-based cultural activities designed as much to stir the hearts of homesick Scots as to pique the interest of visiting Italians.

Alongside the 60 or so Scottish dance organisations, which can organise a good strathspey and reel from Brighton to Watford, and a handful of Scottish-themed pubs with impressive selections of malt whisky behind the bar, a clutch of societies and clubs still survive as living links to the heyday of Scottishness in the capital.

In one respect, the twenty-first century has nothing on the nineteenth. For though the Caledonian Club, the St Andrew's Society and the London Highland Society are still going strong, the Scot of the early twenty-first century who wants to celebrate his nationality in the company of fellow Celts has nothing to compare with the astonishing wealth of clubs, clan societies and organisations which were on offer to his contemporaries more than a century ago. As the Victorian era was coming to an end, whether his interests were scientific, philosophical, nostalgic or cultural, the London Scot could easily move in a world which was, effectively, a home from home.

In fact, so proud of this flowering of indigenous Scottish culture were the London Scots of the late nineteenth century, that they celebrated them in a dedicated newspaper.

On Saturday, 7 January 1888, a Scot on the Strand who had a penny burning a hole in his sporran could have invested in a new newspaper designed to reassure and remind him that he was living in a city thronging with his fellow countrymen. The *London Scotsman*, which went on sale on London news-stands as the new year began, launched its first edition with a clarion call:

OOR AINSEL'S

That there is a 'call', and a loud one, for such a journal as THE LONDON SCOTSMAN, is sufficiently apparent when we state that in this vast metropolis, the Scottish is the only nationality unrepresented by a newspaper specially devoted to their interests; while the need for such a representative journal is further attested by the large number of letters we have received from Scotsmen of all ranks in society as soon as our projected project became known. The lines on which we intend to conduct THE LONDON SCOTSMAN, and the purposes we have in view, may be briefly enumerated as follows:-

1st. To knit our countrymen in the metropolis more closely together.
2nd. To give them an independent voice in all matters connected with the city of their adoption.
3rd. To arouse in our brethren a more lively interest in the traditions of their fathers.
4th. To supply Scotsmen in London with special reports of the doings of their fellow-countrymen in London, as well as regular news of their native land not obtainable through the ordinary sources of information.

But the new publication didn't just aim to keep the Scots in London abreast of developments back home. In keeping with

London's role as the gateway of the Empire, dispatching young Scots to India, Hong Kong and Canada, the newspaper had an international dimension too.

> In carrying out this programme, we shall earnestly endeavour so to conduct our journal that it shall be a welcome guest in every Scottish family in the Metropolis, and also be a pleasant reminder of the 'land of the mountain and the flood' for Scottish kindred in the Colonies and America.

This international dimension of Scottishness would become more pronounced as the newspaper went on, but the inaugural edition of the *London Scotsman*, a professionally produced monthly illustrated with cartoons, packed with news and shot throughout with a strong vein of pawky humour, drew mostly on the interest and dedication of the British Scottish Establishment of the day.

William Gladstone offered a typically sober message of support, noting the intrinsic value of celebrating 'local pride'. The Earl of Aberdeen sent good wishes and Robert Cunninghame Graham, co-founder of the Scottish Labour Party, expressed his hope that the newspaper would draw on the twin Scottish traditions of idealism and good fellowship, noting, 'It was much needed as a means of bringing Scotsmen together in this great desert of arid Conservatism and materialism.'

Perhaps the only sprig of wry scepticism in this forest of laurel garlands came from Edinburgh's Emeritus Professor Blackie, who declared, 'I cannot promise to do more than keep an eye on your doings, and not grudge you a weekly penny when I happen to have an idle one in my pocket.'

The first newspaper itself was well worth the penny of the slightly cynical professor, who that year would publish his life of Burns. Alongside the expected celebrations of the new publication, many written by its own staff, the *London Scotsman* also carried serious articles, such as one on Thomas de Quincey, whose long residence in Scotland made him as much a Scottish opium eater as an English one, and a surprisingly radical article on land use which would mark the beginning of a lengthy debate on the 'Crofter's Question'.

But, understandably, much of the first issue was given over to broad self-congratulation. Noticeable amongst these pieces of self-puffery is a rather hackneyed little playlet in which four broadly drawn London Scots congratulate themselves on their foresight and ability. Alec Stirling, a stereotyped Aberdonian, declares:

> We all thocht there wis no four clever chiels within the suroroundings of the muckle conglomeration o' bad bricks and ditto lime that could haud a cannel tae us. In proof, we've never found a fifth we thocht o' sufficient grit or sufficient cleverness tae gie him the richt hand o' fellowship and mak him a member o' the Thistle.

With their new accomplice, the four resolved to create a new newspaper: the *London Scotsman*. But the newspaper wasn't just an outpouring of locally based Scottish genius; it also gave vent to feelings of nostalgic longing for a Scotland which had been left behind. The *London Scotsman* provided a regular outlet for a very sentimental brand of poetry, most of which revolved around a narrow axis of national pride and intense homesickness. This, from the first edition, gives an indication of the tone and style of most of the poetic offerings.

THE LONDON SCOTSMAN, 7 JANUARY 1888

> Beyond a rampart of eternal hills,
> Our home lies far beneath a northern sky;
> And ever as our daily task we ply,
> 'Mid London streets, the thought of Scotland stills
> The din around us; and we see again
> The blue mist rise above the mountain glen,
> And hear the music of the mountain rills.
>
> Kind Scottish hearts! since thoughts of home can cheer
> The thronging loneliness of London ways,
> And shed a brightness over London gloom –
> In Scotland's name give us your welcome here,
> And turn aside, amid your busy days,
> To listen for the voice that speaks of home.– FRG.

116

But though the *London Scotsman* was larded with enough hoary tales, coincidences and sentimental declarations of loyalty to Her Majesty the Queen to satisfy the most dedicated of its London-based Scottish readership, it wasn't to last, and was just the precursor to what would truly become one of the most successful newspapers dedicated to any native group in the capital.

The true *London Scotsman*, retaining the name of the original, but typical of its audience not only in its sentimentality but also in its financial stability, would only emerge a decade later. This second manifestation of the paper relaunched in November 1897. The new *London Scotsman* appropriated the most successful elements of the first, but reduced the amount of radical political comment and purely sentimental coverage to leave a paper which was more Establishment- and Empire-minded. It was also more financially secure, since it was underwritten by a thriving network of Scottish clubs and societies. Its frontispiece, part acknowledgement and part boast, serves as an astonishing indication of the liveliness of Scottish London life as the nineteenth century came to a close.

After confidently boasting that 'this newspaper will especially appeal to the Members of the Scottish Associations of London, and to those of the similar societies in Liverpool, Manchester, Birmingham, Leeds etc.', it listed the Scottish Associations which were then extant in London. Even now it is an impressive list.

There was the London Aberdeen Banff and Kincardine Association, the London Argyllshire Association, the London Ayrshire Association, the Borders Association in London, the Breadalbane Association, the London Caithness Association, the Caledonian Society of London, the London Camanachd Club, the London Dumfries-shire Association, the London Fife Association, the London Forfarshire Association, the London Galloway Association, the Glasgow and Lanarkshire Association of London, the Gaelic Society of London, the London Highland Athletic Club, the Highland Society of London, the London Inverness-shire Association, the Liddesdale Society, the Loudoun and Galston Association, the London Morayshire Club, the London Ross and Cromarty Association, the Royal Scottish Corporation, the London Scottish Border Counties Association, the North London Scottish Association, the Robert Burns Club, the London Scottish Choir, the London Scottish Rifle Volunteers, and the Viking Club, incorporating the Orkney, Shetland and Northern Society.

There had been Scottish societies in London since the end of the eighteenth century. The Highland Society of London was instituted in 1778 with the aim of:

> Preserving the Martial Spirits, Language, Dress, Music and Antiquities of the Ancient Caledonians; Rescuing from oblivion the valuable remains of Celtic Literature; The Establishment and Support of Schools in the Highlands of Scotland, and in other parts of the British Empire; Relieving distressed Highlanders at a distance from their native homes; and Promoting the Improvement and general Welfare of the northern parts of the Kingdom.

The Highland Society had enormous political as well as social clout, which was shown as early as 1782, when it succeeded in securing the repeal of the Act which made it unlawful for Highlanders to wear the kilt, and as recently as the 1950s when it persuaded the Secretary of State for Scotland to appoint a Gaelic-speaking member to the Crofters Commission.

But the Highland Society wasn't a mere pressure group; it was also a place of learned enquiry. James Logan, the 'English' secretary of the Gaelic Society of London, who coordinated events in the English language, noted in an 1840 history of Scottish Societies in London that:

> There have been accumulated upwards of 260 volumes and tracts, and 44 interesting papers, on various subjects, have been read at the meeting. In forming the library an opportunity occurred of securing, by purchase, a unique collection of tracts and pamphlets on the state of feeling and proceedings during the Rebellions of 1715 and 1745.

And in keeping with the reputation of a society which in 1807 published the fraudulent poems of Ossian in the 'original' Gaelic, with a learned commentary by Sir John Sinclair on the controversy, the Highland Society became a place where the culture and economics of the Highlands received serious discussion and active support. As early as 1786, it had instituted an 'Association for the purchase of lands, and for forming free towns, villages and fishing stations in the Highlands'. An Act of Parliament in the same year incorporated it under the title 'The British Society for Extending the Fisheries and Improving the Sea Coasts of this Kingdom'.

The historian Michael Lynch has termed the Highland Society 'an Ossianic branch of the Enlightenment' – at its best, it embodied an Enlightenment seriousness about philosophical and literary matters and a romantic Ossianic sentiment. Appropriately, in December 1817, *The Times* reported that Prince Oscar of Sweden, 'in recognition of the fact that he has the same name as Ossian's hero', had been admitted as a member.

The Highland Society also gave something of a lead in indicating the ideological justification for many of the Scottish societies in London: Sir John Sinclair, a member of the Highland Society and the first president of the Board of Agriculture, wrote, in the history of the society, that one of its aims was to preserve the 'local distinctions of English, Scots, Irish and Welsh'.

But though the Highland Society ran continuously from its beginnings at the end of the eighteenth century, it was the second half of the nineteenth which saw an explosion in the number of Scottish societies and clubs in London – an explosion which was not confined to the English capital. During the same period, Edinburgh and Glasgow bristled with gentlemen's clubs, ladies' clubs, associations for promoting the Bible, missionary societies, scientific and philosophical institutions and charitable bodies. Edinburgh, too, had its Aberdeenshire, Caithness and Galloway associations, evidence of strong local identities which were sufficiently distinct from that of the Central belt to fuel clubs and organisations dedicated to their continuation.

In London, these local interest clubs flourished as places of debate, discussion and gossip, and as a lifeline back to a community which had been left in favour of pastures new. An evening at such a society would typically include a speech from a local boy made good, or a visitor from home with vital updates to pass on, followed by questions and vigorous debate from the floor, a smoke, perhaps a meal, then a few drinks. Nor were such organisations exclusively Scottish affairs: the Scottish local clubs had their counterparts in the London Jersey Society, founded in 1896, and other associations from Ireland, Cornwall, Wales and various far-flung parts of Britain. But the Scottish clubs were remarkable for three reasons: there were more of them than for any other national group; they had more members (an average of 200 subscribing members and an active membership of between 80 and 100); and they were supported by the Scottish Establishment in London and at home.

Of the twenty-eight clubs proudly listed on the front page of the newspaper, the presidents of five were Scottish MPs, eight were members of the House of Lords, with the Marquis of Tullibardine serving as president of the Highland Society and the Highland Athletic Club, and five were knighted. Four presidents were clan chiefs and His Royal Highness the Prince of Wales was president of the Royal Scottish Corporation. Yet, despite their prestigious figureheads, these organisations weren't simply opportunities for the Establishment to play.

Even those organisations which would come to be seen as mercantile hubs, places where successful Scottish businesspeople could conduct commercial activities in informal surroundings, opened their doors with an announcement that they were dedicated to the continuation of a Scottish sense of community and self-support.

The first edition of the original *London Scotsman* had celebrated the plan to open a Caledonian Club with the aim of 'providing a recognised centre, where Scotsmen of good social position will find the traditions of their country encouraged and upheld, and which will be the recognised headquarters for gentlemen who interest themselves in the many Scottish Societies and benevolent institutions'. The club, which opened its doors in St James Square in 1891 and moved to Halkin Street in Belgravia 26 years later, was from the outset intended to be a home from home for Scots. Bedecked in tartan carpets and military regalia, and festooned with stags' heads and clan pennants, it resembled, even in its early years, a heavy, old-fashioned Highland hotel in which staff would creep discreetly around the members' rooms, serving drinks to the military men and wealthy merchants who used it as their London base. From the very beginning, the club also proved a usefully central venue for Scottish societies to meet, joining the Royal Scottish Corporation in Fetter Lane and Church of Scotland properties as places where clubs and organisations could arrange their events.

But the patchwork of associations, which numbered about 30 in the early 1890s and accounted for between 4,000 and 5,000 people, ran the risk of duplicating their efforts (a few had already complained about the strain which annual events like individual Burns Suppers and St Andrew's Night celebrations put on them). The biggest upheaval in the world of the London Scottish societies, however, was yet to come.

In the February–March edition of 1898, the newspaper announced that a committee proposed that all the London Scottish societies should federate and band together with certain key aims:

> To promote amongst other things, the formation of:
> 1. An Employment Bureau
> 2. A Register of Lodgings
> 3. Reading and Recreation Rooms
> 4. A Debating Society

Debating societies were a distinctive hallmark of Scottish life, with local branches in even the smallest towns in Scotland dedicated to heated, formalised discussions of the political, moral and philosophical issues of the day. The Glasgow University Union, which would become such a crucible for Scottish politicians, was founded in 1890 after a five-year fundraising campaign, and local clubs which had failed in their search for a guest speaker would often devote the evening instead to members' debates, in which Scottish businessmen, apprentices or clerks would stand up and hone their rhetorical skills.

But the other aims of the federated Scottish societies – the employment bureau, register of lodgings and reading rooms – reveal the extent to which expatriate Scottish London society of the late nineteenth century was geared towards the encouragement of new emigrants and the support of those who had made the leap. This practical manifestation of what was effectively patronage in a kinship-based society also showed itself in the extent to which the London Scottish clubs were just that – clubs for Scots. The Caledonian Club, a club of a slightly different sort, declared in its rules for admittance that potential members must have a Scottish parent or grandparent, or, in exceptional circumstances, be strongly identified with Scotland. Gentlemen's clubs can set their own rules, of course, but so did most of the London Scottish societies, some of which specified that to join, an applicant had to prove that he was born in the area to which the club was dedicated.

For the Scottish Masonic lodges in London the rules were even tighter. The Thistle Lodge admitted only Scots; English Masons were barred, although fraternal connections were encouraged. Unsurprisingly, some London critics believed that such clubs were incestuous and self-serving, and there were certainly examples of committees perpetuating their tenure of power, or of businessmen inviting favoured clerks to join their particular society, even if that meant lengthy journeys by tram, in order to introduce them to those who would help their career.

Indeed, the promotion of new arrivals from Scotland was one of the underlying principles which kept such societies together, and incomers from Scotland who joined local interest societies could quickly find themselves introduced to successful Scots in politics, industry and commerce. In 1889, the Dumfries-shire Association had an 'at home' as guests of Mr Robinson Souttar, MP for the county, and his wife.

> The proceedings of the evening were characterised by a charming lack of formality, and good humour and good feeling were omnipresent. Perhaps this was in no small degree due to the two short but significant words at the bottom of the invitation card, 'morning dress'. Like other London County Associations, the Dumfriesshire knows no class distinctions, and in dealing with Dumfriesians Mr and Mrs Souttar know no difference between High and Low. So far as one could judge from appearances, the guests were drawn from very varied classes, say from Sir Robert Reid, a valued member of the late Government and one of our foremost lawyers, to the youth just come to the mighty city from his native

country, whose possibilities of advancement must be regarded as infinite.

At its best, that combination of patronage, respect for a hierarchy which prided itself on its approachability and conviviality and, above all, the prospect of a fellowship which united the humblest recent arrival and the most prosperous London Scot, was a powerful incentive to join Scottish societies, to keep attending in the face of rival attractions and to perpetuate the same principles into the next generation.

At their worst, though, these organisations could be stuffy and self-congratulatory. Women tended to be invited only as guests for balls and fundraisers, and dinners were all-male affairs at which military or pseudo-military hierarchies were observed. In 1893, a group of Scottish clerks, balking at the pompous tone of many of the Scottish societies, decided to form their own – the Scottish Clerks' Association – which was a slightly more relaxed affair and became a place of fevered debate about Scotland and London life.

But while members of the 30 or so Scottish societies were celebrating their own version of the kinship system, they were also intensely preoccupied with larger arguments about the place of Scots in the United Kingdom and, an inevitable concern for Scots of all ages, the precise nature of Scottish identity.

In November 1898, the Revd John Watson, who, as 'Ian McLaren', had become a literary celebrity for exiled Scots with his novel, *Beside the Bonnie Briar Bush,* published four years earlier, spoke at the St Andrew's Day celebration of the Liverpool Caledonian Society on the subject of 'Scottish Character':

> When the Scot went to a foreign country, he had a keen sympathy with the political struggles of that country, and was not inclined to quarrel with its political traditions; but left to himself, nine Scots out of ten reverted to that just and strong democracy which was created by John Knox, who found a number of nobles and their retainers and left a consolidated and independent nation. (Applause) Nothing was so

indomitable as the Scots accent, which travelled before
a man and which, in its hold of the letter 'r', gave pledge
of success in every department of life.

Aside from the prominence given to the influence of Knox, and
the emphasis on the powerful Scottish 'R', it is a flattering view
of Scottish identity which many would agree with today.
Strikingly contemporary too is the argument which gripped the
small world of the London Scottish societies in the last years of
the nineteenth century: a fierce debate over the use of the word
'English' where 'British' was meant.

This, of course, was one of the longest-standing points of
tension within the Union. In the 1750s, English patriots had
grumbled at the surrender of their beloved word 'England' and
its submergence within 'Great Britain', and it became the subject
of petitions to Lord Bute, the Scottish-born Prime Minister.
Though on the surface it seemed to be a petty argument about
words, it was in fact a serious dispute about status. In practice it
took much of its heat from the fact that Scots tended to believe
they were being deliberately insulted by the use of 'England',
and many English people, who used the term in the widest
sense, to include, not exclude, Scotland and Wales, gave the
impression that they couldn't see what all the fuss was about.
Scots, stung by the implication that they were being touchy,
bridled at the insult; and so it went on.

More recently, one of the points taken up by the National
Association for the Vindication of Scottish Rights in the 1850s
had been that 'The United Kingdom of England and Scotland
should be always designated "Great Britain", and not by
implication "England"'. But in 1898, it became such an issue in
Scottish civic society that Her Majesty Queen Victoria, whose
celebration of tartanry at Balmoral led many Scots to believe
that she was intrinsically sympathetic to their aims and values,
was presented with a petition on the subject. Addressed to Her
Majesty from her 'loyal Scottish subjects', it did not pull its
punches, arguing forcibly that when 'England' is used instead of
'Britain', 'the Treaty [of Union] is violated and the honour of
Scotland is attacked'.

Lord Balfour, the former Secretary of State for Scotland,
responded in terms so high flown and legalistic that many were

left confused as to which side he stood on, justifying the then famous slogan, 'You seldom know what Balfour means'. As a sign that the issue was not purely the preserve of cranks, Sir Arthur Conan Doyle, who kept his crankiness for the subject of spiritualism, wrote to *The Times*:

> Why . . . should the races upon whose bones this Empire has been largely built up – the Irishmen, the Highlanders, the Welshmen – be excluded? . . . It may seem to the Anglo-Saxon to be a mere matter of sentiment. But then the whole question is open to that criticism. To the man with Celtic blood, who inherits, amongst other qualities, a certain sensitiveness of disposition, it appears to be a very practical matter, and his support or his opposition may depend on how far he is recognised or ignored.

It is easy to view these as minor, even petty complaints, and Hugh MacDiarmid famously sent them up in a poem about the London Scots, but the sense of exclusion or of being taken for granted is still an important part of the repertoire of feelings many Scots have about their place in the British firmament. In recent years, debates about the economics of Scotland's place in the Union may have taken a larger role than ones about sentimentality, but even these discussions were foreshadowed by a late Victorian concern about whether Scotland was a net subsidiser of, or subsidised by, the English economy. An editorial in the *London Scotsman* of 1898 tackled the issue head-on:

> A few weeks ago, a Scottish contemporary proclaimed, with a great flourish of trumpets, that the good, kind, senior partner of the firm of Britain and Co. was so liberal to its junior, that it was actually paying a greater proportion in taxation, per head, than was Scotland . . . we confess we put our tongues in our cheeks when we heard the good tidings. For we remembered that, as long ago as 1888, it was clearly shown by Messrs. Wm. Mitchell and MacNaught, of the Scottish Home Rule Association, that, at any rate previous to that date, the

generosity had all been in the other direction, and that during the previous 25 years Scotland had been paying in taxation from 2s 6d to 12s more per head of her population than had been contributed by England. In 1871, for instance, to quote Mr McNaught's figures, the taxation per head was: Englishmen £2 2s 11 1/2d.; Scotsmen £2 12s 61/4d.; Irishmen £1 6s 01/2d.; Scotsmen thus paying 10s per head more than Englishmen, and more than double what was paid by Irishmen.

Mr Mitchell adds, 'from the fact that Scotland contributes, relatively to its population, the largest proportion of the revenue of the United Kingdom, it is clear that so far the balance of advantage arising from the Union is financially very much on the side of England'.

But these very modern-sounding concerns also sat beside pieces which now seem to come from the glens of Scottish kitschery: earnest debates on how exactly the kilt should be worn shared pages with disputed economic analyses of Scotland's relationship with England, or laments at the disproportionate numbers of Scots killed fighting for the British Empire. The former, not the latter, hit the most anguished tone, with the habit of wearing the kilt so it covered the whole knee pan being dismissed by one correspondent as a 'degenerate and effeminate custom. What distinguishes the kilt from a mere petticoat is that the former is worn so as to clearly show the whole of the knee.'

But it is the classified advertisements and announcements which give a real flavour of the richness of London Scottish life, whether they note the retirement of much loved Scottish policemen who had kept order in the East End, or the demise of Mr J.R. Gibson, the Aberdeen actor, renowned for his performance of Baillie Nicol Jarvie:

> Mr Gibson was in early days a cabinet-maker, but twenty-four years ago he went on the stage. In Newcastle and Glasgow he was a very great favourite and some ten years ago he took a capital position in London, having for a time a good place in Mr Henry

Irving's company at the Lyceum. For several years past,
however, he has been pretty constantly an invalid and
he died on the 23rd ult., at the age of forty-five.

Or that 'Mr Alfred S. Edward RBA, whose picture, "The
Birthplace of Cuyp" was reproduced in the *Scots Pictorial* recently
is a Moray loon. He stays in the North of London.' Such pride
in the success of Scottish boys made good might strike us today
as rather quaint, but it was an important part of fostering the
sense of a British society studded with successful Scots, and gave
reassurance that Scottish success in London would be cheered
by the expatriate community, who would take it as a sign of the
triumph of their able natives.

Benedict Anderson, one of the most influential writers about
modern nationalism, devoted a whole book, *Imagined
Communities,* to the subject of how newspapers help to create a
community of readers, bound together by the knowledge that
they are a coherent group and that they share a sphere of
interest and concern. The *London Scotsman,* though, seemed to be
a window on a world which was already a powerful community,
vividly real, united by ties of commerce and community, and
able to celebrate the serious and the light-hearted, with earnestly
political discussions about the affairs of the day sitting next to
sentimental reflections on old Scotland.

But why would the Victorian era (the time of 'North Britain'),
the apparent Scottish contentment at the state of the Union
(certainly the absence of anything like the Home Rule
movement in Ireland), and the intense Scottish pride at the
Celtic contribution to the British Empire also see this flowering
of Scottish sentiment at the heart of the British capital?

The answer perhaps lies partly in the Empire itself, which,
whilst it celebrated British unity and the global reach of British
power, was also fascinated by the local, the individual character
of parts of Britain, the distinctive speech of Devon men or
Highland women, and the sense that their vivid local lives were
as much part of the dominion of the British Empire as those of
Indian peasants or Canadian Mounties. The Scottish societies
in London did many things, but they also provided and
maintained local 'colour', commemorating the dress, speech

and concerns of communities far from London. When the North London Scottish Society holds a 'herrin' supper' and notes that 'local dress [is] optional', it is not just dressing up, as modern Scots who put on their kilt for St Andrew's Night are dressing up, it is also showing that metropolitan mores haven't entirely obliterated local loyalties and memories. Modern Scots, hypersensitive to tartanry and trained to wince at the excesses of Victorian kitsch, often find these kinds of events arch and embarrassing, but they were enormously successful, and they drew in some of the most powerful and sophisticated London Scots of the day. The men who scaled the highest branches of the British army, ran surgical wards in the East End, or wrote leader columns for Fleet Street newspapers were many things, but they weren't fools. And they were happy to spend a night only speaking the Doric for fear of incurring a nominal fine, or singing the traditional songs they remembered from their boyhoods.

Another reason for the pride in such Scottishness might be that in Victoria's reign it seemed to be sanctioned from the very top down. The Empress of India, from the moment she decorated Balmoral in a triumph of tartan in 1848, had declared her deep love of all things Scottish. The same year she visited the Balmoral Gathering, cementing a tie between the Highland Games and the Royal family which still exists today. She famously preferred Scottish servants; her relationship with John Brown continues to fascinate, as the success of the film *Mrs Brown* demonstrates. And Victoria's sentimental attraction to all things Scottish also provided surprising routes for advancement to her loyal Scottish subjects.

When in 1881 her Scottish resident medical attendant, Dr William Marshall, retired, she charged her factor at Balmoral to find a new one, not from Harley Street, but from the North-East. She made her requirements clear: she wanted a Scotsman, preferably an Aberdonian, and one who could speak German, in case any of her visiting relatives fell ill while in Ballater. The factor asked a friend who recommended his nephew, Dr James Reid, who had been educated at the Aberdeen Grammar School and had found his way to Vienna via Paddington. At the age of 31, Reid was appointed the Queen's personal doctor, and quickly became a trusted confidant as well as employee. He

128

'I shall have a place, for I'm his Cousin'; a London-based Scots laird dispenses largesse to his kin. (Unknown artist, *The Caledonians Arrival in Money-Land*, 1762, etching, 20.1 x 33 cm image. Courtesy of the Lewis Walpole Memorial Library, Yale University, 762.5.0.4.)

Demonic figures tip Scots onto English soil.
(Unknown artist, *A View of the Origin of Scotch Ministers and Managers*, 1793, etching and engraving, 5 x 10 cm image. Courtesy of the Lewis Walpole Memorial Library, Yale University, 763.4.8.5.)

A Flight of Scotchmen fall towards England and the colonies. (Richard Newton, *A Flight of Scotchmen*, 1796, etching with hand colouring, 31.2 x 45.6 cm image. Courtesy of the Lewis Walpole Memorial Library, Yale University, 769.3.1.)

'A Scotch Louse always travels Southwards' – a comparatively late piece of anti-Scottish propaganda from 1818. ('C.W.', *Making a Compass at Sea – or the Use of a Scotch Louse*, 1818, etching with hand colouring, 21.3 x 32.2 cm image. Courtesy of the Lewis Walpole Memorial Library, Yale University, 818.0.14)

The London Scotsman opens its doors. An 1888 cartoon by 'Mons Meg' in the paper's first edition that year. Despite the exuberance of the image, the first incarnation of the newspaper for London-based Scots lasted only a handful of issues.

PARLIAMENTARY VIEWS Nº 6 A SCOTCH NIGHT *THE CROFTER'S BILL HAS ITS FLING.*

SSENCE OF PARLIAMENT.
EXTRACTED FROM
THE DIARY OF TOBY, M.P.

which it is to be hoped they will sedulously observe. CHRISTOPHER got through the ceremony of introduction with that simple grace and dignity that distinguishes his every movement. Evidently fearful that Sir THOMAS MAY wanted to shake hands with him. He steadily

The passage of the Crofter's Bill, portrayed as a Highland
extravaganza at Westminster, in Harry Furniss's cartoon from *Punch*.
(*Punch*, 3 April 1886. All *Punch* images courtesy of the Punch Library.)

The cricketing Scotsman
on the Make; J.M. Barrie
in his whites.
(G.R. Halkett, *Punch*,
17 December 1902.)

"Oh, I'm no good except as a change bowler."

A WEIGHTY REASON.

Rob. "THEY 'RE TELLIN' ME THAT TAM STIRDY 'S TURNED OOT A GREAT POET SINCE HE GAED TAE LONDON."
Allan. "POET! HOO COULD TAM STIRDY BE A POET! MAN, HE WAS AT THE SCHULE WI' *ME!*"

'Ah kent his faither.' The bemused resentment of the stay-at-home Scots against their successful brothers. (*Punch*, 23 April 1902 by Alexander Stuart Boyd, who was, of course, Scottish.)

THE ALL-CONQUERING SCOT

Old Scotsman (to his son, who has just returned from a business trip to London). "Weel, laddie, and what dae ye think o' the English noo?"
Son. "Oh, I didn't have much of a chance to study them. You see, I only had to do with the heads of departments!"

The successful emigrant returns to crow over the English.
(Welshman Bert Thomas's cartoon from *Punch*, 4 May 1910)

Three kilted Tory Scots admire the portrait of their King; Michael Cummings' view of Alec Douglas-Home, Harold Macmillan and Iain MacLeod as Scots on the Make. (*Sunday Express*, August 1961. Courtesy of Express Newspapers and the Centre of Cartoons and Caricature, University of Kent at Canterbury.)

Close Encounters of a Scottish Kind. One alien invader explains his ambitions to another. (Adrian Teal, courtesy of cartoonstock.com.)

dedicated the rest of his professional life to the service of the Queen and would attend her on her deathbed. Discreet, dedicated and willing to stand up to her wilful moods, he became a vital figure in the Royal household and a living symbol of the centrality of Scots to British national life. When he married in November 1899, he was the subject of a 'Pindaric Epithalamium' written by Lord Rosebery:

> Arise Aberdonian Muse, and sound
> Thy Bagpipes o'er thy classic ground:
> (Let it not be said she tarried
> When her darling son was married.)
> Sound the tabret and the lute,
> The dental harp that Hebrew use;
> For the man would be a brute
> Who his music would refuse,
> Loud enough to wake the dead,
> When our cherished Reid is wed.

From practice in Aberdeen to the bedside of a queen, from the obscurity of the north-east of Scotland to the subject of a truly appalling poem by a member of the House of Lords, famous Scottish trajectories like this encouraged the belief that the world was full of possibilities for Scottish men of talent and that one day, the call might come which would lead from the provinces to the very centre of Empire, of the very world.

Victoria's fetish for all things Scottish seemed to justify Scottish pride that the country was an equal partner in Britain and a foundation stone of the Empire. It also, of course, served to cement the appeal of the Royal family in Scotland, a role performed in the twentieth century by that other 'Scottish' member of the Royal family, Queen Elizabeth, the Queen Mother, who stubbornly asserted that she had been born north of the border even when it was proved that she had entered the world in the back of an ambulance in Berkeley Square. After her death, the mantle passed to Princess Anne, with her devotion to the cause of Scottish rugby, and may perhaps pass to Prince William with his St Andrews University education and fondness for Edinburgh's style bars.

But if national pride and Royal recognition were two powerful pillars in the London Scot's sense of importance, the third was sport. Appropriately, one of the most successful Scottish clubs in London was dedicated to rugby, a game which excited the passions of former Scottish private schoolboys as much as their English counterparts. The London Scottish, who took the field in the St Andrew's colours of a blue jersey and white knickerbockers, made suitably British by the addition of red stockings, were founded in 1878 out of the St Andrew's Rovers, a club whose name attracted many Scottish players, but was in fact a body open to stocky Welsh scrum-halves as much as English wingers.

The new club, though, was unashamedly partisan, and admitted only Scottish players. The brainchild of four successful London Scots – George Grant, Neil MacGlashan, Robert Arnott and D. Begbie Gibson – the club profited from a regular influx of talent from north of the border, and in 1880 was boosted by the organisational acumen and fantastic kicking ability of W.E. Maclagan, an Edinburgh Academical who came garlanded with five Scotland caps and would add a further twenty while playing for the London Scottish.

Maclagan was one of the sporting all-rounders occasionally produced by Scottish schools. He had been captain of cricket and rugby at the Edinburgh Academy and was a man of commanding ability on and off the field. When in 1886 he retired as captain and accepted that his playing days were behind him, he threw his energies into the organisation of the club and, with 47 years of continuous service behind him, died in 1927.

But even this den of Establishment Scots wasn't immune to outbursts of Scottish patriotic feeling. In 1884, a committee member recommended that the red stockings, which saw the London Scottish play in the colours of the Union flag, be replaced with blue ones, making it clear that the team was Scottish through and through. The controversial measure was passed seven votes to six, but for much of the following year the argument raged. Were the London Scottish Scottish first or second? The blue stockinged players romped to victory and defeated all the other teams in the London league in 1884, but by the beginning of the 1885 season the red stockings were back. The argument seems arcane, but the Union colours were appropriate for an organisation which had strong links to Empire, and which would welcome back figures such as 'Jock Wemyss of Gala', who played against Ireland and Wales in 1914 and returned to the field after the Great War minus an eye, a handicap which didn't seem to affect his kicking ability in a successful match against France in 1920.

Rugby wasn't the only sport that London Scots celebrated. Long after the death of Victoria, London-based Scots celebrated their distinctive cultural identity in Highland Games. A year before the British Exhibition of 1951 (in which, incidentally, the British love of hobbies and voluntary societies was a major theme), visitors to White City were able to see for themselves a curious tableau which showed the complexities of multinational Britain: a Highland Games, complete with marching bands, bagpipers, little girls doing the Highland Fling and huge sweaty men tossing the caber. The first Caledonian Games was an enormous hit, and ran for the next five years.

They were serious sporting events, too. At the first, the record for the 200-yard dash was broken, and the news coverage was respectful, if slightly amused.

By May 1951, though, reporters had grasped what an unusual event this festival of Scottish sport truly was. *The Times* report was tongue in cheek:

> The programme . . . was – to purely London eyes – a strange medley of events. There were athletics, strictly according to AAA rules, a demonstration from Mr J.M. Wilson's world famous sheepdogs, tugs of war, tossing the caber, Highland dancing and pipe-playing competitions. The one innovation, a five-a-side football match between Glasgow Rangers and Celtic, might well prove to have started something in the South.

The journalist had clearly never seen anything like Mr Wilson's world-famous collies, but the year before they had thrilled the crowd at White City by rounding up a flock of dizzy sheep in under two minutes. Despite, indeed perhaps because of, the caber tossing and tugs of war, the Caledonian Games became a huge hit at White City. Hundreds of thousands of pounds went to charity and, in 1953, the event was watched by the Australian, Canadian and New Zealand prime ministers, who were in London for the Commonwealth Heads of Government Conference, but were united in the celebration of another commonwealth – Scottish internationalism, which connected the 'land of the mountain and flood' with the rest of its Scottish Empire. It was the high point of a Scottishness wedded to Britain and the outside world, and a culmination of all the work of London's Scottish societies over the years. What lay ahead for them was retreat, retrenchment and decline.

CHAPTER 6

Paved with Gold?

On 12 June 2003, the oldest Scottish society in London threw a party to celebrate its new facelift. For months, the Royal Scottish Corporation in Covent Garden had been shrouded in a tarpaulin while painters coloured its frontage saltire blue and transformed its foyer into an impressionistic collage, symbolically depicting modern Scotland with hills, oil rigs and the faces of Scottish pop stars. Tonight, the wrapping was due to come off.

Inside, guests picked at a cold buffet and listened to speeches celebrating 400 years of glorious history. Founded by Charles II, the son of James VI, the corporation was created to offer relief to the families of Scots who had travelled to the capital in the Scottish King's wake and had found London life harder than anticipated. Since 1660, it has been continuously looking after Scots who have found themselves down on their luck and has supplemented its remarkable financial generosity with a thriving programme of cultural activities and personal encouragement.

On the surface, all seemed prosperous and secure. Trustees who had served in the 1960s were in attendance, alongside clients who had enjoyed the corporation's support since shortly after the Second World War. The meeting room on the ground floor was alive with Scottish voices, medals gleamed from blue-blazered chests and in the crowd actors recognisable from television sitcoms jostled with retired Scottish investment bankers, insurance men and Church of Scotland ministers. A client of the corporation recited his own poetry and a piper played, deafeningly in the enclosed space.

It was an old-fashioned kind of affair, the sort which doesn't happen much in Scotland nowadays, and it seemed particularly incongruous in a Covent Garden swarming with Italian teenagers and street performers. It was like the gathering of an old Scotland in exile, one which took its responsibilities seriously, and which saw them as part and parcel of its public life. Yet for all its signs of vitality, the corporation represents a kind of Scottishness which is dying and it is unclear what is going to take its place.

'I call it London's best-kept Scottish secret,' says Willie Docherty, the corporation's new chief executive. 'The clients themselves call it a society and they don't pass it on. We've been sitting here in Covent Garden in splendid isolation. The corporation hasn't invested in PR for a long number of years. They haven't been required to fundraise, and fundraising itself is kind of PR. Only in retrospect can I see how that happened: they moved from Crown Court in Fleet Street, where they had been since 1870, and in moving they were no longer a nexus point for Scots in London. When they moved here, they assumed that everyone would move with them. No doubt that did happen in the early years, but it's 30 years ago now and people have forgotten about us.'

Docherty has come to the corporation with an outsider's eye and professional expertise gained in development work in Edinburgh's Wester Hailes, one of the most deprived housing estates in Europe. He was born on a Scottish peripheral housing scheme himself and until the age of 35 was a labourer and machine operator. It's a background which could be expected to give him an important insight into poverty and the ways it can be tackled. But Docherty is up against 400 years of tradition in an institution infused with very particular values. Two of his predecessors at the corporation were wing commanders. He doesn't say it, but he'd be forgiven if he found his new job a bit of a culture shock.

'Our activities are set out by a Royal Charter of 1665 which has been renewed three times. That charter prescribes whom we can deliver a service to: people born in Scotland, their sons and daughters, and their widows. We want to extend that to widowers too but we need an Act of Parliament to do it. And [to be eligible] you must live within a 35-mile radius of Charing Cross.'

It's an old-fashioned set of rules and though he can see the potential of the organisation he now heads, Docherty is conscious that the corporation's glorious history is a burden as well as a blessing. Its traditional Presbyterian-based model of poor relief, which until recently had needy Scots getting handouts at the door of its Covent Garden headquarters, isn't as applicable in the twenty-first century as it was in the seventeenth. The country-dancing evenings which were a staple of corporation life have fallen away, and the network of well-meaning, largely voluntary visitors who called on the corporation's pensioners – and in the 1970s ran errands to replace broken irons and wirelesses – has been phased out after it was discovered that they spent most of their time stuck in the London traffic.

But though Docherty may be uncomfortable with some aspects of the corporation's ethos, he can thank its trustees for the extraordinary reserves of cash which underwrite the organisation's activities.

According to publicly available figures, as of November 2002 the Royal Scottish Corporation was £31.3 million in the black, a sum which most charities would look on with astonishment and envy. These reserves have been built up through a combination of Scottish fiscal prudence and compound interest. When the corporation was receiving bequests and donations in the 1880s, it invested in property and a portfolio of bonds and stock; by 1916, it was worth £92,000.

That enormous surplus opens up huge possibilities and means that it is able to broaden and deepen its operation, moving away from the relief of needy individuals to developing a systematic approach to dealing with the issue of poverty amongst the descendants of Scots in London.

But the biggest challenge facing the corporation may be defining its ethos. Docherty, a graduate of urban regeneration programmes in Scotland and the public sector in London, has inherited the running of a protestant warhorse; the public-service side of an old Scottish Establishment which worked through the Caledonian Club, the Church of Scotland and the army. Once it had considerable financial, organisational and moral resources available to it, but it's an unfashionable world now.

The Victorian Scots had a less troubled sense of their priorities. The Royal Caledonian Asylum was formed by prosperous Scottish businessmen in 1815, after the Napoleonic wars, with the intention of supporting the descendants of Scottish military men who had died or fallen on hard times. From its inception, it was a favoured charity of Scottish aristocrats and landowners, and at the beginning of its life it received a boost from a fundraising drive organised by the Highland Society in London under its president, the Duke of Kent.

The Scottish novelist John Galt was called upon to act as secretary of the new institution. He wrote a poem and dedicated it to His Royal Highness, the Prince Regent at a fundraising dinner at the Freemasons' Tavern on Saturday, 4 March 1815:

TRIUMPHAL GLEE
By Mr Galt

To Him the Regal Victors came,
The blest avengers for the fame,
When the great war was won;
They came – they own'd the cheering aid,
Nor till this generous homage paid,
Deem'd their high duty done.

The fam'd Exile, the Royal Guest,
With Rights restor'd and wrongs redress'd –
The rival of his power –
Departing, honour'd, o'er the wave
A nobler sight to England gave
Than Edward's proudest hour.

The Caledonian Asylum lived up to its aims, educating its charges according to the traditions of the Church of Scotland. Classes stressed the importance of devotional duty, alongside writing and arithmetic. An ethos of responsibility ran through the asylum. Boys were taught that they should be responsible for their behaviour before God, as trustees were responsible for those who, by God's grace, were less blessed than they were. Even in peacetime, demand for the support of the asylum vastly outstretched supply. In order to decide who should be supported, the asylum initiated a system where trustees would vote on who was the most deserving.

A document from 8 October 1838 indicates the way in which the asylum gathered support from its benefactors. It also gives an incidental insight into the way Scottish members of the Imperial armed forces could expect to be scattered around the globe; if they were injured or killed, their children fell on poor relief.

NOTICE IS HEREBY GIVEN, that pursuant to the resolution of the General Court, on the Seventh of June last, an election by ballot for EIGHT BOYS to be admitted into the Institution, will take place on the Quarterly General Court, to be held at the FREEMASONS' TAVERN, GREAT QUEEN STREET, on Thursday, the Sixth Day of December next. The Poll to commence at Twelve o'clock, and to close at Three precisely.

CANDIDATES
FIFTH APPLICATION
James Alexander Burnett, aged nine years. The father was a native of the Parish of Benholm, in the County of Mearns: served upwards of 19 years in the First Regiment of Life Guards. He died in March, 1835, leaving a widow and two children totally unprovided for.

FOURTH APPLICATION
James Miller, aged seven years. The father, a native of Dundee, was a Ship-master, and had sailed for many years by the port of London in the West-India Trade. He was lost at sea in January 1834, leaving a widow and seven young children wholly unprovided for. One of the children died lately. The widow at present keeps a small Public-house. Residence 79, Wapping Wall, Shadwell.

Subscriptions will be thankfully received by the Secretary and the Collector at the Institution, and by

the following Bankers:- Messrs. Coutts and Co.;
Messrs. Drummond and Co.; and Messrs. Smith,
Payne and Smiths, in London; and by the British Linen
Company at Edinburgh.

This ballot for worthy orphans, sent out in the post for Scottish
benefactors to consider as they chewed over their breakfast,
seems a little macabre now, but advertising their deserving
charges was an important part of the charity's work. In addition
to postal ballots, the boys who were the intended recipients of
charitable donation were marched around the hall during
annual fundraising dinners and balls, so that their benefactors
could see exactly whom their money was going to support.

And many of those who were educated at the Caledonian
Asylum did go on to a life outside the trap of congenital poverty.
Though the emphasis was on imparting practical skills, the
asylum also produced at least one visionary. The poet James
Thomson, who was placed in the asylum after his father died,
went on to write disturbing Blakean poetry about the capital.
Others leaving the asylum chose to go home to Scotland, where
they were supported by their families. Some went on to become
tradesmen. Most disappeared from the public record.

Those disappearances are symbolic, because for every Scot who
goes to London to make a name for himself, there are others
who end up anonymous, invisible, disappeared.

In January 2004, a 17-year-old mystery was laid to rest. The
King's Cross fire, which ripped through London's busiest
underground station on 18 November 1987, had left one
question behind. Thirty of its victims had been mourned,
grieved and commemorated, but 'body 115' remained
unidentified, lying unmarked in a pauper's grave in Finchley
Cemetery.

The police believed that '115' was a middle-aged man, a
heavy smoker and possibly a brain surgery patient. Seventeen
years after his death, the man was identified as Alexander
Fallon, a Scot who, after his wife died, lived in hostels in
London as a virtual vagrant.

But the identification of Fallon's body left another Scottish
family heartbroken. The sons and daughters of James Brown

had pinned their hopes on the theory that their father, who disappeared in 1987, had been '115'. When their father vanished, Kathleen Wilson and Jim Brown, his adult children, travelled to London and scoured the streets around Blackfriars, but they failed to find him. James Brown's whereabouts are still unknown.

Two Scots, both homeless, both vanished, both believed to be lying in a pauper's grave. They stand as modern symbols for the men and women who come to London and simply vanish, and as fragile modern examples of the problem of Scottish homelessness which has been a feature of London life for at least the last 400 years.

Henry Mayhew's *London Labour and the London Poor of 1851-66* contains many references to the Scottish emigrants who were living rough on the streets of Victorian London and supporting themselves by busking or begging. Mayhew devoted a whole section in his book to street performers and describes many Highland bagpipe players supporting themselves by playing music on street corners or in pubs. In one section, devoted to the 'Wandering Tribes of England', Mayhew interviews a blind Scots musician who plays the pubs around Marylebone:

> I am one of the three blind Scotchmen who go about the streets in company, playing the violoncello, clarinet, and flute. We are really Highlanders, and can all speak Gaelic; but a good many London Highlanders are Irish. I have been 30 years in the streets of London; one of my mates has been 40 years – he's 69 – the other has been 30 years.

By the 1880s, the Scots were even more obvious; when the *Strand* magazine devoted a special edition to cataloguing London street performers, the Scottish bagpiper was prominent amongst the hurdy-gurdy players, accordionists and singers. Many of these bagpipers were former army men, discharged into a world which had no need for them anymore, and desperate to use the skills they had learned in the service of Britain to earn money on the streets of the capital. But charity workers were also noticing a rise in another phenomenon; mobile Scottish homelessness, as those who had been sleeping rough in Edinburgh or Glasgow somehow found their way to London to start again.

Victoria bus station is often the first stop for many Scottish arrivals in London today. Thronging with travellers clutching their luggage, it is also home to a shifting population who aren't going anywhere: Scottish refugees who still arrive daily, hoping that London will give them the chance which Scotland didn't.

'We had a man here last week who came here straight off the bus. He'd had a row with his wife and his brother in Glasgow and decided he'd rather go to London. He didn't even have his wallet with him. In the morning, when he arrived at the bus station, he decided he wanted to go home.' Eileen Ward, the director of Borderline, a charity for homeless Scots based a few hundred yards from Victoria bus station, is the first point of call for many of the Scots who come to London and need help almost the minute they arrive.

Behind a securely locked double-door and a buzzer entry-phone system, Borderline tries to find homeless Scots a hostel bed or a permanent place to live. Inside, the charity looks like a local authority housing department, with contact numbers pinned up on the board and bulging client files spilling out from the shelves. Every year they deal with thousands of Scots who find themselves homeless in the capital. One age-old solution to the problem is to help them go back.

'We do try and resettle people to Scotland, and we do that in two ways, either through planned resettlement with our second chance programme or through emergency situations – just help them get the tickets back to Scotland type of thing. The planned resettlement is something we would like to expand. If you don't do it properly, they'll go back up and it won't work and we get what we call shuttle homelessness, so we are trying to work much more closely with agencies in Scotland. Getting someone accommodation isn't the end to all their problems, so we want to get them to a situation where they can cope with budgets, and if they have children, where they're near enough to them.'

Borderline's annual reports list the hundreds of private reasons which make their clients homeless. It's a predictable catalogue of broken homes, abusive step-parents, atomising relationships and the rest, with the dark undertow of drink and drug abuse. But these aren't necessarily reasons to come to London: why do so many Scots think that their most cherished dreams will be answered in the south? Eileen Ward believes that Scots really do believe the myths about London.

'The streets really are paved with gold in their eyes. They think they will find success here. These days people believe there are jobs, but even if there are, it's hard to find a job and pay accommodation.'

So deep rooted is the desire for success that those who have made it to London, but failed to find success there, will nonetheless pretend that they have hit the big time in order to keep face with those whom they have left behind.

'Sometimes an odd thing happens; a member of the family comes down [to London], pretends that they are successful, gives the success story at home and so someone else – a younger brother or somebody – thinks that they are going to have a good time and comes down to join them. It's only when they arrive they realise that it's not true. It means that those most in need of giving up, or of going home to Scotland, are the last people to do it.'

So keen are some Scots to escape from their situation that they will leave without even the identification necessary to claim benefits; one of Borderline's most popular services is liaising with the Records Office in Scotland in order to get a copy of their client's birth certificate, so they can start again in the new city.

But new birth certificate or not, growing up in Scotland is not necessarily the best preparation for living in London. 'Quite a lot of them can't cope with the fact that Scotland is so white and London is so multi-ethnic,' said one caseworker. Others report clients saying to them, 'Why should these Pakis get a house before me? I'm Scottish!'

But whether they feel entitled to privileged treatment or not, Eileen Ward believes that many are simply swamped by the experience of living in London. 'They come with problems and they don't have the support network. A lot of them are very lonely. I've learned in the last few months that there aren't the same Scottish communities as there are Irish communities, there isn't the same feeling that this is a Scottish area, like Kilburn or Camden are Irish communities. Borderline is run by the two

Churches of Scotland in London and for a lot of people there, that is their community. Both of the churches are very lively and have a lot going on, and unless you have that kind of community it can be very lonely.'

In the face of such a fragmented southern society, Borderline is a kind of Scottish Embassy, in the sense that it's where you go when your wallet has been stolen.

I met one of Borderline's successful clients in the charity's waiting room. James was an intelligent, good-looking man in his early 30s who, two years before, had been sleeping in the doorways of shops on the Strand. 'They were good friends there, you know. I remember lying there one night in the cold and thinking I was going to die. I still see some of the guys I was there with, they're still sleeping rough, and I go and speak to them. There's a real camaraderie, a real sense of something in common. A lot of the Scottish guys, you'll see them again and again. You'll be walking along the street and they'll call out to you and you'll speak to them, and it turns out they'll still be in the situation you left them in. Time just goes by so quickly.

'Sometimes when you are in Scotland people will talk about a good place to go and stay next time you're in London, a hostel or something, so there is a kind of network. And some of the guys will be down here and think, "Oh, I fancy going up to Scotland for a while and see my pals", and so they'll go up there and be homeless there for a while, and then come back here.'

When James was living on the street, he became addicted to drugs and eventually received a sentence for possession. But now, a star of the Street League, a football league for homeless people, he is offering his services to others, coaching the team and helping to organise tournaments. He's streetwise, an old hand. When we had finished speaking, he offered some advice and some cigarettes to two pale teenagers who had just arrived at the door and were waiting for guidance about what to do next. They said that they were in their late teens but they looked about 15. It was hard to tell from their expressions whether they were scared or were quite enjoying their adventure in the big city.

Whatever happens to them, they won't be alone. Fourteen per cent of the London homeless are Scottish, with 40 per cent of those coming from Glasgow. The continuing influx of Scots, who arrive in London with nothing more than a sense of adventure and the hope that it will offer them a better chance, seems to defy sense. Could it somehow be that desperate Scots are hardwired to believe that London might hold the solution to their problems? For some that's undoubtedly true, but London is also a bolthole for those who find they can't even be themselves if they stay at home.

London has long been one of the favoured places for Scottish gay men to relocate to. In the 1950s, the 'two Roberts', Colquhoun and MacBride, made their careers as painters in Soho, drinking in a louche set which also included the Scottish poet W.S. Graham. They had been an openly gay couple at Glasgow School of Art, but they would have found it hard to live together in Glasgow's West End.

In the 1980s, the gay Scottish singer Jimmy Somerville and his band Bronski Beat had a top-three hit with a song about the experience of being gay, being brought up in the provinces, and being desperate to escape. Somerville, a politicised Glaswegian cherub with a soaring falsetto, sang 'Smalltown Boy', a disco track with a confessional lyric about the experience of having to escape the provinces. It was based on his personal experience. In an interview in the 1990s, Somerville described leaving Glasgow and experiencing London life as a release:

> Got here in the summer of '79. Only meant to be for the weekend. First stop, Earls Court. Oh, my! So many men. A return ticket, two days and so little time. This was my chance to start afresh, find out who I was. I could make up any old shite and who'd know what I was, wanted and needed. Of course, wasn't so romantically simple. Contrary to myth, the streets are not paved with gold. No money, no address and no shame.

It's an experience which many gay men identify with. Amongst other Scottish incomers, London is the natural home for thousands of homosexual Scottish men who grew up in towns in Scotland in which it seemed impossible to be gay, and where the only hope of self-realisation was in going away and seeking a new life in the company of other men, in London.

Fraser Serle, now in his mid-30s, grew up in Edinburgh in the 1980s. 'When I came to London,' he says, 'I was living in a flat with a lassie from Port Glasgow. One night the dance company DV8 were on the telly and everyone was laughing about these poofs on the TV. She said "No one's gay in Scotland" and I said, "Well, I'm from Scotland and I'm a poof". She was really shocked, but we all started talking about it. There must have been gay people from where she was from. Not every gay man in Scotland is down here.

'But she was right in a way. If you were gay in Aberdeen, or Glasgow, or Edinburgh, it would only be a matter of time before someone saw you coming out of a disco and then realised you were gay. I remember when I was in Edinburgh all my parents' friends would laugh about the gay bars, and make it seem really sad and tacky. And one time a girl at my work saw me coming out of Fire Island, the big gay disco that used to be on Princes Street, and she said, "I know you're gay, but it doesn't bother me", so you always felt really exposed.'

Serle's work with the health needs of gay men has brought him into contact with a lot of Scots. 'When I worked with a street health project, a lot of the guys who were working as male prostitutes were Scottish, and they didn't have a clue about health. A lot of the homeless guys are gay, and they act as prostitutes to get by.

'London is a city of exiles and a lot of men come here who are gay and can't be out at home. A lot of them are young and potentially vulnerable, and they might come here because they can't be open in their own community. But their loneliness can make them vulnerable too. I took a group of them around some of the gay bars in the West End and I started talking about Dennis Nilsen. [Nilsen, who was from Fraserburgh, is one of Britain's most prolific serial killers. A low-grade civil servant, he would meet gay men and take them back to his flat, where he would butcher them. Some of his 15 victims were young Scottish men.] I realised that these guys I was talking to were too young to remember Nilsen and that could make them so vulnerable. I had to tell them that if they were leaving a bar with someone, they should at least make sure and speak to the barman so if anything happened somebody would remember who they were with. I think Nilsen played on the fact that a lot of the guys he was with had no friends and no contact with home. It meant that they weren't missed, and nobody at home in Scotland even realised that they were gay.'

The gay historian Bob Cant, who edited oral histories of gay life in Scotland in the 1980s, is now working in London at the University of the South Bank. He agrees that London is a target for many lonely and isolated gay men. 'When I first came to London, I was struck by the number of Scottish barmen in the gay bars. That was the job they could do and they used it as a lifeline to get them out of Scotland. I think a lot of those smalltown-boy stereotypes were true for people growing up in Arbroath or wherever, and though I think it must be easier for people to grow up gay in Scotland today, it's certainly true that many older men have come to London simply because London gives them the chance to be themselves, maybe for the first time.'

But migrants or not, there is no formal network for Scottish gay men in the capital. 'There was a Gaelic-speaking group but that was very small and it closed down,' Cant says. 'And I've heard of Irish, Jewish and Asian groups, but no Scottish ones. There are certainly plenty of us down here and the experience of older gay men in particular is very different from people of my generation; just like I suppose the experience of gay men in their late teens and early 20s is very different from mine. Scotland might be another country now, but to tell you the truth I think most Scottish gay men are just glad to be here.'

The gay Scottish men who can only be themselves when they leave Scotland, or the homeless Scots who came looking for a new chance in the British capital have more in common with their high-achieving countrymen than it might at first seem. In fact, their attitudes are surprisingly close to those of the capital's high-profile Caledonian success stories.

They all share a fundamental belief that Scotland somehow isn't *enough*; that the range of opportunities it offers is too narrow, or too proscribed, and that the only way in which they can achieve their full potential is by leaving.

It's not that the men and women who end up sleeping rough on the streets of London necessarily have the wrong dream; they have exactly the same dream as the many Scots who make it. What they lack is the support, the confidence, the contacts or the sheer blind luck to transform their dream into a reality. And that makes the Scot in the doorway, or the Scot who hangs around Piccadilly Circus at night the spiritual twin of the one who slides by in his chauffeur-driven car.

Because the Scottish homeless are often questioned about their experiences, they provide raw data about Scottish emigration and Scottish attitudes to London which are invaluable, and which relate closely to the broader dreams of the Scots diaspora. How strong would the dream of success have to be to make anyone take a risky leap in the dark? Exactly how bad would things have to be at home to make it seem worthwhile?

CHAPTER 7

Scots Wha Hae

During the week, the skyscrapers of the City of London are alight into the early hours, the sandwich shops open early and close late, and the streets are black with pinstriped suits rushing to and from work. But when the working week is done, London's Square Mile becomes a high-tech ghost town, where the traffic lights blink from red to green and back again, keeping guard over deserted intersections and vacant roundabouts. It's easy to imagine this empty cityscape as the setting for a low-budget British science-fiction film, in which the hero wakes to discover that somehow he's the last man alive in London. A few miles north, the busy West End is alive with weekend crowds, frantic clubs and noisy conversation, but now, on a Saturday night in late August, the biggest financial centre in the world has packed up and gone home for the weekend.

The flowered balconies of the flats in the Barbican Centre make it look heavy-lidded in the drizzling rain, and the taxis race by with no one aboard. But suddenly, an incongruous sound echoes through the concrete gullies. Someone is playing the bagpipes.

In a square opposite the gates of Smithfield Market, a handful of wet figures are clustered around a plaque which has been set into the wall of St Bartholomew's Hospital. Some are swathed in tartan; others are dressed in black. As a few bewildered bystanders look on, the faithful band enact a sombre little ceremony. As the pipes play 'The flo'ers o' the forest', wreaths of fresh flowers are laid alongside dried bunches of heather. The tone is respectful and reflective. The men in the kilts and the women with the tartan shawls seem utterly out of place here, but still very much at home.

Albion Way and a narrow close called Little Britain may be just around the corner, but this is a part of London that will be forever Scotland. In 1305, this spot saw the bloody execution of William Wallace, the Scottish patriot who would achieve worldwide fame 700 years after his birth in the form of an Australian actor who had taken American citizenship. Waging spirited war against a collection of effete English villains and challenging his wavering compatriots to fight in the name of Scotland, *Braveheart* – written by Randall Wallace, an American Scot whose CV includes running the animal shows in Nashville's Opryland, as well as screenplays for *Pearl Harbor* and *The Man in the Iron Mask* – transformed Wallace's Scottish struggle into a universal tale of bravery and chutzpah.

The global power of Hollywood blasted *Braveheart* to global success and the fourteenth-century Scottish patriot is now international property, cited by Amazonian Indians and Tamil nationalists as an inspiration for their struggles against tyranny. Thanks to the film which dramatised his life and struggle, and burned an image of Wallace, his face painted blue and white, onto the retina of the world, 70 per cent of Scots questioned in a recent opinion poll have a mental image of Wallace as a handsome man, despite the fact that no pictures of him exist, and Mel Gibson's rallying cry of 'Freedom' echoes, sometimes ironically, around bars and sports stadiums from Brisbane to Brechin.

Yet even if Wallace now has a post-celluloid life in the imagination of the world, there are more tangible memorials to him, too. The Wallace Monument in Stirling, its massive tower pointing towards the sky, or the bronzed statue of him in Aberdeen, which keeps watch over Rosemount Viaduct, convey something of his power as a warlord and symbol of Scottish national pride. But this place, a small square beside one of London's most famous teaching hospitals in the very heart of the City of London, is a different kind of memorial to the Scottish patriot. Serious and sober, this modest site is ground zero for Wallace enthusiasts. Braveheart was butchered here.

Wallace streaks across Scottish history like a meteor, appearing from a dark sky before being snuffed out less than a decade later. He marched into the pages of history at the end of the thirteenth century, fully formed as a formidable warrior who, though only around 25 years old, already seemed to have military experience and daring in abundance. In 1297, he led a Scottish army to an improbable victory against the English at Stirling Bridge. The highly trained English army was estimated at 50,000 well-armed troops; Wallace's rag-tag Scottish fighting force numbered only 10,000.

Seven hundred years on, the facts are hard to come by, but Blind Harry, Wallace's chronicler, writing a century and a half after the battle, already had a Wallace mythology worked out. According to Harry's fantastically successful account, which had gone through 23 editions by 1707, Wallace used a kind of Scottish judo to defeat the English forces: their own weight counted against them when a Scot concealed in a wicker basket below Stirling Bridge pulled out a pin, collapsing it as they marched across. Many were killed and injured in the fall, the rest fell victim to the Scottish troops. In fact, the outcome of the battle seemed to have more to do with English impatience than Scots ingenuity; the wicker basket and the concealed peasant are inventions, the fact that the Scots were able to drive through the centre of the English troops having more effect.

Either way, the victory was a characteristic bit of Wallace daring. Blind Harry celebrated the collapsing bridge as a symbol of the élan of the charismatic commander: its cheekiness was well captured in *Braveheart*, along with the bared bottoms of the Scottish troops, contemptuously mooning at the English in the cause of Scotland's freedom.

The defeat of the English expeditionary force at Stirling Bridge came as a jolt to political opinion in England. Its soberest minds decided that Wallace's home-grown army couldn't be a genuine peasants' revolt. Wallace, chroniclers wrote, was merely the puppet of Scotland's ruling classes; Robert Wishart, the Bishop of Glasgow, and James the Steward, two ex-Guardians of Scotland, were pulling the strings.

Puppet or not, Wallace pressed his victory in the late autumn and winter of 1297 by invading northern England, taking time along the way to sign a letter to the mayors and commonwealths of Lübeck and Hamburg informing them that Scottish ports were free again to undertake foreign trade. But England was unlikely to tolerate such open mockery for long. The following year Wallace's forces faced the English army again, but this time, at Falkirk, they were routed by the superior side, and Wallace was forced to watch impotently as his cavalry quit the field.

In the aftermath of the battle, Wallace vanished almost as suddenly as he had appeared. At Falkirk, he had lost some of his closest friends and most valuable military strategists. Blind Harry has Wallace's wife dying there too.

Whatever the truth, for the next seven years Wallace all but disappears from history. Some later historians believe that he spent that time travelling around Europe, drumming up support for Scotland and engaging in complex diplomacy with the leaders of foreign powers. He may have been in France, negotiating with Philip IV, though no mention is made of him by the Scottish diplomats who were already at the French King's court. His discussions with the Pope may have provoked a letter to Edward I in which the Pope criticised the English King for his savage treatment of Scotland. By 1305, with his European missions completed, Wallace was back in Scotland.

The road which led Wallace to the high gallows erected at the gates of Smithfield Market began on 3 August 1305. At the beginning of August he was near Glasgow, possibly to meet with Robert Wishart, the Bishop of Glasgow. He planned to sleep the night in a barn near Bishopbriggs. At about midnight, his sleeping place was surrounded by soldiers and Wallace was taken into the custody of Sir John Menteith, a Scot who had gone over to Edward's side in 1304 and been rewarded with a crown appointment as Sheriff of Dumbarton. The captive spent that night in Dumbarton Castle, and in the morning was taken by back roads to the Solway Firth.

There, Menteith handed over his precious prisoner to Sir Aymer De Valence and Sir Robert De Clifford, who bundled him away to Carlisle and into the hands of Sir John Segrave. Segrave had led the English attacks on Scotland in 1303; taking possession of a captive Wallace must have given him huge satisfaction, and on his uncomfortable journey to London, Wallace must have had ample time to reflect on the irony of his situation. The Scottish freedom fighter had been delivered to the English via the hands of a Scot who had signed up with the enemy power.

Once in the custody of the English, Wallace's fate was never really in doubt. After a meeting with the King, when, tradition has it, Edward would not look his irritating enemy in the eye, Wallace was taken to face the might and cruel majesty of English justice.

After a show trial in Westminster Hall, Wallace was convicted of rebellion, sedition, arson, robbery and sacrilege. During the trial, in front of the Mayor of London, sheriffs, aldermen and other officials, the Scottish patriot was forced to wear a crown of laurels, 'since he had reportedly said in the past that he deserved to wear a crown in that hall'. Wallace was forbidden to speak, but was able to blurt out that he had never been a traitor to the King of England because he had never sworn his allegiance to the King. It was a spirited point, but it had little influence on what followed.

Sir John Segrave, Wallace's captor, read out the inevitable sentence of the court. Wallace was to be quartered and the four parts of his body dispatched around the kingdom.

Once the sentence was declared, Wallace was lashed to a wooden pole suspended between two horses' tails to be dragged to his execution place at Smithfield. A large crowd formed to watch Wallace as he was dragged from Westminster Hall, past Parliament Square and along the modern-day Strand.

From there, jeered all the way, he was dragged along Fleet Street, into Ludgate Hill, north to Aldgate, then to Cheapside, Newgate and, finally, Smithfield itself. The route had been specially chosen to loop through London, passing along the north bank of the Thames before following the boundary of the old city up to the north, so that Wallace could be seen by as many Londoners as possible. In all, the Scottish patriot was dragged for nearly five miles, battered by the uneven road.

At Smithfield, he was pulled up to the high gallows and hanged. While he was still alive, he was cut down, his genitals were cut off and his bowels were pulled from his body and burned in front of him. Finally, his head was cut off and his body was cut in four. A crowd of thousands attended this public torture, but, in case anyone had missed the show, his head was displayed on London Bridge, where the seagulls would have pecked at it, the Guardian of Scotland reduced to food for the London birds.

The dismembered body was entrusted to Sir John Segrave, who was granted ten shillings to dispatch the pieces around Scotland. One quarter was displayed in Newcastle, another in Berwick-upon-Tweed. An arm went to Stirling. In Perth, they received a leg. Some claim that Aberdeen received another arm which is buried in the cathedral wall, but the evidence seems shaky.

The savage dismembering of Wallace seems to have been intended to obliterate his memory. In fact, his betrayal, the cruel death, the posthumous dispersal of the body around the kingdom and the crown of laurels serves to impress the idea of Wallace as a sainted, even Christ-like, figure. As Blind Harry wrote, 'a martyr Wallace was'.

The site of Wallace's execution, once open fields, is now the heart of one of the biggest cities in the world, and the dedicated band which has gathered to mark the anniversary of Wallace's death is reaching the climax of their ceremony. After a few words about the martyr and a spirited rendition of 'Scots Wha Hae' sung from damp songsheets, the London branch of the Scottish National Party adjourns to a nearby pub.

'It's a very important part of our calendar,' explains John Green, the acting convenor. 'If it wasn't for Wallace, Scotland would just be a region of England. When they hung drew and quartered him, they created a Scottish martyr and that martyr is celebrated today.'

Over pints of London Pride Bitter, the younger members are sheepishly apologetic about not wearing their kilts. 'You get such hassle on the tube.'

Wallace would have taken such hassle in his stride. The strapping warlord towers above Jim Sillars, Alex Salmond and the Ewing clan in the pantheon of Nationalist heroes. Uncontaminated by modern-day political machinations, Wallace's heroic struggle against overpowering odds and his eventual martyrdom has long stirred Scots to patriotic raptures. It may have taken Mel Gibson to bring Wallace to a wider audience, but the commemoration of 'Wallace Day' long predates *Braveheart*.

Burns wrote about Wallace as a symbol of Scottish resistance. His name was invoked in the early nineteenth century as a symbol of Scottish national identity and the very formation of the National Party of Scotland was announced on 3 June 1928 at the Wallace Monument in Stirling. These commemorations of Wallace's life often provoked popular appeals to raise money for statues: one of the earliest was erected in 1814, overlooking the Tweed in Dryburgh, and within 40 years it was joined by one in Falkirk and two in Ayrshire. In 1856, an estimated crowd of 20,000 turned out to watch a procession led by a pipe band though Stirling demanding that a Wallace monument be built there.

But though modern nationalists have fastened on to Wallace as one of their martyrs, at different times Scots of almost every political belief have championed him as a hero. The bourgeois Scots who fronted the money for the construction of the Wallace statue in Aberdeen in 1888 were patriots, certainly, but few would have voted for the modern SNP.

Unionist Scots like the sculptor Sir Joseph Noel Paton, who proposed the construction of a national monument to honour Wallace and Bruce in Edinburgh in 1859, championed Wallace for contributing to equality under the Union with England. Had Wallace not fought for Scottish independence, so the argument went, the Scotland which entered the Union in 1707 would have been so weakened that the Union would have been a takeover of Scottish society and not the partnership which many Victorian Scots believed in. Nationalists, who tend to see the Union in exactly those terms anyway, have little truck with this, seeing it as a bit of Unionist doublethink. Their Wallace is the hero of 'Flower of Scotland', who sent Edward packing 'tae think again'. The Unionist cult of Wallace weakened in the twentieth century, though the distinguished historian Geoffrey Barrow, writing about the cult of Wallace the nationalist democrat, judged that 'politically and constitutionally, Wallace was a conservative'. It was noticeable that the Conservative Secretary of State for Scotland Michael Forsyth wore a kilt to the premier of *Braveheart* at Stirling Castle, even whilst ungraciously declaring Wallace a 'loser'.

Nor are Wallace statues confined to Scotland. Ballarat in Australia has one, raised by public subscription, alongside a statue of Robert Burns and one of Queen Victoria. In Westminster itself, an inscription marks the spot where the treacherous Scot was put on trial. But the Smithfield plaque, the focus of an annual Nationalist pilgrimage for nearly 40 years, was put up in the 1960s by a band of Scottish patriots who raised £3,000 to tell their version of Wallace's life. Its sentiments are echoed on the front of a T-shirt worn by Morag Kerr, the membership secretary. To them, Wallace was a 'patriot', a 'freedom fighter' and a 'nationalist'.

But now the patriot in the T-shirt is chivvying new members of the party to pay their subscriptions and helping to organise a prize draw. A buffet appears from the back room of the pub, of the kind peculiar to Scottish political meetings wherever they occur: wet egg sandwiches, chicken drumsticks as sinuous as hurdlers' thighs and oily mini-pizzas, fluorescent with glowing cheddar. No one rushes to eat.

The guest speaker, Bob Purdie, a Scots exile who teaches at Ruskin College, Oxford, delivers a scholarly paper on Hugh MacDiarmid, another Nationalist hero, who, with Compton Mackenzie and others, formed the National Party of Scotland in 1928. Everyone listens politely as Purdie anatomises the complex politics of Scotland in the 1920s and tries to explain MacDiarmid's schizophrenic political beliefs. In 1923, MacDiarmid had written 'Programme for a Scottish Fascism', an article which proffered lavish praise for Mussolini's Italy. This polemic, though it argues for many things that modern nationalists might agree on, like the need for land reform and the importance of a cultural element to the Scottish political debate, is also a historic embarrassment for the party, and divining MacDiarmid's precise meaning is something of an after-dinner game for intellectual members of the party.

'Was MacDiarmid a fascist?' Purdie asks, and though nobody believes that he could have been, 40 minutes later everyone seems relieved to hear that he was not.

'The real problem is recruitment,' Kerr explains when the speeches are done. 'There may be plenty Scots living in London, but they don't have stars against their names in the phonebook to let you know they are Scottish. In a branch at home you can put up a stall in the High Street, but there's not much point doing that in Oxford Street.' Instead, to attract new members, the branch relies on word of mouth and leafleting at Scotland rugby matches and Runrig concerts. 'Standing around like a lemon,' as Kerr puts it.

On paper, the SNP shouldn't have any trouble raising the troops from the thousands of Scots who make up such a healthy minority in this city of exiles. But then Scots who choose to live in London might not necessarily be the kind who join the Scottish National Party, since London and Scottish nationalism have a historic problem with each other.

MacDiarmid encapsulated the issue when he referred to London as 'that teeming sore'. In 2003, a cache of uncatalogued papers at the National Library of Scotland was found to contain a poem in which MacDiarmid seemed to be gloating at the bombs which were then falling on the East End of London.

MacDiarmid wrote:

> Now when London is threatened
> with devastation from the air
> I realise, horror atrophying in me,
> that I hardly care.
> The withering in me of the nerve of horror
> Is only I see, as it were,
> A foreglimpse of the elimination
> Of earth's greatest horror down there.

MacDiarmid, who listed one of his hobbies as 'Anglophobia', may have been one of the finest Scottish poets of the century, but he could turn out political doggerel like this by the yard. But though the policy of the SNP nowadays is to be publicly polite about the English, with the former leader Alex Salmond pointedly declaring one of *his* hobbies as 'Anglophilia', modern Nationalists share MacDiarmid's view, expressed elsewhere in the poem, that London is a 'pirate's cave' packed with Scotland's wealth. As part of their critique of the British state, Nationalists believe that the United Kingdom is structurally unbalanced and that Gordon Brown's exchequer drains Scotland of its oil revenue. If the streets of the City of London are paved with gold, presumably it's Scotland's gold.

And the fact that they live in London seems to be a matter of considerable embarrassment to many of the members in the Rising Sun pub. Pending a radical change of policy, the SNP doesn't field candidates in Hackney or Brent, and so many London-based activists are put in the curious position of devoting a considerable amount of their free time to campaigning for a party they are unable to vote for. It's a conundrum which some solve by casting their votes for the Greens, who also support Scottish independence, and a few committed members bend the rules to stay registered at their parents' homes back in Scotland or as phantom tenants of flats they haven't lived in for years. Most explain that they are only visiting London, though it turns out that some of the visits have lasted for decades, and others dismiss their sojourn in the south as nothing more than a wearisome necessity.

'I've been to America, and I've worked in Brussels. I'm just doing what Scots have always done – I'm seeking to expand my horizons,' says David Munn, the branch organiser.

'I feel separated from Scotland, though hopefully not divorced,' confides Fiona Nerberg, one of the branch's younger members, who sheepishly confessed that her interest in the SNP grew out of a political crush on Alex Salmond.

A psychologist would have no problem diagnosing the fact that some are suffering from a pathological case of homesickness. They speak rather wistfully about Paul Martin, the former convenor of the branch who had decided just the week before that he would 'go back'. I assumed that Martin had just gone north for a few days. My mistake: he hadn't gone back; he had Gone Back for Good. It may be only four and a half hours away by train, but Scotland suddenly feels like the other side of the world.

There is an old Tennant's lager advert in which a decanted Scot tires of getting jostled to bits on the tube and then finally realises what he's missing and gets on the train and comes back to Edinburgh. It's an image which strikes a chord with the Nats, who clearly feel temperamentally out of tune with London life.

'About 50 per cent of the branch say they'll go back, but they've been here too long. They've been assimilated,' says Green, who contested Aberdeenshire West and Kincardine in the 1997 general election, and after a career spent in Russia and Europe, is making firm plans to return to Scotland.

Why would a Scot living in London join the SNP? Some are Nationalists already from university, but an interesting few find their Nationalist horns growing when they find themselves in London. 'Quite a lot of people who come to live in England find that they hadn't realised before the enormous cultural gulf that exists between Scotland and England,' Kerr explains. 'They are the butt of a lot of anti-Scottish jokes and after a while they start to feel more Scottish.'

There is no shortage of radical political movements in London, but this must be one of the gentlest. Within a 20-mile radius, militant cells are hard at work plotting the overthrow of global capitalism, freedom for West Kashmir and ultimate victory for Al-Qaeda. In the Rising Sun pub in London, the SNP's London cell are mulling over the relative merits of Hearts and Hibs. A Scot who uses the pub as his local refuses the nationalist call to arms and prefers to nurse his pint rather than stray out into the rain. Beyond a little joshing, he is left to enjoy his drink.

And that is the problem. Most London Scots, faced with the bewildering array of attractions that the city has to offer, find that politics is low down on their list, below drinking and work. If they are feeling terribly homesick, then there is always the Caledonian Club, which plays host to wealthy Scottish businessmen, and the Army and Navy Club, where military types can drink the night away.

In contrast, Irish societies in London have active memberships five or six times that of the SNP. But the Irish always seek each other out, band together and socialise with one another, and modern London Scots have shied away from the kind of social clubs which their Victorian forebears so enjoyed.

But the branch was once energised by a sense of history in the making. When, in the second 1974 general election, the SNP succeeded in getting 11 MPs elected to the House of Commons, the SNP's London branch became the willing hands and legs of new MPs who were strangers to Westminster, and in some cases were living in London for the first time. Older members look back with nostalgia on the time when the United Kingdom seemed on the verge of separating and Nationalists walked the corridors of power in London with a spring, and a sense of destiny, in their step. But that was exactly 30 years ago.

Now, though the SNP is the official Opposition in Holyrood, its intake of Westminster MPs has a low profile, and their voices are seldom heard outside the Scottish news bulletins. Once Nationalists could pack the Usher Hall in Edinburgh and demand independence 'now', but the tide of SNP support seems to have receded, leaving its island of London support high and dry.

Besides, the SNP as a whole seems discomfited by the present dominance of Scots in senior positions in the UK Government. Though the party has an argument ready against 'assimilated Scots' who seek 'British power', they have historically served as a useful safety valve in those moments when Scotland has seemed furthest from the concerns of Westminster government. The SNP has always had an ambivalent relationship with those Scots who hold power within the British system. John MacCormick, one of its founders, was slated as the party's Ramsay MacDonald, too keen by far to establish happy relationships with the Establishment of the day, and too easily bought off by expressions of pro-Scottish sentiment from those who had no intention of turning those easy expressions into hard political decisions. As branch members readily admit, the SNP's day will come again when England elects a government which is politically opposed to the one in Holyrood, allowing the Nationalists to apply leverage to the constitutional crack. For the moment, its London representation seems marooned by history.

In the interim, the branch has fought back from a reputation in Nationalist circles as 'eccentric', as a senior party member delicately puts it. In the last general election, the branch generated four candidates to stand in Scottish constituencies, but as one member gloomily conceded, 'We never get given ones that we can win.' For the rest, telephone canvassing is the best way to make them feel part of the political protest. 'I canvassed 998 voters in Peterhead in the election,' Bob Purdie explains. 'Our call centre is the envy of the party.'

If it took film to make Wallace famous, it has taken telephones to help the branch carve out a meaningful role in the modern party. It has convinced the SNP in Scotland that it has an important role to play and looks forward to the party conference where it can show its worth again. And in the meantime, there are fundraisers to plan, earnest discussions to be held and the hope of 'going back' is enough to keep the spirits up.

But in the absence of independence, many in the SNP London branch have been gripped with a new enthusiasm. In time for the 700th anniversary of Wallace's death in 2005, the branch has thrown its weight behind a campaign to set up a permanent monument to the Scottish patriot.

Mayor Ken Livingstone has created the 100 Public Spaces

Programme, which aims to create in London the kind of public areas associated with Paris, Barcelona or Berlin. The branch believes that the site of Wallace's execution could qualify for such funding and provide a place of focus for Scots exiles in the city. Beside the Wallace plaque is a small square of grass in the concrete heart of the City. The plan is to enlarge the green and create in front of the Wallace plaque a space of 'historical, environmental and social benefits'. As well as the patriotic benefits, those behind the scheme also hope that patients from the nearby St Bartholomew's Hospital could benefit from the improved public green space.

But the plan, which aims to create a focus for Scots in London, is also a sign that the Scottish community in London currently lacks a heart. Though the branch has identified a tartan patchwork of Scottish clubs and societies in the capital, many of them seem to be disconnected, isolated, and, it must be said, rather bemused by the Wallace plan. Could Braveheart, that tabula rasa on which so many Scots have written their own meaning, be about to acquire a new one, uniting the Scots of London as he once did the Scots of the fourteenth century? It would be ironic if the Wallace who stood shoulder to shoulder with Bruce and the Scottish freedom fighters, who was championed by patriotic Scots in Stirling, Perth and Aberdeen, and who was dismembered in an attempt to dissolve Scottish opposition to English power, found his ultimate destiny as a focal point for the Scots in London, realised through the civic-minded schemes of Red Ken.

Soon the pub sings with the kind of abusive banter that enlivens many an Edinburgh howf in the early hours, and members shake their heads wearily at the iniquities of England's tight licensing hours.

As I leave, the party has moved up a few gears, fuelled by London Pride Bitter, and as I go down the stairs they have broken into a song made famous by the advert for another brew entirely. 'Caledonia, you are everything I've ever had.' It's a surprise to find that outside the door, London life goes on as normal.

CHAPTER 8

The Scottish Version

In one of the most famous, and most widely quoted, passages in modern Scottish fiction, Duncan Thaw, the hero of Alasdair Gray's *Lanark*, tells his friend McAlpine that no one imagines living in Glasgow: ' . . . when our imagination needs exercise, we use [it] to visit London, Paris, Rome under the Caesars, the American West at the turn of the century, anywhere but here and now'.

Thaw and his friend are art students, and this sounds exactly like one of the sweeping, pretentious comments that students have always made to one other. But Gray's hero is at least partly right: alongside the Wild West or *fin de siècle* Paris, London has always been a place in which the Scots have imagined living, and, alongside a thousand practical skills, city living demands the full play of the imagination. In *Soft City,* one of the cult books of the 1970s, Jonathan Raban argued that 'living in cities is an art, and we need the vocabulary of art, of style, to decide the peculiar relationship between man and material that exists in the continual creative play of urban living'.

For most temporary visitors, of course, practical details take precedence: a well-thumbed A–Z is the essential guide to London city life, but even the most famous image of London, the schematic underground map first devised in 1933, is a fiction, with any sense of London's real geography twisted in order to create an aesthetically pleasing image. As an imaginary map of London, it is responsible for almost as many people missing their train as catching it, preferring to wait for the unreliable Northern Line at Tottenham Court Road, for example, rather than walk the short distance to King's Cross; it's a 15-minute stroll, but on the map it looks like miles.

Henry James once noted that London is an interconnected sequence of villages, and that his sense of the city only unfolded when he discovered the ways in which they connect up; before then, he wrote, he had been 'crushed' by the city's 'inconceivable immensity . . . The city sits on you, broods on you, stamps on you.' In one sense the underground, which opened in 1863, made it easier to negotiate around the already vast and rapidly growing metropolis, in another it encouraged the sense of geographical atomisation: for many Londoners, the city exists as a series of islands which surround the tube stops, and they have little idea of what lies between them.

In the face of the city's bewildering size, it's not surprising that Scottish writers who have spent longer in London than a weekend have coined their own Scottish versions of the city, transforming it in their imaginations; imaginations which are hungry to make sense of a new environment and which often colour it in the distinctive shades of the country they have left behind.

One of the earliest Scottish portraits of London comes from 1501, when the Scottish poet William Dunbar was sent as part of a court delegation to London to arrange the marriage of James IV to Margaret Tudor, a dynastic union which he celebrated in 1503 in 'The Thrissill and the Rois'.

Dunbar was a worldly and sophisticated man who had visited other European capitals in the service of his King, but in 'London', the poem he wrote about his visit, he seems unable to overcome his astonishment at the bustle and size of the English capital.

> Above all ryvers thy Ryver hath renowne,
> Whose beryall stremys, pleasaunt and preclare,
> Under thy lusty wallys renneth down,
> Where many a swanne doth swymme with wyngis fare;
> Where many a barge doth saile, and row with are,
> Where many a ship doth rest with toppe-royall.
> O! towne of townes, patrone and not-compare:
> London, thou art the floure of Cities all.

That theme of admiration of the material richness of London tempered with an awareness of the temptations which it offers runs right though Scottish poetry about the city, from Dunbar's verse to *The Seasons* by James Thomson, the man who wrote 'Rule Britannia', to the work of his namesake, James 'B.V.' Thomson, who, in *City of Dreadful Night*, transformed London into a Blakean realm of hell.

The flower of all cities, a modern paradise or a vision of hell: these imaginary portraits of London seem almost as real as the metropolis of bricks and mortar. But while most of London's residents take their own private version of the city as the real one, a few have seen that their version of London can only ever be a partial grasp of the almost incomprehensible whole.

James Boswell, who had a great love affair with the city, realised that the London in his head was quite distinct from the reality. In his journal entry of 27 January 1786, he wrote, 'Imaginary London, gilded with all the brilliancy of warm fancy as I have viewed it, and London as a scene of real business, are quite different.'

Boswell was to become the patron saint of the London Scots, but whilst in his imagination he bestrode the city like a colossus and dared to pen the definitive portrait of one of the great literary men of his day, he found the practicalities of succeeding in London harder to negotiate. His partial understanding of the difference between his own version of London and the demands exercised by the real one may even have made his eventual disappointments in the city harder to bear. He desperately wanted to be a success there, and the city became his playground and his dream world, the place in which all his hopes would be made to materialise; the reality was sourer, smaller and more agonising.

The journal entry in which Boswell realised this dilemma was written in Edinburgh, where he had returned in order to fret over his decision to relocate permanently to London. His earlier visits southwards had been convivial and happy, and allowed him to fraternise with a network of transplanted Scots. Boswell was desperate to make the leap for good, but at the last minute his nerve had deserted him.

He worried about money, he was concerned that his

knowledge of English law wasn't good enough to make him a successful English barrister, and he was uncertain about how to accommodate the needs of his family in Scotland.

In the journals which Boswell wrote before 1786, London is a place of delight, excitement and stimulation. After 1786, when he goes to live there more or less permanently, the imaginary London competes with the practical one, and slowly the necessities of earning a living, developing a reputation and carving out a legal practice in a foreign jurisdiction begin to dent Boswell's confidence. In his earlier journals, Boswell is an impetuous force of nature, brimming over with misplaced *joie de vivre* and inappropriate enthusiasm; it is impossible not to love him as he bounces around Edinburgh, trying to make his mark in politics, literature and law, whilst being constantly put down by the dour and sober men who ran the place. But in the London journals a darker note creeps in. In London, Boswell is constantly twisting and turning, trying a new strategy, devoting his energies to buttering up yet another potential patron; he desperately believes, he needs to believe, that there is a key to London and if he can find it then his earthly dreams of success and self-respect will be magically unlocked.

As Boswell's biographers have noted, the London journal of this period makes painful reading, particularly when, in an attempt to get up to speed with the English Law, he takes a place as a junior on the Northern Circuit. By this time, Boswell was a successful author of travel books and essays with a respectable literary reputation. He was also 46, middle-aged and overweight. But as a junior barrister in the provinces, he was essentially a dogsbody in a wig; he was charged with writing letters, keeping accounts and other small bits of administration. That he threw himself into the work and enthusiastically recorded the charm of the Yorkshire ladies he met at balls and parties only adds to the pathos of this talented man who dreamed of making a huge success of London life and has been temporarily forced to the bottom of the heap by relocating to England.

One factor in Boswell's failure was his own undisciplined and mercurial personality, which would see him soaring into enthusiastic raptures at one moment and plunging into the depths of lethargy and despair the next. But there was another reason why Boswell found it hard to prosper in London. On the eve of his departure, Lord Thurlow, the Lord High Chancellor, wrote to Boswell to warn him that the English Bar was not an easy option and that he would have to succeed there on his own merits, and not hope for assistance from those in a position of power.

Thurlow had put his finger on one of Boswell's weaknesses: he was perpetually in search of a patron, someone who would be able to promote him to the level of authority he felt he deserved. Johnson would become a combination of patron, friend and surrogate father, but whereas Johnson had a good deal of affection for Boswell, as any reader of the journals quickly realises, Boswell's more political patrons tended to be an unappealing and inconsistent bunch. In this period, Boswell was unsuccessfully trying to entice the interest of the Earl of Lonsdale, an obnoxious political kingpin with the personal grace of Robert Maxwell. For months, Boswell debased himself in front of Lonsdale in the hope that he could be secured a place in the House of Commons. The fact that the MPs Lonsdale commanded were known to be little more than puppets didn't matter to Boswell; the honour did. Whether Boswell's experience of Scotland, where patronage and kinship were an accepted principle of political advancement, had ill prepared him for London or whether he simply didn't have any contact with the patrons who would perform the equivalent role for him in England is debatable. Lonsdale let him down, as in a way London let him down, but Boswell eventually earned his immortality through the London of his imagination, not the London of hard politics, back-scratching and worldly success. But the image of Boswell, desperately striking around for some strategy which would make the city work for him, is a telling one. He wouldn't be the last Scottish writer to fantasise about the one successful approach which would make the city fall at his feet.

Forty years after Boswell took the leap and moved to London, in *Babylon the Great*, a great prose hymn to the city, the Scottish journalist Robert Mudie describes the capital as a leveller of pride:

> The pursy provincial, who takes upon him to insult his
> neighbours because he happens to possess a few

thousand pounds, becomes a mere cipher in Cornhill or Threadneedle-street; the provincial bashaw, who ranges the whole village with his equipage, is outshone upon the drive by a slopseller or dealer in old books, and the Adonis who conquers and then abandons half the fair in a remote country, cannot in Bond-street distinguish the fine gentleman that the tailor made from the tailor that made him, and thus he is humbled in the sight of both.

This tendency to restrain within narrow limits all the adventitious grounds of human vanity, and to drive man back for his vanity upon that which belongs to him as man is one of the most valuable features in the character of London. It gives a man fair play, clears the arena for him, and so places him, that if he does not triumph, the fault is wholly his own.

Mudie was an embodiment of industry, dedication and eclectic learning who did everything in his power to improve his prospects. The son of a weaver, born near Forfar in 1781, it quickly became clear that he was destined for a different kind of life from his father. An autodidact, he taught in a village school in Fife after his four years of militia training, but he wanted something better.

Glenfergus, the novel which he wrote in the evenings after school, was published in 1819. A triple-decker in the fashion of the day, it is an interesting hybrid of Highland fantasy and the upper-class novel of ideas. In it the weaver's son, eking out a living in a Fife schoolroom and working by the light of a candle in the evenings, created a cast of leisured aristocrats. He made one of them, Saville, express this sophisticated opinion on British life:

> I have often thought, that if British subjects gave themselves less trouble about politics, they would be both happier and wiser. I doubt much whether that noise of applause and that depth of censure, which are so liberally poured forth upon every man and every measure, do not, to a very considerable extent, distract the judgement, and fritter away time which might be

more usefully employed. We hear one man praising and another censuring, not from any conviction of right or wrong, for they will not stop to think of that, but merely because the action was, or was not, done by a member of that party with which they fancy themselves to be enlisted.

Determined not to fritter away any more of his own time, Mudie left for London in 1820, where he was employed as a reporter on the *Morning Chronicle,* the newspaper which would later employ both Charles Dickens and Henry Mayhew. He covered George IV's visit to Edinburgh for the paper and, sensing an upturn in interest about Scotland, turned the opportunity into a book intended for English readers called *The Modern Athens,* which introduced the architecture, history and noteworthy characters of the Scottish capital to a London audience.

Buoyed with the success of the Edinburgh book, he accepted a commission to write its counterpart: a book about London for an implied Scottish audience. The book he produced was less a guide to London's history than a spiritual love letter to the city of his adoption:

> London may be considered, not merely as the capital of England or the British Empire but as the metropolis of the world, not merely as the seat of a government which extends its connexions and exercises its influence to the remotest parts of the earth's surface, not merely as it contains the wealth and the machinery by which the slavery of nations are bought and sold, not merely as the heart, by whose pulses the tides of intelligence, activity and commerce, are made to circulate throughout every land, not merely as possessing a freedom of opinion, and a hardihood in the expression of that opinion, unknown to every other city, not merely as taking the lead in every informing science, and in every useful and embellishing art, but as being foremost and without a rival in every means of aggrandisement and enjoyment, and also of neglect and misery – of everything that can render life sweet and man happy, or that can render life bitter and man wretched.

166

After Athens, Babylon: Mudie believed that London could only be compared with one of the other great cities of antiquity, but in his self-created role as intermediary between the Scottish and English capitals, explaining each to the citizens of the other, Mudie also seemed to be trapped, an outsider to both. Temperamentally, he was in favour of Scottish emigration and in 1832 he wrote *The Emigrant's Pocket Companion*, a collection of practical advice and stirring descriptions intended for a readership of Scottish émigrés contemplating life in North America or Australia. His description of London also has the air of a book written to soothe the worries of potential emigrants.

> Notwithstanding the crowds by whom you must every day be elbowed, you may pass through them as unheeded as you would by the trees of the forest or the billows of the ocean; and though in one vigorous day's journey you might encompass nearly fifteen hundred thousand human beings, yet it might be possible for you to spend your whole life among them without any of them so much as asking your name.

The fear of being swallowed up by such a city and of losing your individuality in the process is a common Scottish anxiety, but Mudie's solution to the worry eventually killed him. Though at one time the editor of the *Sunday Times*, financial security eluded him and he fell into the pattern of writing huge slabs of prose for publishers on demand. Eventually he wrote more than 90 volumes on art, politics and science, and allegedly dashed off one, on a scientific subject, in eight days of feverish writing. But even such superhuman industry wasn't enough to save him. He died in Pentonville on 29 April 1842, imprisoned as a debtor, leaving behind a widow, one son and four daughters. It was an ironic end for a man who had counselled readers of his books on emigration to practise 'thrift, saving and sense in the use of money'.

The idea of London as a place which would level petty social ambitions and then allow the man of talents to rise was a common one at the time and a fundamentally attractive one for Scots. In *A Glance at London, Brussels and Paris by A Provincial Scotsman*, published in 1829, the author observed:

> A man from the country discovers himself to be a small
> person indeed amid such a congregation of excellence:
> where he is surpassed by thousands and tens of
> thousands in every quality and accomplishment for
> which he was wont to give himself credit. Is he vain of
> his riches, capacity, figure, knowledge? At every corner
> he meets with throngs that excel him in all these
> particulars: and what is worse, who never heard of him,
> his connections or residence, and will live all their lives
> careless about such information.

But, as the extract above shows, the competitive nature of
London society, and the erasure of carefully built-up Scottish
social status, was also profoundly threatening. The writer who
best grasped the possibilities and threats implicit in the
relationship between London and Scotland was John Galt, who,
in a series of Scottish novels published between 1820 and 1832,
set out to portray Scottish rural communities under threat of
change. Change in Galt's novels tended to come in the guise of
money, the promise of money, or political power.

In his *Autobiography*, Galt described the peculiar form he had
decided to write in: 'The novels would be more properly
characterised as theoretical histories . . . I do not think I have
had many precursors, in what I would call my theoretical
histories of society . . .'.

Galt's novels, often written in the first person by unreliable
narrators, read as attractively modern today, even if he had a
terrible weakness for heavily symbolic names. But leaving aside
the farmers called Byres and the ministers called Swapkirk,
Galt's reduction of Scottish society to a few symbolic traits, or
more accurately symbolic activities, allows him to penetrate to
the heart of a profoundly unsettling and dynamic time in
Scottish life. In 1804 Galt left Greenock for London, where he
enjoyed no huge success. He found financial security in Canada
16 years later when he served in pioneer settlements as secretary
to the Canada Company, and even gave his name to the town
in Ontario. This colonial success was to be short lived, however;
he was recalled from Canada for negligence and even served a
term in a debtors' prison in London.

Perhaps because of his precarious financial fortunes, Galt's novels are often concerned with the allure and the unsettling power of money. *The Ayrshire Legatees* is a novel in the form of letters about an Ayrshire minister and his family who go to London to collect a legacy. If the legacy was a kind of wish fulfilment, so too was the theme of his next novel, *Sir Andrew Wylie*. Wylie, by name and nature, is a Scot on the make who carries all before him, and the novel about the rise of a 'humble Scotchman in London' plays on the idea of the wily provincial who hides his intelligence behind blunt talk and an artificial 'simplicity'.

Galt was particularly sensitive to the opportunities which being a Scot afforded him, and the threat which outside opportunities represented to the Scots who stayed at home; his novels are full of scenes in which Scottish propriety is tested against ambition, and the old Scottish civic order appears to be threatened by the new culture of mercantilism and easy money.

In his novel of 1826, *The Last of the Lairds*, Mailings, the Laird of Auldbiggins, is threatened by Mr Rupees, a man who has returned from India, a country where so many Scots vaulted up the pole to worldly success. Mr Rupees, whose name suggests that he has been literally transformed by, and into, money, wants to buy himself a place in landed society. Mailings borrows money from Rupees and when Rupees calls in the loan he risks losing his entire estate.

There is nothing particularly Scottish in the contrast between the old impoverished aristocracy and the thrusting, wealthy arriviste (it is the source of the comedy in the television series *To the Manor Born*, alongside other less sophisticated entertainments), but Galt's novel is really a drama about the conflicts between the Scots who stayed at home and saw their fortunes quietly stagnate and those who went off to seek them elswhere. Galt portrays the drama as a symbol of an age in which 'every man of sense and talent seeks his fortune abroad, and leaves only the incapable and those who are conscious of their deficiencies at home'. It is a challenging idea, and it challenged the author too; Galt's *Autobiography* is remarkable for the amount of space it devotes to the Scottish activity of 'getting on'. Whether by design or not, Galt portrayed the writing of novels as just another way of succeeding in the world. After a period of neglect, his novels started to be reprinted in Scotland in the 1970s; they, and the town named after him, are his testament.

In 1823, Galt had fallen out with his Edinburgh publishers Blackwood's and transferred to another in the city, Oliver and Boyd. In January 1832, after a similar break with Blackwood's, the 'Ettrick Shepherd' James Hogg travelled to London, partly to secure a new publishing deal. In common with many visiting Scots, he spent much of the time in the company of his countrymen, who hailed him as a visiting genius, and Hogg took time to catch up with Thomas Carlyle, the painter David Wilkie and the poets Alan Cunningham and Thomas Hood.

The centrepiece of Hogg's visit, though, was an address which he gave to a Burns Supper at the Highland Society of London. There, in front of an audience of the Scottish aristocracy, Hogg spoke mischievously about 'a nobility whose titles no king or government can bestow, and no king or government take away – the chiefs of the Highland clans'.

But Hogg's journey was essentially devoted to business, not pleasure. After the break with Blackwood's, he was anxious to establish connections with London-based Scottish publishers and eventually signed a deal with James Cochrane, who, ironically, was to go bankrupt after publishing only one volume of Hogg's collected *Altrive Tales*, plunging the writer into even more precarious financial straits.

The search by Scottish writers for London publishers and the relocation of Scottish publishers to London was a theme of the first two decades of the nineteenth century. David Craig notes that two of Blackwood's six sons were sent to London to learn their trade, while John Murray, a London Scot, founded his own eponymous publishing house in the English capital in 1768, which would go on to publish the works of Charles Darwin, Jane Austen and Lord Byron – now part of the Hodder Headline conglomerate, it still exists as an imprint. Daniel Macmillan came to London by stages after periods in Stirling and Glasgow, and Archibald Constable had been an apprentice in London and in turn apprenticed his son there in 1811.

This cultural brain drain worried Scots. Thomas Carlyle left Scotland in 1834 and, though he occasionally complained about London in letters to relatives, stayed there more or less for the rest of his life. George Davie ranks the 50 years after 1830 in

Scotland as characterised by a 'failure of intellectual nerve'. But Carlyle was able to use his position at the centre to dominate Victorian letters and thought. The Sage of Ecclefechan was the first Scot since Walter Scott to exert such a powerful influence over the tastes and values of Britain. And he would not have been able to do that from Ecclefechan.

More than a century later, George Gordon, the Scottish president of Magdalen College, dismissed Scottish writing after Burns, arguing that 'Scotland . . . continues to produce its occasional writer of genius but not one of them has kept his roots there and stayed where he was planted.' But physically abandoning the country did not necessarily mean leaving Scotland behind. As Scots began to dominate the popular press and newspapers of the Victorian period, a generation of Scottish writers who had left their country of birth found an outlet in London for distinctive tales about the Scotland they remembered from their boyhoods.

After a two-year period as a newspaperman in Nottingham, J.M. Barrie returned home to Kirriemuir in 1884 and began writing stories about his home town, fictionalised as 'Thrums', in the *Cornhill Magazine* and the *St James's Gazette* . In early 1885, Mr Greenwood, the editor of the *St James's Gazette,* rejected a Barrie manuscript with the note, 'but I liked that Scotch thing – any more of those?' When Barrie wrote back expressing his desire to relocate to London, Greenwood advised against it. But Barrie left the next week on the night of 28 March 1885. His imagination had been preparing for the trip for years. When he was a boy, Barrie and his mother had pored over maps of Bloomsbury. Finally, he felt ready to turn the imaginary London into reality.

In a biographical extract, Barrie describes waiting 'on the brink' of life in London:

> Only asset, except a pecuniary one, is a certain grimness about not being beaten. Pecuniary asset, twelve pounds in a secret pocket which he sometimes presses, as if it were his heart. He can hear, as you may, the hopes and fears that are thumping inside him. That bigger thump means that the train has reached St Pancras Station.

He reached London on the morning of 29 March. As he dragged his luggage to the left-luggage office, he saw a placard advertising the previous evening's *St James's Gazette*.

On the cover was starred the title 'The Rooks Begin to Build', the piece that he had sent from Dumfries. Later, he wrote, 'In other dazzling words, before being in London two minutes he had earned two guineas.'

Though Barrie rewrote his arrival in London as a humorous augury of the riches that were to come, in reality he found his early months in the city hard. His first novel, *Better Dead*, which he published at his own expense, is a slight work, often ignored by critics. In fact, it is a fascinating example of the Scottish writer with a pet strategy of how to succeed in London life.

Its hero is Andrew Riach of Wheens. Riach is a transparently autobiographical character and *Better Dead* dramatises his London adventures. Its first line is a parody of the hopes of Scots who think that London will open its riches to them immediately: 'When Andrew Riach went to London, his intention was to become private secretary to a member of the Cabinet. If time permitted, he proposed writing for the press.'

On the night he arrives, Andrew sees a murder being committed by the banks of the Thames, and after following the murderer, he falls in with his gang. Instead of killing him, they invite him to join a secret society, the SDWSP – 'the Society for Doing Without Some People'.

The murderer asks him:

> You are miserable? . . . You say that London has no work for you, that the functions to which you looked forward are everywhere discharged by another. That does not drive you to despair. If it proves that someone should die, does it necessarily follow that the someone is you?

The society is exactly the kind of criminal organisation, seemingly got up on a whim, that Sherlock Holmes, whose first adventure would appear the following year, would have been pleased to get his teeth into, though Barrie's book is written more in the style of the Chesterton of *The Man Who Was Thursday*.

It hardly needs stressed that Barrie's flippant novella offers one solution to the frustrated ambitions of the able Scottish immigrant: simply murder those who get in your way – '. . . take the world of letters. Why does the literary aspirant have such a struggle? Simply because the profession is overstocked with seniors.' Barrie lost £25 on this first publishing venture. Clearly there were some people to be cleared out of the way before he was going to make it.

But though Barrie modelled himself in these early days as Anon., the writer without an identity, before too long he was making a name for himself. The *St James's Gazette* couldn't get enough of his work, a collection of which was eventually published as *Auld Licht Idylls* in 1888.

He was also making friends. As a shy young man, he automatically gravitated towards those with whom he had something in common. Many were transplanted Scots like the *Daily Telegraph* reporter Alexander Riach, who became editor of the *Edinburgh Evening Dispatch* and gave Barrie two columns there. Another was W.E. Henley, famous now only for his poem 'Invictus' and as the inspiration behind Stevenson's Long John Silver, but then a Victorian titan, a journalist of prodigious energy and determination who, at the time Barrie met him, was editing two newspapers as well as churning out essays, poems and plays. Henley joined Riach as an admirer and champion of Barrie's work and began to publish him too.

But the most influential Scottish influence on Barrie's life, aside from that of his mother, was William Robertson Nicoll, an ordained minister of the Free Church of Scotland, a graduate of Aberdeen University and the editor of *The Expositor*, a homespun and hugely successful compilation of religious and occasional articles, published by the house of Hodder and Stoughton.

But for all his growing success, Barrie had an unusual combination of personal characteristics: a capacity for immense hard work and focus combined with a fey otherworldliness. For many years as a highly successful journalist he never had a bank account and would give his friends cheques to cash, carrying the crossed ones around in an inside pocket. Playful and light-hearted with friends, he could also be a martinet, writing stiff letters to tick off any actor who dared to ad lib in his plays.

Barrie's real success was to sell a version of Scotland to the English reading public shot through with a vein of sentimentality but also underwritten by a harsh practicality, a hard-nosed Celtic realism which those who saw no further than the boys who never grew up, and the fairyland fantasies, missed.

His books and plays also took an oblique look at the English society of his day. Barrie's *The Admirable Crichton*, the class-inverting parable about life on a desert island where the practical servant transforms into something of a despotic autocrat, ordering his pleasure-loving English employers about before meekly submitting to the social order on his return to normality, can be seen as a parable about the Scot in English society, not doubting his greater capacity for practicality but accepting the social hierarchy unless an emergency demands his focus and action.

Barrie died in 1937, leaving a fortune of £173,000. He was a knight of the realm, a favourite of the little princesses, and forever associated with Peter Pan. Like Stevenson, Barrie was often seen by his contemporaries as a boy-man, somehow adolescent and sexless whatever his true age. (His height, only 5 ft 2 in., which he was conscious of throughout his life, may have added to the image, and the fierce black moustache which he sported in later life didn't entirely dislodge it.) But Barrie was also a conspicuous literary success, adept at walking the lines between sentiment and sentimentality, sensitive to the public mood and, like a good journalist, more than willing to cut his copy to match the appetites of the day.

It was a technique which brought him the admiration of Nicoll, the father of the Kailyard, who marshalled Barrie, S.R. Crockett and the minister John Watson, who wrote as 'Ian McLaren', into one of the most commercially successful publishing operations of its time, all the more successful for not being cynically done. The Kailyard was essentially hoed up in order to satisfy the tastes of Scottish emigrants in North America, and the English reading public. But it was also written by emigrants, educated Scots who, while negotiating their way around the world of the London publishing scene, also had a keen enough sense that what they had to sell was an image of a time just passed, when community, society and pawky religious piety were the dominant notes. But another standard character in the Kailyard novel came close to representing the experience of the writers who created it: the talented lad o' pairts, dedicated to getting on in the world.

Nicoll could be at turns sentimental and tyrannical, renowned for bullying his authors and for exacting work which would above all sell. In his autobiography, *People and Books*, he detailed the advice he gave to journalists:

> Count the number of your words, and adapt them to
> the usual requirements of the periodical. See that your
> subject is in line with the subjects in the paper. Above all
> things, be sure that what the editor prints is what the
> editor likes.

That combination of hard-nosed business sense overlain with a moralistic gloss became one of the hallmarks of Scottish newspapermen; John Junor came to embody something similar, and DC Thomson turned it into an art form.

The Kailyard was a genre for the middle-, lower-middle- and 'decent' working class. Novels about Scotland appealed to the homesick and the deracinated, whether Scots in Canada or the United States, or Scots, Irish and English provincials in London. Home, belonging, simple pieties, warmth, comfort: all were themes guaranteed to appeal to those who might find themselves vulnerable and severed from their roots, or indeed comfortable enough, but a little homesick.

It also provoked its own antithesis. *The House with the Green Shutters*, the anti-Kailyard novel by George Douglas Brown, took aim at the sentimental excesses which had come to dominate images of Scotland. If the Kailyard was sentimental, yet ultimately settled and conservative, Douglas Brown's book depicted a society which was stagnated, self-satisfied and ruled by small-town despots. John Gourlay, who dominates his family with a rod of iron in order to uphold his social status as the only man in town who can afford a house with green shutters, is a classic malign Scottish father, crushing the life out of his emotional and imaginative son. When the son finally kills his domineering father while drunk, he is tormented by his imaginative memory of his father and eventually kills himself.

As a Grand Guinol version of the couthy Scottish pastoral novel, *The House with the Green Shutters* is occasionally, and unconsciously, hilarious. But those critics who fastened on it as, at last, an end to the sickly confections often forget that Douglas Brown's broadside was fired from a house in St John's Wood, against writers living in South Kensington, King's Cross and Ladbroke Grove.

This idea of London-based Scottish writers fighting over a fictional version of the rural Scotland which they have left behind them, but still feel in psychic thrall to, recurs again in the twentieth century when Leslie Mitchell, writing not in London but in Welwyn Garden City as Lewis Grassic Gibbon, created a world in *Sunset Song* in which the social order of the Mearns near Aberdeen is battered by successive waves of history: the First World War, international Marxism and the rise of the city. Gibbon's world is heavily schematised, with an artistic structure lain over the real landscape which his father worked as a ploughman and tenant farmer. As if to show that the reality of the Mearns wasn't enough for the imaginative burden he was going to put on it, he even creates an imaginary city, Duncairn, where Chris and her family move, mirroring Scottish migration from the countryside to the city.

Duncairn, rather like Welwyn Garden City itself, is a place built to a schematic plan: Gibbon's plan of how to create a city which embodies all the worst soul-destroying features of capitalism. At the end, when Ewan, the son of the central character Chris Guthrie, leaves the Mearns to go on a Communist-led hunger march to London, he isn't just leaving Scotland for London, he is marching out of a fiction into a fact.

While Barrie, Crockett and Co. were producing sentimental visions of Scottishness to sell to a London audience, another exiled Scottish-born writer, Arthur Conan Doyle, of Irish ancestry but born in Edinburgh, was monopolising the periodicals market. Sherlock Holmes, Doyle admitted, was inspired by his old professor at Edinburgh University, Dr Joseph Bell, a pioneer in forensic medicine. But Holmes' debt to Scotland goes deeper than that. On the surface, this may sound like an odd claim; Doyle is the source for one of the most powerful portraits of Victorian London, and Holmes' adventures tended to be confined to the city, with a few expeditions to the Home Counties. But Doyle's London is a surprisingly compact and comprehensible place. Even given the detective's tendency to slip off to one of the secret addresses which he maintained in the city, Holmes has the unerring knack of knowing the hidden nooks and crannies of every dingy London neighbourhood he comes up against. Elaine Showalter has argued that Dr Jekyll's London house in Stevenson's *The Strange Case of Dr Jekyll and Mr Hyde* is modelled on Edinburgh, where genteel and lawless areas are cheek by jowl; Doyle's London is similarly Edinburgh-sized, and his detective, with his tendency to change appearance and don disguises, is a displaced protean Scot.

Perhaps the last Scottish writer to unironically embrace the Victorian ideal of the Scot who by dint of hard work and steely character can create an entirely new, and better, model of himself was John Buchan, described by the critic Gertrude Himmerfarb as 'the Last Victorian'.

Buchan, who began his life as a son of the United Free Church manse and ended it as Lord Tweedsmuir, Governor General of Canada and pillar of the British Establishment, is a conspicuous Scottish success story who became as unpopular a writer in the years immediately after his death as he had been popular before. But recently, partly as a result of Andrew Lownie's authoritative 1995 biography *The Presbyterian Cavalier*, Buchan has started to emerge again as a writer of interest, shrugging off his reputation as nothing more than a writer of boys' adventure stories and a nascent anti-Semite. On the first count, Buchan may have added to his own misfortune, as he was always happy to describe his most popular novels as 'shockers' and confessed a love of 'the second-, third- and even the fourth-rate on sentimental grounds', but even, perhaps especially, the most popular of his books are interesting in their own right.

In retrospect, the career of the man who wrote *The Thirty-Nine Steps,* and was bracketed shortly after his death with Dornford Yates as a writer of cheap thrillers, can be seen as a peculiar, skilful negotiation of Scottish and British themes. The alternating focus of Buchan's imagination can even be seen in a list of his published books: his biography of Montrose was followed by one of Cromwell, and that was followed by one of

Walter Scott. The novels *Midwinter*, set in the Jacobite uprisings, and *Witch Wood*, the story of a seventeenth-century minister's attempts to stamp out the vestiges of witchcraft in his parish, sit alongside essays on 'Lord Balfour and English Thought' or histories of the South African forces in France.

Buchan provides a good illustration of the kind of split identity which T.C. Smout refers to in his *A Century of the Scottish People 1830–1950*: he exhibited 'a kind of dual ethnic consciousness, composed partly of loyalty to the actuality and opportunity of modern Britain; and partly of loyalty to the memory and traditions of Scotland'.

In the beginning, the Scottish side was dominant. As a boy, Buchan wrote in his autobiography, *Memory Hold-the-Door*, he and his siblings were tiny Scottish patriots:

> We resented the doings of Edward I, Henry VIII and Elizabeth as personal wrongs. The brutalities of Cumberland after the 'Forty-five seemed to us unforgivable outrages which had happened yesterday. We early decided that no Englishman could enter Heaven, though, later, our delight in the doings of the Elizabethan seamen forced us to make an exception of the inhabitants of Devon.

Adventure and bravery would always be a key ingredient in Buchan's patriotic feelings about Britain and was one of the forces which led him out of what he came to see as the parochialism of his Scottish upbringing. After a first degree at Glasgow University, he took a place at Brasenose College, Oxford, as a Snell Exhibitioner, and after a journey southwards, in which he registered first that the border country on the English side was very like the border country on the Scottish, he came into the presence of what would become his new love: 'I came under the spell of [Oxford's] ancient magnificence and discovered a new loyalty.'

Oxford was a formative influence for Buchan and had a huge effect on the man he would become. It enlarged his sense of possibilities and introduced him to some of the successful friends whose careers would parallel his own. He was already a recognised writer, having published his first novel *Sir Quixote of the Moors* when he was only 20; the *Oxford Magazine* noted, 'It is not easy to prophesy how far he may go.'

Writing 50 years after these events in his autobiography, Buchan describes falling in love with England's magnificence, unbroken history and traditions of power.

After leaving Oxford, Buchan lived in London for the first time, although at first he found it dingy, lonely and depressing. But those feelings soon gave way to delight as:

> The spell of London wove itself around me . . . Fleet Street and the City had still a Dickens flavour, and Hollywell Street had not been destroyed. In the daytime, with my fellow solicitor's clerk, I penetrated into queer alleys and offices which in appearance were unchanged since Mr Pickwick's day. On foggy evenings I would dine beside a tavern fire on the kind of fare which Mr Weller affected. Behind all the dirt and gloom there was a wonderful cosiness, and every street corner was peopled with ghosts from literature and history.

Buchan's apparently easy sense of his national identity, the Scottish sitting within the British, and the British within the Imperial, is hard to replicate today. But Buchan, the cultural nationalist and political Unionist, who could write sentences like 'I had lost any wish ever to leave England, for it seemed to me that I could not exhaust the delights *of my own country* [author's italics]', could also devote his energies to documenting the history of his own country, Scotland, in a series of novels which are faithful in their historical grasp and engaged in a passionate argument with the land, and landscape, of his boyhood and youth.

Buchan's Scottish novels are more than just an exercise in historical empathy or re-enactment. *Witch Wood*, which Buchan believed to be the best of his novels dealing with the landscape of his boyhood, also fits with his view of Scotland. The young minister David Semphill is struggling to assert the Christian gospel in his parish and simultaneously struggling against a coven of witches and a divided presbytery. On the surface, the story fits Buchan's publicly held beliefs that Scotland, by subduing its irrational, emotional self and submitting to order,

179

authority and rationality, had become part of the settled British order. In fact, the book is more complicated than that. Many of David's Christian flock are also members of the coven, one of his Kirk Session is the 'King-Deil' and, most worryingly of all, the witches have a sexual seductiveness about them which makes the slightly priggish minister hot under the collar.

The rational side of Buchan was able to separate the sentimental allegiance to Scotland from the rational practical appeal of England, but his feelings could easily well up, particularly when he was away from England itself. Then, rather like his first sight of the English side of the border, Buchan tended to see Scotland wherever he went.

In South Africa for the first time, while he disliked the town-dwelling Afrikaners, the temperament of the veld farmer was entirely familiar to him:

> He had many of the traits of my Lowland Scots, keen
> at a bargain and prepared to imperil his immortal soul
> for a threepenny bit, but ready to squander pounds in
> hospitality . . . I was a Scot, a Presbyterian, and a
> countryman, and therefore was half-way to being a
> kinsman.

To ease these conflicting senses of his own Scottishness, Buchan often hived them off into minor characters. Richard Hannay may have been South African, but he famously spends the climax of *The Thirty-Nine Steps* rolling about the Scottish hillsides, and Buchan gave him a Scottish sidekick in Sandy Arbuthnott. Buchan created a retired grocer, Dickson McCunn, and his collection of street urchins from the Gorbals, and put them in *Huntingtower, Castle Gay* and *The House of the Four Winds*, and Sir Edward Leithen of *The Power-House, John MacNab* and *The Gap in the Curtain* is paired with Sir Archibald Roylance, the Scottish laird and keen birdwatcher.

Buchan found embodying his Scottish identity in other characters who were important, but not entirely central, to the plot of his novels such a useful and compelling strategy that in his last book, *Sick Heart River*, set in Canada, he creates Lew Frizell, a Native American Scot, who embodies something of the hybrid nature of Canadian life. Buchan, who was famously photographed in the headdress of a Native American chief, could understand that kind of hybridity because he had lived with it all his life.

By the time he came to write *Sick Heart River,* Buchan had reached the climax of his public life as Governor General of Canada, a role which, at least at first, he relished. As it had when he visited South Africa a half-century before, the foreign landscape and culture reminded Buchan of home. But then in many ways the culture of Canada *was* Scottish, so Scottish that when he toured Canada's island provinces in the east he was repeatedly spoken to in Gaelic, a language he didn't have, about which he felt rather ashamed.

But Buchan's time as Governor General of Canada was not an unalloyed success. The Canadian Prime Minister Mackenzie King had first championed him for the role, arguing, 'He is the style of Governor-General who would greatly appeal to the university men and women and students, to authors, poets and the like – the Intelligentsia.'

At first it seemed a prescient view. Soon after arriving, Buchan was asked to become honorary president of the Canadian Authors Association, and accepted, happy to promote Canadian nationalism through literature. But ironically, by the end, the man whose ideology of Empire had envisaged a great Scotland of the mind, stretching into Canada and South Africa, found that he had become a symbol of the past to the very people who were expected to approve of him. The political and cultural landscape of Canada was shifting.

Towards the end of his tenure, Buchan became preoccupied with what he saw as the infuriating attitudes of Canadian Rhodes Scholars, who, far from falling in love with Oxford as he had done when a young man, were returning to Canada suffused with anti-British attitudes. The issue wasn't purely academic, or rather it was, since many Rhodes Scholars went on to hold university chairs or become leading journalists. In a letter to the King, Buchan blamed the men, not the times: 'I think that something will have to be done to discover a better type of Canadian Rhodes Scholar.' The man who saw himself as a friend to developing Canadian cultural nationalism came to be seen as a symbol of British power. He had become a relic, to be swept away.

Buchan's blend of Scottishness, carefully synthesising English power and Scottish sentiment, was a high-wire act, but a highly influential one. For a time, his was seen as an exemplary Scottish career, loyal to his past but engaged with the practicalities of carving out a successful future. The fact that Buchan was so alive to the potential tensions in it, while all the time carrying off the role of a British public servant, make him a more appealing character than he might appear on the surface. Re-reading Buchan's novels, it is noticeable how obsessed he is with borders and frontiers of all kinds, a natural preoccupation for a man who crossed so many, and with such success.

But Buchan's influence is also related to the temperament, attitude and *joie d'esprit* of his books. When his autobiography was published, one of its more critical reviews complained that it was full of pen portraits of his friends. It was entirely natural for him; friendships were one of the great themes of his life. He remained on good terms and in close contact with friends from Glasgow and Oxford, and struck up close relationships with many of the leading political and cultural figures of his day. His air of self-deprecation – whatever his formal, even grim, public manner – helped, but so did his sense of life as an adventure, to be experienced with as much travel, dash and commitment as he could muster.

Though Buchan remains in vogue with more romantic and old-fashioned Tories, his is not a terribly noticeable influence on current Scottish writing. There is perhaps a little of Buchan's sense of dash in the novels of William Boyd, but Boyd, another London Scottish writer out of Glasgow and Oxford, has a greater sense of comedy, and his early novels, like *A Good Man in Africa*, are clearly influenced by Evelyn Waugh.

Buchan died in 1940, still in office as Governor General of Canada and Chancellor of Edinburgh University, in which role he had succeeded J.M. Barrie.

Richard Hannay worked for the Foreign Office as a freelancer, an amateur offering his services to the State. But by the time Ian Fleming, son of the Scottish banking dynasty, came to create the secret agent who would bring him immortality, professionalism, albeit of a maverick kind, was the order of the day. When James Bond appeared in the middle of the sweat and excitement of a casino at three in the morning, in the opening pages of *Casino Royale*, lighting his 70th cigarette of the day, he was a glint of steely glamour in a world of 1950s food rationing and currency restrictions. But though the social climate was gloomy, Bond knew no such restrictions, either in his prodigious consumption of dry martinis, the glittering array of technological gadgets on loan from Q division, or his globetrotting adventures.

When the Bond novels were turned into films, this fetishistic excess threatened to take over, with each new Bond gadget (invisible cars, indeed) threatening to tip the whole franchise into comedy, but whatever his flashiness, Bond, like his creator, was a Scottish boy at heart. Educated at Edinburgh's Fettes College, where he left too early to be an inspiration to Tony Blair – though he may have served as an inspiration to Dame Stella Rimington, who graduated from Edinburgh University in the 1950s – Bond has more than a love of golf to link him to his father's homeland. Given flesh in the form of Sean Connery, Edinburgh's most famous former milkman, who had to conceal his 'Scotland Forever' tattoo with heavy make-up during the obligatory love scenes, Bond walks through the world of temptation with a stern Calvinist's eye.

As John Pearson, the former *Sunday Times* journalist who has the honour of being biographer of both Fleming and Commander Bond, has pointed out, the villains in the Bond books are always wealthy men, and though Bond is surrounded by the appurtenances of worldly success, he is in spirit a warrior monk who travels light. Small wonder that Fleming begins *You Only Live Twice*, his own covert nod at Scottish dualism, with Bond in training at a Japanese monastery, living as a monk and honing his martial-arts skills, while the world mourns, or celebrates, his apparent demise.

Bond has cast a long shadow, influencing every subsequent spy hero, some of whom are little more than pale imitations, but Fleming too is an inspirational writer. Philip Kerr, the Edinburgh-born and London-resident writer, is happy to claim him as an influence. Kerr's novels, which began with *A Philosophical Investigation*, an intellectual thriller which combined time travelling and the philosopher Ludwig Wittgenstein, have always shown a Flemingesque love of gadgetry, as well as tight plotting and pacing.

During his lifetime, Ian Fleming was a less famous writer than his brother Peter, the travel writer who was married to Celia Johnson and who explored the Brazilian rainforests. Something of that sense of excitement and potential has informed the writing of William Dalrymple, son of the Dalrymples of North Berwick and relative of the many Dalrymples who made their fortune in India. In *White Mughals*, his bestseller of 2003, Dalrymple revisits the scene of some of his family's greatest adventures and discovers that Scottish and British officers in India weren't the stereotypes of *Carry On Up the Khyber*, but were instead more likely to go native and marry Indian women. Dalrymple is fascinated by the boundaries between cultures and sits on the boundary between England, Scotland and India with ease. 'I'm not sure how important nationality is to my identity,' Dalrymple explains. 'I was born in Scotland but I feel equally at home in England and India. It's the places where cultures are in dialogue which interest me – the points of contact.'

The Victorian era, with its promise of possibility for young Scottish men, still exerts a residual pull on some Scottish writers. Appropriately enough, to signify that he has made it in London, Kelvin Walker, the hero of Alasdair Gray's 'fable of the 1960s' *The Fall of Kelvin Walker*, buys a new wardrobe of mock Victorian clothes: high boots, dove-grey trousers and waistcoat, a cut-away tail coat with a high collar and a cravat. Gray's short novel, which comes furnished with Barrie's 'Scotsman on the make' as its epigraph, is a Victorian fable of Scottish ambition set in a swinging London replete with cruel painters, promiscuous miniskirted doxies and sticky-tabled coffee bars.

Walker, whose Christian name, taken from Glasgow's second most-famous river, suggests that he can literally walk on water, is a post-Presbyterian Scot empowered by his reading of Nietzsche to believe that London lies at his feet, as long as he shows enough will and determination. At first, Kelvin follows the unofficial rule book of Scottish advancement in London to the letter. After posing as a famous London Scot, Hector McIvor, who happens to come from Kelvin's hometown of Glaik, Gray's hero bluffs his way into a series of interviews for jobs for which he has no qualifications. Most of his interviewers see through the ruse immediately, but a message sent out on the bush telegraph of London Scots secures Walker an interview at the BBC, where he is taken on as a Scottish version of Ali G, a *faux naïf* guaranteed to ask the most embarrassing questions to politicians used to fending off the more polished barbs of professional interviewers.

Like many London novels by Scottish writers, Gray's book was almost a self-fulfilling prophesy. Inspired by a meeting with Huw Weldon, he sold the play to the BBC, where it was broadcast on BBC Television. It led to a profitable 15-year relationship in which Gray sold radio and television plays to the Corporation, but the arrangement eventually dried up. Gray went on, of course, to write *Lanark*, the novel which bemoaned the lack of creative possibility in Glasgow, then helped create it, kicking off a renaissance in the form of Booker Prize winner James Kelman, Janice Galloway, A.L. Kennedy and others. But Gray has always been preoccupied with power as well as art, and *The Fall of Kelvin Walker* is consciously a novel about London, portrayed as a place where money is power, gifted with the capacity to transform, rejuvenate and enliven. Money is juice here, liquid joy, even sex. When Kelvin arrives and sits on a bench in Trafalgar Square, he can feel the money 'humming behind the ancient and modern facades, throbbing under the streets like silver-electric sap or semen'. In short order, he moves in with a girl he meets in a coffee bar, stays on her couch, meets her hellish soulmate Jake (she, naturally, is called Jill), falls in love with the girl, loses his virginity to her and lands a job as presenter of *Power Point,* benefiting from a vogue for new on-air talent with regional accents. Gray's chapter titles, 'The Discovery of London', 'Securing the Base' and 'The Conquest of London' make clear that Kelvin's life is a campaign, as focused as a military expedition and driven by sheer self-belief.

In the end, Kelvin, after a lightning ascent of the summit, is destroyed by his Scottish roots, or, more accurately, by the appearance of his Scottish father, the religiously minded session clerk of a small Presbyterian church. In the interviewee's seat for once, he is horrified when his father appears from the shadows and berates his successful son for his worldly desires. The chastened Kelvin quails in the face of this onslaught from the archetypal forbidding Calvinist father and suffers a nervous breakdown on live television. In the epilogue, 'Anticlimax', Jill and Jake (it turns out his surname is Whittington, another provincial striver) marry and settle down to a happy, unfaithful marriage while Kelvin, realising that he is part of God's plan, returns to Scotland and to Glaik, a place equidistant from Aberdeen, Edinburgh and Glasgow, to become a spokesman for a particularly repressive form of Scottish Calvinism. Kelvin's 'demonic', amoral energy has been tempered into something harder, more restrictive and less exciting, but at least he has pleased his father. Jake and Jill, who stay in London, have at least one thing over Kelvin: they are happy. But then 'it is easier for them. They are English.'

A demonic Scot features in another novel of the 1960s, Muriel Spark's *The Ballad of Peckham Rye*. But whereas Kelvin Walker is a stiff, buttoned-up figure who triumphs partly because of his inflexible nature, Dougal Douglas, Spark's hero, is the protean Scot personified, carrying a faintly sulphurous scent. Hired as a graduate of Edinburgh University to serve as the 'arts man' at a factory in south London, he arrives as a lord of misrule, a mercurial father confessor who soon has the dissatisfied residents of Peckham Rye spilling out their unhappinesses and small sorrows. And are the small bumps on his head the remains of two cysts, as everyone believes, or the stumps of horns, as he claims himself?

When Douglas applies for another job, he quickly slips into a Scottish accent after perceiving that his interviewer is a Scot, and is asked if he is any relation to Fergie Dougal the golfer. But Douglas isn't interested in playing the Scottish card when he can slip with ease into the tones of a priest, a psychiatrist or a trusted friend. Douglas claims that he has the power to drive devils out of those he talks to, but he might be the devil himself. Having sown his chaos, he is happy to depart, leaving the community to talk endlessly about him, until their stories become almost as blurred, contradictory and confusing as he is himself.

More than a decade before the publication of *The Ballad of Peckham Rye*, Muriel Spark herself had walked away from a job, one in which she was persecuted by conservative members of the Poetry Society. She had been elected to the job of general secretary of the society and editor of its magazine, *The Poetry Review*, in 1947. She dedicated herself to cleaning out the stables of what, as she describes it in her autobiography *Curriculum Vitae*, was a nepotistic and mediocre organisation, whose magazine was dominated by a clique of bad poets.

In *Curriculum Vitae*, incidentally one of the least revelatory autobiographical works ever published, she notes that the archive of the society, now housed at the University of York, contains no record of her time there. Luckily, she had preserved many of the poisonous letters exchanged with enemy members and quotes from them at length, their unpleasantness undiminished by the intervening half-century. Some bridled at the fact she wouldn't publish their poems, one complained that his name had been kept off the cover, others accused her of having an affair with the chairman, another even dug up the details of her divorce from her husband. Eventually she had had enough and allowed herself to be sacked, with three months' pay. Anyone looking for the reason why the betrayal of Miss Jean Brodie is so agonisingly drawn in Muriel Spark's most famous novel might see the roots in the treacherous atmosphere of the Poetry Society in the period 1947–9.

It was an unpleasant interlude, but in Muriel Spark's novels of London life not everything is unpleasant. In *The Girls of Slender Means* and *A Far Cry from Kensington*, London life is full of possibility, excitement and the dream of escape for a young woman.

London also appealed, of course, as the place where a young man's destiny could be transformed from potential into reality. Gordon Williams, who was shortlisted for the first Booker Prize alongside P.H. Newby (who finally won) and Iris Murdoch, was born in 1934 and worked as a journalist before writing *From Scenes Like These*, a dark novel set on an Ayrshire farm. Another farm made Williams famous: his novel *The Siege of Trencher's Farm* was turned into the film *Straw Dogs*, which famously fell foul of the British Board of Film Classification over its extended graphic rape sequence.

Straw Dogs, filmed by Sam Peckinpah, was only one of Williams's flirtations with film. His previous book, *The Man Who Had Power Over Women*, was also filmed by Hollywood, and Williams worked in the 1960s and '70s in journalism and television, co-writing the Hazell novels with football manager Terry Venables and living a boozy life around Soho. One of the great lost talents of Scottish writing, Williams is still alive, and reportedly about to complete a new book.

Emigration and escape, whether actual or dreamed of, were common themes in Scottish novels of the 1950s and '60s, and London was often the desired place to escape to. Alan Sharp's *A Green Tree in Gedde* ends with his central character, John Moseby, thinking about escaping from Scotland; his inspiration is a friend Harry Gibbon, a modern wandering Scot who is planning a series of adventures abroad. Sharp failed to live up to his promise as a novelist. *A Green Tree in Gedde* was planned as the beginning of a trilogy, but Part Two was judged to be disappointing and Part Three never appeared. Ploughing his energies into film, he emerged as a successful Hollywood scriptwriter. After his success with *The Hired Hand*, his first film, he became a hired hand himself, with five screenplays going into operation in five years. After a further success with the Liam Neeson vehicle *Rob Roy*, he is currently working on a biopic of Robert Burns, a figure who embodies his earlier themes of rampant sexuality and railing at religious restriction.

In James Kelman's novel *The Busconductor Hines* it is Australia, not London, which beckons, and the Scottish renaissance of the 1980s also seemed to give London a body swerve, at least at first. Gray's *Lanark* had been rejected by London publishers and the Scottish settings of the novels which followed it seemed likely to limit their reach into the English market. In the 1840s, Francis Jeffrey had reviewed Scott's *Waverley* and described it as 'composed, one half of it, in a dialect unintelligible to four-fifths of the country'. The same complaint was made by a Booker judge about James Kelman's work, 'written in unintelligible Glaswegian'. But in the 1990s such 'incomprehensible' Scottish speech seemed to be less of a barrier than ever before to an English publishing scene suddenly alive to literature written in Indian and Afro-Caribbean versions of English. Through the agency of Robin Robertson, the Aberdeen-born editor at Jonathan Cape, A.L. Kennedy, Duncan MacLean and Janice Galloway signed to the English house.

Polygon, the Scottish publisher which had begun as a student-run press at Edinburgh University and had published Kelman's early work, was eventually sold to Birlinn as an imprint and secured a surprise 2003 bestseller with *The No. 1 Ladies' Detective Agency* by the Edinburgh law professor Alexander McCall Smith. Canongate, the Edinburgh publisher that had taken a risk with *Lanark* in 1981, was bought out by an internal bid from Jamie Byng, who broadened the base of its catalogue, drawing on a long-standing interest in black music to set up the Payback Press, which published gritty black urban fiction. In 2003, Canongate won the Booker Prize with *Life of Pi* by Yann Martel, the first Scottish publisher to do so. To date, Byng and his company have resisted the allure of London.

Other Scottish writers found a home in the London literary scene which nonetheless allowed them to pursue their interests in Scottish themes. Andrew O'Hagan, who left Strathclyde University in Glasgow with a first in English literature in 1990, worked on *The London Review of Books*, itself founded by deracinated Scot Karl Miller, and went on to write *The Missing* and the Booker shortlisted *Our Fathers*.

O'Hagan has used London as a base to continue to write about Scottish culture, critiquing Calvinism in alliance with the Scottish-based composer James MacMillan and taking advantage of the increased interest in Scotland which has followed devolution.

Meanwhile the most successful children's writer in the world chooses to live in Edinburgh's Merchiston, while her book, fished out of Bloomsbury's slush pile, helps keep the company afloat. Appropriately, the *Harry Potter* films are largely shot in Scotland.

Harry Potter's creator is a neighbour of two other best-selling British writers: Ian Rankin, creator of the hard-boiled Edinburgh detective John Rebus, and Alexander McCall Smith, whose gentle fables starring Mma Ramotswe have brought him international fame, and an unexpected conclusion to a career as a Professor of Medical Law at Edinburgh University. Since Robin Cook and Transport Secretary Alistair Darling have chosen to live in the neighbourhood too, Edinburgh's Merchiston can hold its head up with the most sophisticated Parisian *arrondissement*.

These success stories and others seem to show that the issue which has bedevilled Scottish publishers since modern publishing began – the difficulty of securing Scottish bestsellers which break out of the Scottish market – can be bypassed, with sufficient ingenuity. Not just Scots, but English and international readers too, have thrilled to the adventures of Harry Potter, though J.K. Rowling has maintained that she was told by her first editor not to set her novel in Edinburgh for fear that it would confuse readers. 'Edinburgh is Edinburgh, but London is anywhere.' It is a lesson which Scottish writers have reluctantly acknowledged for years.

PART 3
As Others See Us

CHAPTER 9

'Traditional Sarcasms' – Scotophobia from Dr Johnson to Boris Johnson

In the end, it was the trolls that did it. A mere nine months after it had been created, the Welsh Assembly turned aside for one morning from urban regeneration, the travails of the education system and the plight of the Welsh language to tackle a slur on the pride of the principality: racism against the Welsh.

In February 2000, eighteen Assembly members drawn from all four Welsh political parties signed the Assembly's version of an early-day motion calling on regulatory bodies to combat 'persistent anti-Welsh racism' in the UK media.

Ever since King Edward I abolished the Welsh legal system with a swipe of his pen in 1284, the Welsh have had a lot to put up with at the hands of the English. Now, in the very months when the Welsh Assembly was finding its feet, the country had come under another onslaught, as fearsome in its way as that of the English armies who ransacked it at the end of the thirteenth century, only now the hostile columns were in the national newspapers.

The first shot in this renewed war against the Welsh was fired in 1998 when A.A. Gill, the *Sunday Times* restaurant critic, who glories in his image as a caddish English toff – Terry-Thomas with teeth – took time out from a damning review of a Welsh restaurant to offer the view that the natives were 'loquacious dissemblers, immoral liars, stunted, bigoted, dark, ugly, pugnacious little trolls'. It was an interesting view for a Celt to hold, since, despite his image, Adrian Gill is Scottish. Ioan Richard, an independent councillor in Swansea, said: 'If Mr Gill had been writing about blacks or Asians then he would have been locked up by now.'

Gill was reported to the police for his troubles, though they took little interest in this outbreak of inter-Celtic rivalry. Undaunted by the thought that one of their number had just escaped becoming the Cardiff One, the first political prisoner to be tried in the reformed United Kingdom for crimes against a devolved country, other voices joined the throng.

On the BBC Television programme *Room 101*, Anne Robinson consigned the whole Welsh nation to the eponymous hellhole: 'What are they for?' she asked. 'They are always so pleased with themselves.' To complete the unholy trinity, Jeremy Clarkson snipped Wales off the map and put it in a microwave oven on national television.

So serious was the trend that Ian Hargreaves, the English former editor of the *New Statesman*, contacted Channel 4 and sought to present a television programme on the troubled relationship between the English and the Welsh. *Enter the Dragon*, a title which owed more to Bruce Lee than to the inhabitants of Tiger Bay, was aired in February 2001. But Hargreaves' argument that Wales 'has shown matchless ingenuity over the centuries in retaining its identity and national purpose' fell on deaf ears: the Welsh, dismissed as the sheep-loving inhabitants of 'Goatlandshire' in the nineteenth century and still looked down on in the twenty-first, were too good a target to miss.

But this late surprise-flowering of Welshophobia wasn't the only sign of anti-Celtic sentiment in the early months of devolved Britain.

In 2002, *The Guardian*, normally the home of politically correct cultural awareness, also found itself in the unusual position of being reported to the police for racism after a piece by columnist Julie Burchill condemning London Mayor Ken Livingstone's decision to promote St Patrick's Day events in London. Burchill slammed 'the Hitler-licking, altar-boy-molesting, abortion-banning Irish tri-colour'. John Twomey, a social worker at the London Irish Centre, complained to police that the article contravened the Race Relations Act, but the Metropolitan Police dropped the case because of lack of evidence.

Did these apparently disconnected instances of English journalists being rude about their Celtic cousins show the dark side of the rise in English nationalism, first noticed in the 1996 World Cup when the flag of St George began to take its place in the windows of pubs and flutter on the aerials of a million black London taxis? Or had the Welsh and Irish simply lost their sense of humour?

There is, of course, a long history in Britain of humorous attacks against the Celts; indeed humour, rather than physical assault, has tended to be the weapon of choice for those who dislike and resent them, not least because it allows the perpetrator to maintain that his victim has suffered a sense of humour failure when he objects to the joke. The complaint by the Welsh Assembly members about their national image did wonders for the stereotype of the dour and touchy Welshman who just doesn't get English humour. When Charles Jennings's book *Faintheart*, a light-hearted travelogue around Scotland, was published by Little Brown in 2000, the reviews it received in Scotland were similarly po-faced. The *Sunday Herald* led the pack with its dismissive review: 'Oh good, another pathetic, snivelling, suburban Londoner has decided to trundle around Scotland in a hired Seat for no good reason other than to pour snot, scorn and plagues of expletives for the consumption of readers in, oh, let's say Surbiton, wherever that may be . . .'.

But humour isn't an innocent or innocuous weapon. As Freud observed, humour and anger are root cousins. Were the English growing increasingly angry at the attention being paid to the Welsh, the Irish and, by implication, the Scots?

Almost inevitably, the Scots soon joined the Welsh and the Irish as targets for the ire of politically minded English journalists. In an article entitled 'Cronies and Sleaze: Why do we pander to the Scots?' published in the *Daily Mail* in November 2001, journalist Simon Heffer used a slur on Scottishness to get at New Labour: 'The ruling ethos in New Labour is a Scottish one, rooted in a culture of corruption and low moral standards.'

But though these attacks seemed to show a pattern, they also show the distinctions which English critics have always made between the countries with which they share these islands.

The Welsh have endured many years of being derided, not

least because the country is divided in two by a linguistic line: the aspirational Welsh from the south (Geoffrey Howe, Michael Heseltine, Roy Jenkins, Michael Howard) can easily pass themselves off as English but the 'Welsh' Welsh from the north, like Neil Kinnock, have been labelled as blathering rugby-playing boyos, beery and boisterous. One group is seen as disingenuous and dissembling, the other as defiantly unmetropolitan and unsophisticated. Smooth sophists or sheep-loving bumpkins, from the Welsh Wizard to the Welsh Windbag: neither of the two extremes of Welsh identity, as viewed from England, is terribly flattering.

Scotland has its own north–south divide, of course, and the Victorians made a very clear distinction between the characteristics of the inhabitants of the unreformed Highlands and the settled Lowlands, but whereas Victorian Britain took great pleasure from its images of whiskery Scotsmen befuddled after too many glasses of the 'wheesky' or lost in King's Cross after missing the last train to Inverness, for much of the last century the Scots have come off fairly lightly from the sarcastic barrage which has periodically been directed at the Irish or the Welsh.

Indeed, much of modern Scottish self-image has been built on a complacent belief that no one could dislike us at all:

> As I travel around the world I hear no ready animosity
> expressed about Scotland in any of the countries of
> Europe, nor elsewhere. Nothing in the long sacrifice of
> our pioneering generations seems to have stored up ill
> will or given us the name of unreliable or dishonest . . .
> the English have stirred up animosity for themselves
> everywhere. They have offended and oppressed most
> of the countries of the world and especially those of
> Europe. Their enemies are now closing in.

When Sir Alastair Dunnett, the moderate, reform-minded former editor of *The Scotsman*, wrote a piece in support of Scottish independence in the *Herald* newspaper in September 1996, during the dying days of the Major Government, his argument for severing the Union rested strongly on the belief that the good relationship Scots have with their neighbours abroad would ensure a welcome for an independent country which had dumped its brash, insular and xenophobic neighbour. It was a powerful view at the time, and to Dunnett's high-minded relief that the Scots' involvement in the British Empire seems to have done no lasting damage to the international reputation of post-Empire Scotland should also be added the conspicuous good behaviour of the Tartan Army, who, on international duty supporting Scotland's football team abroad, go out of their way to be well behaved. Good behaviour isn't always what it seems, though; many Scottish football fans take great pleasure in showing up the behaviour of their English rivals; and Scottish domestic football, as exemplified by the *Clockwork Orange*-style violence of the Aberdeen Soccer Casuals in the 1980s, hasn't always been as restrained. Nonetheless, Scots who have recently returned from abroad will often recount the thawing in relations with their foreign hosts when it dawns on them that their British guests are actually Scottish.

For a country in which so much self-esteem rests on the conviction that no one actively dislikes us, it is potentially devastating to realise that a growing number of people in England are coming to do precisely that. Whilst the attitude of most English people towards Scotland remains benign or neutral, more and more are finding cause to be resentful about Scotland's power within the Union.

'Make no mistake,' Simon Heffer explains. 'If I was Scottish I would be a member of the SNP. If a nation decides it wants to be independent in the modern world then it should have that right. But what English people understand about the Scots is that when they could get something out of Britain, or the Empire, they were very enthusiastic about Britain. It's only now they can't that they want to dismantle a successful project which has been running since 1707.'

Whereas the Welsh tend to be the targets for personal abuse, in recent history the Scots have been lampooned more for their political culture than for their physical characteristics, though in 1902 T.W.H. Crosland in his book *The Unspeakable Scot* (of which more later) described the Scot in terms not dissimilar to the ones used by A.A. Gill of the Welsh:

> But a Scotchman certainly does make one feel that underneath his greasy and obviously imperfect

civilisation the hairy simian sits and gibbers. Rouse him, thwart him, disappoint him, rally him, and your cross-eyed, sandy-haired, bandy-legged, but withal sleek, smug, moralising man suddenly 'bleezes' and you perceive in him the ten thousand devils of an ancient and arboreal barbarity. Whether he be Highlander or Lowlander or mongrel, as he mostly is, it is just the same. He is Scotch and compounded for the most part of savage.

Such uninhibited abuse of the Celts has a long pedigree: Charles Kingsley, author of *The Water Babies*, thought the Irish were 'human chimpanzees' and anti-Scottish cartoons of the 1760s routinely portray Scots as hairy savages. The legend of Sawney Bean, the supposed Scottish cannibal who lived in a cave in Ayrshire with his feral family and ate passing travellers, leaving their bones strewn around the beach, became a motif for all Scots and 'Sawney in the Boghouse', an anti-Scottish cartoon of the time, has Sawney sitting with his feet in the latrine and defecating on the floor.

But anti-Scottish sentiment in England, though it shares some of the characteristics of the abuse meted out to the Welsh and the Irish, does have a different root. Irish and Welsh societies were, to different extents, marginalised and despised, their citizens viewed as less than truly human. Anti-Scottish abuse is a perverse tribute to Scottish power, not a condescending response to powerlessness, and tends to be at its height when Scots are at their most visible and successful in British society.

As such, many of the roots of anti-Scottish sentiment can be seen as early as 1603, and not all of it was verbal. In the reign of James VI, Scots sleeping rough on the streets of London were routinely beaten up by the Swaggerers, a gang formed exclusively for that purpose. The success of James VI in becoming King of England provoked a storm of anti-Scottish propaganda, some of which took the form of theatricals, which he sought to ban.

An English poet, Francis Osborne, described the Scots who came down to London in doggerel:

> They beg our lands, our goods, our lives
> They switch our nobles and lye with their wives.

And the supposed sexual potency of the Scots (not an image normally associated with Scottish men aside from Ewan McGregor and Sean Connery) would reappear as a propaganda device in the 1760s.

But in the seventeenth century, when the monarch was the centre of political power, it was James's ambiguous sexuality which proved to be one of the most effective ways to smear the King, and through him the nation he came from. The image of the monarch which has come down through history, of the slavering homosexual, his tongue too big for his mouth and his hands forever fondling his crotch or the limbs of attractive young men, comes directly from the pen of Sir Anthony Weldon, a disgruntled English courtier who was dismissed by James after making a cack-handed attempt to flatter his King by denigrating Scotland. After visiting Scotland in 1617, Weldon wrote that the country was 'too good for those that possess it and too bad for others to be at the charge to conquer it. The aire might be wholesome but for the stinking people that inhabit it.' Medieval Scotland was notoriously unhygienic, but Weldon's point was bigger than that. The willingness of so many Scots to leave Scotland has led generations of English people to believe that there must be something seriously wrong with the place, and the tension between the attractions of London and the repulsive power of Scotland remains one of the strongest images about the two.

This idea of the Scots desperate to leave a depressed and depressing kingdom and rubbing their hands with glee at the thought of the English wealth awaiting them in the south recurs again and again in English writing about the Scots. When the Scots flooded into London in the 1760s, taking advantage of the opportunities which Union gave them, they were greeted with a flood of satirical propaganda which portrayed them as money grubbers out to fleece the capital of its cash and secure the best government positions through the agency of their highly placed fellow countrymen. Nor were these English fears without foundation. Linda Colley, in her book *Britons*, records that from 1745, just after the last Jacobite uprising, to 1780, Scots MPs feathered their own nests so successfully that in 1745 none held state pensions, and 35 years later, half were in receipt of one. Arrivals in the 1780s and '90s were able to take advantage of successful Scots who had already established themselves in London political society to give them government positions, partly to ensure a client group of supportive fellow countrymen and partly, one suspects, as a form of wealth redistribution.

But what the Scots saw as simple support of their kinship group, continuing a tradition of loyalty which was an important feature of life in Scotland, the English saw as cronyism of the most blatant kind. 'The Caledonians' Arrival in Money-Land', a cartoon from 1762, shows a line of cheery, bekilted arrivals in the capital. On the right a line of Scots are welcomed in by a prosperous-looking host who promises, 'Come in Laddies, we shall au be Muckle Men.' Another, doffing his cap, declares, 'An it please you my Laird to give Me a gude Post', while behind him a figure announces, 'I shall have a place, for I'm his cousin.'

But if nepotism was one charge against the Scots, the other was sycophancy to the established political order. The broad Scots stereotype, Sir Pertinax MacSycophant in Macklin's *The Man of the World*, is a highly exaggerated picture of the Scot who adheres to Hanoverian government. Government pressure had made Macklin, an Irishman, abandon his original title, *The True-born Scotsman*.

One of the driving forces behind this wave of anti-Scottishness was the speed with which the political position of the Scots had changed. At the beginning of the eighteenth century, the Scots were barely trusted foreigners in England, yet by 1707 they were fellow countrymen, portrayed by propaganda as equal partners in the new country. Daniel Defoe, whose *Robinson Crusoe* was based on the experiences of the shipwrecked Scot Alexander Selkirk and who would serve as an English spy in Edinburgh during the Union debates, portrayed the pre-Union Scots in his satire *The True Born Englishman* as raiders from the north:

> Scots from the Northern Frozen banks of Tay,
> With Packs and Plaids came Whigging all away:
> Thick as the Locusts which in Egypt swarm'd,
> With Pride and hungry Hopes completely arm'd:
> With native Truth, Diseases and no Money,
> Plundered our Canaan of the Milk and Honey.

Recent historical research has paid a good deal of attention to these anti-Scottish cartoons and polemics. One of the most notorious outbursts of London Scotophobia was witnessed and reported by that most famous of the London Scots, James Boswell.

On the night of 8 December 1762, Boswell, who had a fatal weakness for theatricals, and actresses, attended Covent Garden for a production of *Love in the Village*, a light comic opera. Just before the overture was played, two Scottish officers from a Highland regiment came into the pit. The mob in the upper gallery immediately started to bay 'No Scots, no Scots!' and pelted the men with apples. Boswell leaped up on the benches and shouted out, 'Damn you, you rascals!' The crowd screamed back at him.

'I hated the English,' he wrote in his journal. 'I wished from my soul the Union was broke and we might give them another Battle of Bannockburn.'

The men were members of Lord John Murray's regiment. They had been fighting in Havana for the British army. 'And this,' they said, 'is the thanks that we get – to be hissed when we come home.'

That 'home' was at the root of the problem. To many English, the Scots were in *their* home and were occupying all the best seats. The Union of the Parliaments had been sold to Scotland as a way of gaining access to the markets of the south, and by the 1760s, thousands of Scots were making good on the deal. Londoners believed that they were being swamped by immigrants, and the Scots were labelled with many of the characteristics which would later be used against other incomers. They were stealing English jobs and taking the best positions; they looked out for themselves and squeezed English traders out.

The English and the Scots stereotyped each other long before the two unions, of course: in the fifteenth century, Scots believed that their English neighbours had long tails which they kept wound down their breeches and flexed out at night, and children in the Borders played games in which they divided into two teams, English and Scottish. But these rivalries and misunderstandings stemmed from regular, and often violent, contact. The English borders were subject to frequent raids by the Border Reivers; the Scotophobia of the eighteenth century was based on less personal knowledge of who the incoming Scots were. Indeed, many Londoners had only the vaguest notion of where Scotland actually was. On 1 March 1754, the novelist Tobias Smollett wrote to Alexander Carlyle:

> Ignorance prevails to such a degree that one of our Chelsea Club asked me if the weather was good when I crossed the Sea from Scotland. If the truth be told, the South Britons in general are woefully ignorant in this particular. What, between want of curiosity, and traditional sarcasms, the effect of ancient animosity, the people at the other end of the island know as little of Scotland as of Japan.

The ignorance of many Londoners as to where Scotland was and what it was like added to the sense that the Scots who had begun arriving in the capital were an invasion of foreigners. But it was also an invasion which was encouraged by those at the very centre; Scottish loyalty to British institutions could be encouraged by bringing the Scots right into the heart of power.

The Scots scaled to the very top of British politics with astonishing and, to many English observers, suspicious ease. The premiership of the hapless Lord Bute, one of the least appealing or charismatic of the parade of peers who held the post of British Prime Minister in the eighteenth century, was a palpable sign that the Scots had entered the British pile at the top of the heap.

Bute was born in Edinburgh in 1713, educated at Eton and came to London as one of the 37 Scottish nobles allowed seats in the House of Lords under the Act of Union. A chance meeting with Frederick, Prince of Wales at Newmarket Races allowed him entry to the Royal circle and he quickly became a fixture at court.

Bute was a perplexing character, pompous and condescending in person but a skilled political manipulator and a man of wide and unusual enthusiasms. His interest in cards and amateur theatricals seemed slightly at odds with his reserved personality, but he was also a keen botanist, the author of the nine-volume *Botanical Tables Containing the Nine Families of*

British Plants, and a benefactor of Kew Gardens. The Earl of Shelbourne, a political ally, judged Bute:

> . . . proud, aristocratical, pompous, imposing, with a great deal of superficial knowledge, such as is commonly to be met in France and Scotland, chiefly upon matters of natural philosophy, mines, fossils, a smattering of mechanics, a little metaphysics, and a very false taste in everything.

But though Bute seemed oddly composed, he had the ear of the King. He had acted as tutor to George III in his boyhood, and the King relied on Bute to take most of the decisions relating to the organisation of the Royal household. He held Bute to be his 'dearest friend' and consulted him on everything from the choice of his bride to the seating arrangements at Royal functions. Opponents grumbled that George even spoke with a Scottish accent.

Bute's nationality became a focal point for anti-Scottish sentiment. In an attempt to get his political message across, the Prime Minister hired the novelist Tobias Smollett to edit a government newspaper called *The Briton*. It was an inspired choice. Smollett, another Scot, had already shown that he had a peculiar insight into the dynamics of the age. His first novel, *The Adventures of Roderick Random*, was the picaresque tale of a young Scot 'born in the northern part of this united kingdom' who seeks his fortune in the capital. Random encounters more than just random prejudice: Smollett's hero and his companion Strap are roundly abused by almost everyone they meet and mocked in a jibe which comes straight from Defoe: 'You Scotchmen have overspread us as the locusts did Egypt.'

Roderick is comically unaware of the jibes levelled at his nationality. Smollett needed to develop a thick skin too. Reviewers dismissed him as a 'Caledonian Quack' and a 'vagabond Scot'.

In response to such English hostility, Smollett sought and found a group of Scottish supporters in the capital. His relative, Sir Andrew Mitchell, served as a patron, and he introduced Smollett to James Thomson, the Scottish composer of 'Rule Britannia'.

Smollett, who had observed that 'from Doncaster downwards, all the windows of the inns were scrawled with doggerel rhymes in abuse of the Scottish nation', dutifully churned out copies of *The Briton* to support Bute's ministry, but his message could not compete with that of the most virulent anti-Scottish pamphleteer of the century, John Wilkes.

Wilkes was a scurrilous journalist and political campaigner who delighted in mocking the standards of decency of the age. A member of the original Hellfire Club, he delighted in whores, vicious humour and the black arts of politics. For Wilkes, Bute's unpopular ministry was too good a target to ignore. Bute was already suspected of helping his countrymen into positions of power: in 1761, alongside other Scottish appointments, he had promoted Robert Adam to the important sinecure of Architect of the King's Works. Wilkes was able to add allegations of sexual misconduct to those of cronyism. He delightedly propagated a rumour that Bute was having an affair with Augusta, the Dowager Princess of Wales, mother to the King. Though the rumour is almost certainly untrue, it was widely believed at the time and occasioned a series of scurrilous prints in which the Princess is seen in a variety of sexual poses with Bute. In one, with her hand wedged firmly under the Prime Minister's kilt, she is made to remark, 'A man of great parts is certain to rise.'

For a man being slandered as a Scots chauvinist, Bute was spectacularly inept, at one stage presenting a list of sixteen recommendations for public office which contained the names of eleven Stuarts and four MacKenzies. Those Stuarts were also reminders of another awkward political fact: Bute's father had been a supporter of the Jacobites, the family name was Stuart (the French spelling of the Royal Stewart) and so Bute embodied both sides of a developing Scottish stereotype – the British sycophant who also carried the threat of disloyalty to Britain.

All this was grist to Wilkes's mill. One cartoon in *The North Briton* showed a northern witch conveying Scotsmen on her broomstick to the land of promotion. Bute was portrayed as 'Sawney', after Sawney Bean, the notorious mass murderer, or as a boot, a play on his name.

Then John Wilkes went too far. In April 1763, issue 45 of *The North Briton* appeared (the number was a reference to the 1745 uprising). Inside, Wilkes repeated and embellished the references to the sexual relationship between the Prime Minister and the King's mother and claimed for good measure that the King's speech to Parliament that year had contained a lie.

It was too much. Wilkes was arrested and imprisoned in the Tower of London. Even there, he demanded that he be spared a cell previously occupied by a Scotsman for fear of contracting the pox. But as a Member of Parliament he had certain rights, and a week later he was released by Charles Pratt, the Chief Justice of the Common Pleas, his imprisonment viewed as a breach of parliamentary privilege.

An attempt to have issue 45 of *The North Briton* burned in front of the Royal Exchange failed because the crowd seized the pamphlet, assaulted the sheriff and his officers and instead put the familiar boot and petticoat into the flames.

Wilkes was rapidly becoming a symbol of popular resistance to authority. The mob was willing to riot in order to defend him. The King and his ministers were worried lest the situation spiral out of control. By November, to the King's relief, the Commons had decided that seditious libel was not covered by parliamentary privilege and voted to expel Wilkes from the Commons. Wilkes himself decided to flee to Paris.

By this time Wilkes was a hate figure amongst Scots and on his arrival in Paris he was immediately challenged to a duel by an outraged Scotsman. John Forbes was the son of a Jacobite from Aberdeen who had fled to Paris in the aftermath of the '45. He recognised Wilkes from the famous portrait of him by Hogarth and immediately pursued him to his lodgings and demanded a duel.

Wilkes escaped by a characteristic bit of cheek, and placed himself under the safekeeping of a French magistrate. But the Wilkes saga was about to enter its final and most dangerous phase. In February 1768, after being greeted in Paris by Diderot as 'a brother in arms' and sojourning in Naples, with his money running low he returned to London. He immediately wrote begging the King's pardon but was ignored. A few days later, he announced that he would stand as parliamentary candidate for the City of London at the forthcoming election.

In the event he came bottom of the poll but then threw his hat into the ring for the vacant seat of Middlesex. Supported by a violent mob, who hustled passers-by and chalked '45' on the doors of coaches, he was returned for Middlesex and promptly surrendered himself to the Chief Justice, upon which he was sentenced to 22 months in the King's Bench Prison in Southwark.

Where Wilkes went, his mob followed. The prison was surrounded. Houses in Middlesex, including that of Lord Bute, were stoned and the Austrian Ambassador was dragged from his carriage to have the number 45 chalked on the soles of his shoes. Like the dockers who 200 years later would strike in support of Enoch Powell, seamen from the docks came out in force to protest at the incursion of Scottish labour.

The Monarch's response was sharp. On 10 May, he authorised a magistrate to read the Riot Act outside the prison and soldiers were authorised to shoot rioters. Six were killed, including at least one in a case of mistaken identity. When the mob surrounded St James's Palace, the situation seemed dangerous indeed, and at times the King himself feared for his life. As his manoeuvrings became more desperate, a candidate with Royal approval quit his Cornish seat and stood against Wilkes in Middlesex; Henry Lawes Luttrell was defeated at the ballot box by 1,143 votes to 296, but declared to be member for the constituency since the winner was debarred from Parliament. Another riot followed and the new member for Middlesex did not leave his lodgings for weeks.

George's response to Wilkes had created a martyr. In a petition, the King was threatened with revolution. By the time the Wilkes affair died down, Bute's ministry was broken and the first Scottish Prime Minister of Britain was travelling on the continent under the name Sir John Stuart. His replacement, George Grenville, was, for safety's sake, not a Scot.

What do these examples of historical anti-Scottishness have to do with today's situation? They say perhaps that anti-Scottishness is more akin to anti-Semitism than anti-Irishness because it is premised on the belief that Scots are a secret cabal which operates to the advancement of its members. Whilst some Scottish incomers to London, notably the homeless, have always been seen as worryingly violent, drunken and potentially threatening, Scots are mostly seen as peaceable but cliquish, clannish and devoted to their own advancement.

Nor is the analogy with anti-Semitism far-fetched. Like the Jew, the educated Scot could pass in English society unnoticed, adding to fears about infiltration from within. Indeed, Scots Covenanters themselves sometimes made the analogy with Israel, seeing Scotland as a small and yet saved nation, secure in the love of God. Sometimes the comparison between the Scots and Jews is stated explicitly: in 'The Scotsman in London', an article by the pseudonymous James M'Turk esq. in *London*, a six-volume compilation of essays on the capital edited by Charles Knight and published in 1844, the Scots are equated with the chosen people of Israel in their supposed self-regard and their enclosed community within the metropolis:

> If one were to attempt an analysis of what keeps the Scotch, almost as much as the Jews, a distinct and peculiar people in London, this notion that they 'think such a d——d deal of themselves' will be found at the bottom of the English side of this shyness.

But M'Turk's real complaint about the Scots is their clannishness:

> It is scarcely a paradox to say that you meet with more intense Scotch nationality in London than in Scotland. Every strath and valley in Scotland has a character of its own; and in Edinburgh, the capital where representatives of all these districts are brought into contact, the clannish spirit of the people prevents their mixing . . . In London, on the contrary, Scotsmen recognise a common nationality, as they do in any other foreign country, and herd lovingly together. The English part of the community know them as merchants, or lawyers, and, above all, as bakers (for, strange though it may appear to those who have tasted bread in Scotland, almost every baker's shop you enter in London is a Scotsman's); but they know little of them as persons to live with: they are public mysteries, mid-day spectres, things to be seen, not touched, except by each other. 'They herd together': they have their Caledonian Balls once a year, at which some of the

most imaginative appear in the Highland costume; they have their Presbyterian clergymen and places of worship – Scotch Presbyterianism is quite a different thing from English; and they have an annual dinner of the Caledonian Asylum, after which Highland chiefs win all their hearts by dancing the Highland fling.

M'Turk's eyewitness description of the Scots in Victorian London fits in with other historical evidence, though his interest in the devoted service of Scottish boulangeries seems to be a personal quirk. But where M'Turk makes a lasting contribution to the literature of Scotophobia is in his portrayal of the Scots as second-raters, diligent rather than distinguished, bright rather than truly intelligent. Naturals, in fact, to serve a subsidiary role in Britain.

> The Scotch are first-rate second-rate men; as in their own bagpipes the *drone* is more pleasing than the higher and more varied notes to which it is the monotonous accompaniment. They swarm in counting-houses and engineer-shops – in the subordinate departments of government-offices – in the India-house, and so-forth: their triumphs are over the commonplace and narrow-minded of society – the class most alive to the dislike of successful rivals.

This image of the Scot as the perfect number two, a natural second-in-command to the English leader, is a vital imperial idea of Scottishness, where the Scot as engineer, manager or doctor is seen to be in a subservient relationship with his English boss, a relationship which mirrors the pecking order within the United Kingdom. This idea also finds its way into the image of the Scot as the 'upper servant', a superior inferior like Gordon Jackson's Hudson in the television series *Upstairs, Downstairs* set in Edwardian London. There were real-life versions of Hudson, and of Barrie's Scottish butlers: at least one agency in the capital specialised in supplying Scottish servants to Victorian London, and the Queen's enthusiasm for them encouraged the trend.

The idea of the Scot as the ideal second-in-command has appealed to modern writers too: Patrick O'Brian's Aubrey and

Maturin novels, set during the Napoleonic Wars, have a Scot, Heneage Dundas, serving as Aubrey's confidant. Dundas is a scrawny, bad-tempered tyke who serves as a useful sounding-board for his English captain, but the very name of this fictional aide-de-camp serves as a reminder that despite the imperial ideology the Scots weren't always second-in-command: Henry Dundas was, of course, the Scot who served as Solicitor General, Lord Advocate and then president of the Board of Control for India. The key Scottish political fixer of the time, Dundas was justly accused of packing the East India Company's overseas offices with Scots and paving the way to many a Scottish fortune made in the service of the mercantile British Empire. On securing their fortune, these wealthy Scots would return home to Scotland and help secure Dundas's political control over the domestic sphere.

Such imperialising Scots, with their worrying propensity for benefiting from Empire without returning to the London centre, would emerge in time as English anti-heroes, as when the ambitious Donald Farfrae ('far frae' home, presumably) takes over a Wessex town in Thomas Hardy's *The Mayor of Casterbridge*. In India and the Far East, such Scottish mercantile takeovers of whole communities were common.

But the image of the busy Scot, making his way in the world, gets its most savage and pointed critique in T.W.H. Crosland's book of 1902, *The Unspeakable Scot*. A mixture of bile and penetrating insight, Crosland's book is at heart a savage attack on the Scots who by the beginning of the twentieth century had established a central role in English journalism.

Crosland has not been treated kindly by literary historians. He was born in Leeds on 21 July 1865 and carved out a career as a polemical journalist and occasional poet, writing reviews and editing *The Outlook*, *The Academy* and the *Penny Illustrated Paper*. An unlikely friend of Lord Alfred Douglas, Crosland was notorious for his hatred of Oscar Wilde and ghost-wrote Douglas's self-justifying, and self-pitying, autobiography *Oscar Wilde and Myself*. Crosland was a collaborator with Douglas on the revised version of *The Academy*, relaunched in 1920 as *Plain English*, which served as a vehicle for Douglas to propagate his own colourful and objectionable brand of anti-Semitism.

In Aleister Crowley's *Diary of a Drug Fiend*, Crosland is

present at an encounter between Frank Harris and Lord Alfred Douglas at the Café Royal.

> The slight figure of a young-old man [Douglas] with a bulbous nose to detract from his otherwise remarkable beauty, spoilt though it was by years of insane passions, came into the café. His cold blue eyes were shifty and malicious. One got the impression of some filthy creature of the darkness – a raider from another world looking about him for something to despoil. At his heels lumbered his jackal [Crosland], a huge, bloated, verminous creature like a cockroach, in shabby black clothes, ill-fitting, unbrushed and stained, his linen dirty, his face bloated and pimpled, a horrible evil leer on his dripping mouth, with its furniture like a bombed graveyard.

Crosland's book is a curiosity, so unrelieved in its hostility that it is hard to believe it could ever have convinced an undecided Englishman to hate the Scots in his midst. In Crosland's view, the Scot is a man whose personal mediocrity is only made more ludicrous and inadequate by the exaggerated claims made on behalf of his race by Scottish writers. As a savage attack on the smugness and self-satisfaction of Kailyard writing, it is bracing.

> Numerically, the Scotch journalist is unquestionably strong. He possesses, too, certain solid qualities which are undoubtedly desirable in a journalist. For example, he is punctual, careful, dogged, unoriginal and a born galley-slave. You can knock an awful lot of work out of him, and no matter how little you pay him, he may be depended upon to sustain the 'dignity of the office' in the matter of clothes, extended habits of life, and a dog-like devotion to the hand that feeds him and the foot that kicks him.

Crosland has an acute eye for the pillars of Scottish pretension. The Scottish love of learning gets a kicking (all the Scotsmen in his book are labelled 'Dr'). The Scottish pride at being a 'heid o' depairtment' gets pilloried ('second-rate, mediocrities').

Scottish fiscal probity is pooh-poohed ('Scotch clerks and Scotch managers . . . are no more trustworthy and no more to be depended on, and no less human than Englishmen'). And above all, Scots' self-regard is mercilessly lampooned:

> Your proper child of Caledonia believes in his rickety bones that he is the salt of the earth. Prompted by a glozing pride, not to say by a black and consuming avarice, he has proclaimed his saltiness from the house-tops in and out of season, unblushingly, assiduously, and with results which have no doubt been most satisfactory from his point of view.

To find anything comparable to this sustained and unrelenting attack on the Scottish character one would have to go back to the 1760s. Crosland's book (he followed it up two years later with *The Egregious English* written under the pseudonym Angus McNeill, an attempted reply which lacked the drive and spleen of the original) is an oddity which, despite its blunderbuss approach, occasionally hits its target. Its tone of irritation at the self-satisfaction of Scots who claim that Scottishness gives them a superior store of human qualities is its most noticeable feature, and that same note occurs in this piece by Boris Johnson, the ebullient editor of *The Spectator*, and the Conservative MP for Henley:

> Och aye, it's the New Jerusalem! It's a land of milk and honey they're building there in Scotland, laddie. They'll nae be doing it with your horrid Anglo-Saxon devil-take-the-hindmost approach. No, they're just more socialist than us sour-mouthed Sassenachs.

But anti-Scottishness has more to it than just dislike of Scottish self-satisfaction. A cartoon from the 1760s shows two Scottish Highlanders with two separate speech bubbles coming from their mouths. One demands a share of English power and favours, the other threatens to go back and raise a rebellion. The implication is clear: the Scots want it both ways. They burrow to the heart of English society, ferociously seeking out the benefits of membership of the elite, but they are capable, if their ambitions are thwarted, of turning away from English values and threatening to strike out and go it alone.

In modern political times, the threat that Scots would go off and ally themselves with a foreign power to rival England has been negligible (though the neutrality of the Irish in the Second World War is often held against them). In place of the threat of Scottish disloyalty with a foreign power has arisen the prospect of disloyalty at home: nationalism, where the Scot is seen as turning his back on his natural English allies and seeking the unpredictable, and essentially resentful, path of home rule.

This criticism of Scottish nationalism takes two forms: the first is the broadest and the most comic. The novel *Scotch on the Rocks*, penned by the Tory Cabinet minister Douglas Hurd and Andrew Osmond, falls into this category. Written as a fictional response to the rise of Scottish Nationalism in the 1970s, it lampoons the Scottish Nationalist movement and has at its heart a portrait of Mrs Merrilies, a bonkers, high-spirited version of Wendy Wood, the Scottish Nationalist activist and keen supporter of the cultural case for independence, who in the novel drives her Morris Minor at perilous speeds around winding Highland roads. (A Scottish Hillman Imp, like the one which bore the victorious Winnie Ewing to Westminster in 1967, would have been more appropriate.)

Scotch on the Rocks is an entertaining romp with some surprisingly astute barbs at the SNP's Poujadist membership. In a thinly fictionalised Beach Ballroom in Aberdeen, SNP leader James Henderson looks over the crowd:

> These were the folk he was at home with, the street corner chemist, the fifty-acre farmer from West Aberdeenshire, the trawler skipper in his best suit, the small local builder. These were Henderson's people and the muscle of the SNP: men of little substance, with bulky wives, men worried about the future, jealous of the growing wealth south of the border, suddenly conscious and proud of being Scots.

But in the novel, the small-town SNP also contains the militant cells of a fictionalised Scottish National Liberation Army, intent on militarising Scotland's political situation and bombing the

English out of Scotland. In its portrayal of Whitehall's response to the escalating crisis, *Scotch on the Rocks* accurately captures the blend of mystification and irritation which the rise of Scottish Nationalism seemed to create in some sections of the English Establishment:

> Harvey [the British Prime Minister] had always disliked the Scots, a formal, long-winded lot, boasting about their scenery but living in fact in grim damp cities and terrible villages, consumed with unending quarrels and complaints.

In reality, the bombs never came, and it's unclear whether the real-life Scottish National Liberation Army had much of a life outside the imaginations of certain tabloid journalists. Real-life Scottish Nationalist leaders rightly take pride in the fact that no one has been killed or injured in the long constitutional struggle for Scottish independence. In the absence of any armed threat to Englishness, Scots escaped the worst of the hostility which the IRA's attacks on England generated. After the Brighton bombing, Sir John Junor famously compared Irish people to pigs and, after he was confronted on his own doorstep by a group of Irish people, he printed an apology 'to pigs'.

The Scottish form of nationalism is more often seen by English society as an intellectually self-serving conspiracy of organised selfishness in which Scots try to screw more money out of the English exchequer than they deserve. In this cause, Scottish nationalism isn't the preserve of one party; Scottish Labour or Liberal MPs can be 'nationalists' too.

In the election race for Mayor of London in 2000, Ken Livingstone coined a sound bite which was guaranteed to appeal to the *Evening Standard*: 'I don't think it's right that Londoners should pay through their taxes to support a level of services in Scotland that the Scottish Chancellor then refuses Londoners the right to have themselves.' Livingstone, whose high view of the Scots extended to him accusing Scottish Labour MPs of enjoying their time in Westminster because it afforded them easy access to the brothels of London, normally has a keen political antenna, but according to the London Mayoral Election Survey of 2000, only 9 per cent of Londoners believed that the

Scottish Parliament had weakened the Government of the UK, 14 per cent thought it had made it better and 61 per cent believed it had made no difference.

Livingstone's jibe about the carnal tastes of Scottish politicians is only a minor example of another prevalent strain of anti-Scottish comment: the accusation that Scottish politics is itself corrupt, rooted in cronyism and rule-bending. This argument about Scotland dates back to before 1832 and the Great Reform Bill, when Scotland was seen as the biggest rotten borough in Britain and stems from the (not entirely inaccurate) belief that Scottish politics is the preserve of political fixers and managers who pride themselves on their capacity to 'deliver' Scottish votes in return for preferment and promotion.

Journalist Simon Heffer put the case far more concisely. Responding to the resignation of Scotland's First Minister Henry McLeish over bungled expenses claims for his constituency office, Heffer suggested that the tale was symptomatic of a Labour Party in Scotland which tolerated corruption; by extension, New Labour, with its Scottish dominance, was complacent about sleaze:

> We in England ignore at our peril what is happening in Scotland and the actions of those Scots who rule us in England. The peril is not just to our wallets and to our public standards, but to the very basis of our democracy. We have been warned.

In the face of such fierce condemnation, it is almost a relief to turn to the results of an informal survey carried out by the sociologist Isobel Lindsay amongst English students to determine their views about the Scots in the months leading up to devolution. Asked which words and ideas they most associated with the Scots, the students provided a list which few in Scotland would quarrel with: the Scots were a bagpipe-playing, whisky-drinking, rather mean bunch who ate haggis and celebrated Hogmanay with rare relish. Lindsay's research revealed that the gentler Scottish stereotypes which flourished in *Punch* magazine for most of the nineteenth and twentieth centuries still had a receptive audience. There, Scotland is a land of innocent peasants, old men from the Highlands who get 'fou' on 'ower muchle wheesky' and tend to cheek and bamboozle English incomers. The cartoonists who drew these stock Caledonian stereotypes, like George Denholm Armour and Alexander Stuart Boyd, were themselves often Scottish commercial artists who had graduated from work on Scottish daily newspapers in Glasgow and Edinburgh. These broadly comic situations, mild slights at the Scots, got a belated outing in a series of cartoons by Joseph Lee, from the *London Evening News* of the 1930s, in which 'Jock', a stereotyped Scot living in London, conducts his daily life as if he was still living in a small Scottish town. Jock, seen stopping the Inverness express at King's Cross and asking if it can drop off a postcard to his auntie in 'Auchternoustie' or scrawling 'Happy New Year' on the side of the north-bound train 'because it saves the postage', is a canny and benign character, and even the boozy Scotsmen in kilts who crop up in London political cartoons whenever the Scottish football team plays at Wembley do little more than get drunk and wonder when the Circle Line train is due to arrive at Glasgow Central.

These broad comic stereotypes find their natural home on British television and in films, where Scots tend to fit into neat categories, often ones which would be familiar to *Punch*'s Victorian readership. The most obvious Scottish stereotype is the canny technician, Scottie from *Star Trek*, but the Scottish upper servant is there too. Most commonly, the Scot in English popular culture crops up as the natural bearer of a pettifogging sense of authority (Fulton MacKay in *Porridge*, Alec Guinness in *Tunes of Glory*) or an existential miserablism (Private Fraser in *Dad's Army*, Gordon Brown or Victor Meldrew in *One Foot in the Grave*). Interestingly, though, Meldrew, one of the most totemic comic creations of the 1990s, is never referred to in the fictional world of the television programme as being Scottish, though clearly he and his wife, played by Annette Crosbie, are Scottish exiles, and he, at least, draws on a long line of needlessly grumpy Scots.

But even in this gentle realm of Scottish stereotyping there is an awareness that the Scot in English culture could simply be the vanguard of a more serious Scottish takeover: 'Ian Hay' was the pen name of John Hay Beith, a professional humorist who also wrote a series of patriotic books celebrating the efforts of the British fighting forces. An angular, witty man, he was a considerable success as a writer and was fêted by Hollywood as well as the British popular press. In 1917, he published a slim book on the subject of the relationship between the different countries of the United Kingdom. He called it *The Oppressed English*:

> As a Scotsman, the English people have my profound sympathy.
>
> In the comic papers of all countries, the Englishman is depicted – or was in the days of peace – as stupid, purseproud, thick-skinned, arrogant and tyrannical. In practice what is he? The whipping boy of the British Empire.
>
> To a Scotsman . . . the English are a frivolous, feckless race, devoid of ambition, and incapable of handling weighty matters with the required degree of seriousness. So he comes to London and takes the helm. Today a Scot is leading the British Army in France [Sir Douglas Haig], another is commanding the British Grand Fleet at Sea [Admiral Beatty], while a third [Sir William Robertson] directs the Imperial General Staff at home. The Lord Chancellor is a Scot [Lord Findlay]; so are the Chancellor of the Exchequer and the Foreign Secretary. (The Prime Minister is a Welshman and the First Lord of the Admiralty is an Irishman.) Yet no one has ever yet brought in a bill to give Home Rule to England!

As a humorist, Beith is most famous for one coinage. In *The Housemaster*, his novel of 1938, the eponymous hero quizzes a boy, 'What do you mean, funny? Funny peculiar or funny ha-ha?' So, is *The Oppressed English* meant to be funny peculiar or funny ha-ha?

The answer is both. In common with most discussions about the relationship between Scotland and England, it came at a time of growing constitutional crisis. In 1913, the Scottish Home Rule bill had passed its first reading in the Commons by 204 votes to 159. The First World War pushed it off the agenda. But it was not the only constitutional issue which seemed to threaten the integrity of the United Kingdom. Beith's book, though only six chapters long, finds it hard to stick to the subject of Scotland and England at all. Chapters four and five are long diversions on the Irish Question, which gives the clue that, on its serious side, this is a book about Britishness under pressure and likely to fall apart. On the other hand, it's noticeable that the preferred style for anyone who seriously puts the case that the English are being squeezed out of power in their own country by the Scots is humour; to Beith's book should be added a thousand heavy-handed speeches delivered at Burns Suppers. Only recently has the idea been worth taking seriously.

But the most stinging rebuke to the Scots doesn't come from words at all, even rough unfair ones. The worst insult is not to be spoken about at all. In his book *Scotland and Nationalism*, Christopher Harvie quotes an illuminating exchange:

> 'I hope you in Oxford don't think that we hate you,'
> John Stewart Blackie asked Benjamin Jowett in 1866.
> 'We don't think about you,' was the reply.

That feeling of not being thought about, of being utterly superfluous to the national debate, is the one truly mortifying putdown to a Scot. A culture which is based on argument and debate might even take a secret pleasure from being abused by Englishmen, but being overlooked is truly devastating. At the end of his *The Unspeakable Scot*, Crosland has a few rules 'for the general guidance of young Scotchmen who wish to succeed in this country':

> TRY TO FORGET THAT THE BATTLE OF BANNOCKBURN WAS WON BY THE SCOTCH IN 1314. THE DATES OF FLODDEN AND CULLODEN ARE MUCH BETTER WORTH REMEMBERING, THOUGH MOST ENGLISH-MEN HAVE FORGOTTEN THEM.

It's a double whammy: first, forget any claims to being the victorious power in the eternal battle with England, but second, get used to the fact that no one in England thinks these battles are worth remembering anyway. English silence is a much more powerful weapon against Scots than any amount of abuse; there is little silence on the subject of the Scots around at the moment, and that is something which should make even the proudest Scotsman glad.

CHAPTER 10

The State of England

An English radical hero keeps watch over Red Lion Square, a block north of Holborn tube station in central London. Fenner Brockway, the campaigning journalist and orator who was converted to socialism after a single meeting with Keir Hardie in 1907, is caught in mid-speech, his arms outstretched, a clutch of papers held in one hand. On the plinth he is described as a 'liberator'. And on a sunny morning in mid-November 2003, the community hall tucked away over Brockway's right shoulder is slowly filling up with people who have England's liberty on their minds.

Saturdays are always busy in the Conway Hall. The Humanist Women meet upstairs, the Troops Out Movement have taken up residence along the corridor, and the Meeting for World Revolution is due to begin once the yoga class have rolled up their mats.

Inside, the atmosphere is radical, vegetarian, non-conformist and rather dusty. Faded pictures of Bertrand Russell and Michael Foot line the walls, next to photocopied humanist pamphlets and posters advertising earnest discussion groups on Tibet and Ireland.

Today, a brand-new political cause is due to join those listed on the noticeboard. A battered Renault is parked outside, two fluttering St George's Crosses lashed to the ladder on its roof. A man wearing an England rugby top and sporting a close-cropped moustache stands beside the car, speaking conspiratorially into his mobile phone.

Half a mile away, shoppers on Oxford Street may be

plunging into the early Christmas throng, but in Holborn a new political movement is stretching its wings. This is the venue for what is billed as the first meeting in 1,500 years devoted to the subject of England's future. The Campaign for an English Parliament (CEP) hopes that today will be the start of something big.

'We were formed in 1998 after devolution was introduced in Scotland,' explains Mike Knowles, the mild-mannered retired teacher who chairs the movement. 'It's a bit of a shock when you've been brought up to believe that there'll always be an England, to realise that your country no longer exists. Scotland and Wales have their own parliaments now, but constitutionally and politically England isn't on the map.'

Knowles's group isn't the first to note that devolution was a messy compromise, giving domestic parliaments to Scotland and Wales and leaving the government of England untouched, but they are the first organisation to champion the idea of a parliament for England based on the Scottish model. Like the Scottish Parliament, the English one would control key aspects of domestic legislation but leave the reserved matters of defence, foreign affairs and taxation in the hands of Westminster. If the Campaign for an English Parliament gets its way, the United Kingdom should brace itself for yet another seismic shock to its constitution, because so anxious are some CEP members to end the confusion between Westminster's British responsibilities and the governance of England that they would like to separate an English Parliament from the British one entirely, and site the new chamber nearly 200 miles from Westminster in the historic city of York, which last held an English Parliament in 1314 during the reign of Edward II.

As a political movement, the campaign is still learning to walk. So far, it has been a low-key affair, longer on discussion than on action, confining itself to a few symbolic gestures like handing out fliers at Twickenham, coordinating letter writing to England's local newspapers and badgering English MPs. Though it has provoked a few bemused pieces on the features pages of the national press, it has yet to grab the headlines.

Its one attempt at direct action led to an unfortunate brush with controversy when it was accused of a very un-English act: vandalism.

When CEP supporters put red dye in the fountains at Trafalgar Square to mark St George's Day in 2002, London's Mayor Ken Livingstone accused the campaign of vandalising one of London's most important monuments; not only did the gesture fail to galvanise the people of England but the red dye damaged the historic stone of the fountains.

This piece of patriotic pranksterism provoked a waspish exchange in the letters pages of *The Spectator*, where Michael Knowles, whilst disowning the unauthorised dyeing incident, pointed out that Mayor Ken himself had spoken about colouring the fountains green for St Patrick's Day. If Irish green dye wouldn't mark the stones, it seemed a disgrace that English red would. Knowles's letter ended with an open appeal to readers of *The Spectator* to accept the campaign's invitation to come along today and engage in the debate about England's future.

It's hard to tell whether the crowd now filing into the Conway Hall are readers of *The Spectator* or not, but, by the look of things, the wake-up call has been heeded the length and breadth of England. With branches from Northumberland to Buckinghamshire, from West Mercia to the depths of Devon, and with a solitary representative from Scotland, there is plenty of grass-roots support to draw on and all day English patriots have been arriving in the capital on planes, trains and buses.

In expectation of a decent crowd, the hall has been laid out with seating for 350, but it quickly becomes clear that the CEP has underestimated its support, and as the floor has filled up by 10.15, late arrivals are shown up into the balcony.

Along the walls, little stalls sell pamphlets on the constitutional case for the English Parliament, alongside tiny metal St George's Crosses to be worn as lapel badges and home-printed books celebrating England's heroes and distinctive folklore. T-shirts and rugby tops emblazoned with patriotic slogans are selling well, and when the morning session is over, a lunch of diluting orange and ham sandwiches will be laid on for the faithful.

Ignore the subject matter of the pamphlets and mentally add some homemade fudge and tea cakes, and this could be a well-organised church fête, with a controversial AGM at its heart.

The hard of hearing are invited to sit down at the front

where a special loop has been set up to allow them to tune in to what is being said. By 10.30 all the seats are full and the event starts bang on time. The enormous English flag at the back of the hall has obscured the clock, however, so many of the speakers over-run; the sound system seems to have a mind of its own and whelps and howls in counterpoint to the speeches. Michael Knowles welcomes the crowd and thanks the organising committee for their efforts before getting into his stride.

'While Scotland is subsidised by the Barnett Formula, every Scottish man, woman and child is supported to the tune of £30 per week by the English exchequer. This just isn't fair!' The crowd breaks into applause.

But though the sentiments are heartfelt and the crowd is large and vocal, Mike and his colleagues have been disappointed by the lack of interest from the political parties. After a dedicated supporter of the campaign paid the postage out of his own pocket, the CEP sent a letter of invitation to every MP and MEP representing an English seat. Despite that impressive mailshot, only two of England's elected representatives heeded the call. Nigel Farage, the MEP for the UK Independence Party, resplendent in gleaming pinstripes and sporting a military coiffure, is here to deliver a barnstorming speech on the wrongs of the European superstate; and Simon Hughes, the Liberal Democrat candidate for Mayor of London, is due to speak before lunch on how the campaign could turn their dreams into reality.

It wasn't quite the turnout the campaign had hoped for, and the fact that professional politicians are content to snub this grass-roots campaign clearly rankles with the CEP's ordinary members.

'They know that we're here but they are just trying to ignore us,' explains Don Beadle, 'but there is a growing groundswell of opinion. It took Scotland 90 years to get a parliament. I hope it won't take us as long but it won't happen overnight.'

But then one of the successes of the long campaign for the Scottish Parliament was that it persuaded Scots that they shouldn't be afraid of their own national identity. Other nationalisms around the world might be narrow, violent, chauvinistic or harsh, but Scotland's chattering classes formed a consensus, partly in response to Thatcherism, that the country's unique national identity was broad, humane and internationally minded.

Whilst Scottish Nationalists routinely see themselves as internationalists, and heap the blame for everything from the Empire to the poll tax at the door of the English, English nationalism has long struggled with a rather darker image.

Anxious to distance themselves from the strutting patriots of the British National Party, Campaigners for an English Parliament are desperately struggling to wrestle the flag of St George from the pudgy fingers of thick-necked taxi drivers and football hooligans. 'We know that the flag has had a bad press,' confesses Mike Knowles. 'In fact, when we drafted our constitution, we took particular care to make sure that we couldn't be taken over by the far right. But for me, the most important book on English national identity was E.P. Thomson's *Making of the English Working Class*. I was organising marches against the National Front in the 1970s and I got the bruises to show for it, so it really angers me when people make that easy equation between Englishness and racism, because it just isn't so.'

In fact, though entirely white, the crowd at this meeting shows no sign of being racist. An over-enthusiastic reference to multiculturalism from the floor provokes angry glowers from some thick-set men in the balcony, but the supporters attracted by the CEP's open invitation certainly don't constitute a coven of skinheads or a gang of bovver boys.

So who were these people? Aside from their shared colour, they seemed to be a cross-section of English life, mostly middle and lower-middle class, though not exclusively. They listened attentively, clapped enthusiastically and chatted happily during the lunch break. No one was heckled or barracked. On the surface they seemed to be concerned English citizens with a list of grievances at the way British life was going. But the longer the day went on, the more confusing it all became.

In short order, the speakers from the platform rolled out an impressive list of complaints. English pensioners were being discriminated against because the Scottish Parliament has voted for free care for the elderly. English students studying in Wales have to pay higher tuition fees than Welsh students.

At Keele University, students trying to set up an English Society were banned on the grounds of 'tolerance'. And England will have foundation hospitals imposed upon it because of the votes of Scottish Labour MPs, despite the fact that Scotland itself, governed by the decision of the Scottish Parliament, won't have them.

These were all genuinely held beliefs, but it's hard to imagine that the plight of persecuted students at Keele, or even the alleged iniquities of the Barnett Formula, will raise the blood of English voters, let alone lead to the political earthquake that the CEP dreams of.

When Mrs Christine Constable, a member of the English Democrats, a new political party dedicated to putting England's rights first, stands up to speak, the problem becomes obvious. Mrs Constable, a crisply turned-out, formidable-looking woman in her 30s, gave a professional performance devoted to the subject of how England had become a second-rate country, uncertain about its values, but tied by a self-denying decency and restraint which has allowed the wily Celts to run rings around it. English schoolchildren, she argued, are no longer being taught English history in their own schools. Applause. 'Meanwhile we are prevented from celebrating St George's Day while grants are handed out to anyone who wants to celebrate St Patrick's Day.' More applause.

Christine Constable blamed the politically correct BBC, the snooty views and anti-English beliefs of the metropolitan clique who run New Labour, multiculturalism and the 'machinations of politicians who have denied the aspirations of modest people'. Nigel Farage put the blame for the crisis in England's sense of identity firmly at the door of the EU with its plans for a European superstate.

But the biggest cheer of the day went to Neil Herron of the Metric Martyrs, the campaigning group which champions the rights of market traders who prefer to weigh out their fruit and veg in British pounds and ounces, not European kilos and grammes. Herron is a former Sunderland fishmonger who, just before a raid by police and trading standards officers in June 2000, snatched his imperial measurement scales off to a place of safety, and has devoted his life ever since to championing the cause of imperial measures.

Today his speech focused on John Prescott's attempts to persuade large swathes of England to vote for an extensive programme of regional devolution. This is not the kind of devolution the CEP wants, since it represents what they see as the Balkanisation of Britain's backyard into competing, and probably squabbling, assemblies. As Herron portrayed it, John Prescott's campaign to persuade England's regions to adopt devolution was an act of high-handed political manipulation which had already seen rule-bending, dodgy opinion polls and spin aplenty.

As he detailed how, with the aid of a hotline to Companies House and a keen sense of injustice, he was able to frustrate the plans of the Campaign for Devolution in the north-east, it was clear why Herron, an indefatigable and likeable Jack the Lad, had managed to secure the title of European Campaigner of the Year in 2001.

And his portrayal of himself as an ordinary bloke who was unwilling to be pushed around by bullying bureaucrats seemed to hit a real chord with the audience. Herron's brand of Englishness seemed to come straight from the pamphlet on England's heroes. If Robin Hood and Watt Tyler had been invited to speak, they would have spoken like Herron, who embodied the reluctant radicalism of the small man forced to take time out from his private life to combat the bloody-mindedness and bossiness of the State. If English nationalism has a future, this could be it; attractively bolshy, suspicious of authority, cheeky and unputdownable. It would be a hard act to argue against, particularly when carried off with Herron's natural flair.

But the Metric Martyrs represent just one stream in the river of the CEP's support, which also swirls with other currents: anti-multiculturalism, hostility to Brussels, a dislike of Tony Blair and his henchmen, discomfort about immigration, even residual anti-Scottishness, Saxon nationalism and Cromwellian republicanism. Underlying them all is the uncomfortable perception that English people have become second-class citizens in their own country, left without a role because of the conflicting agendas pursued by other parts of the British state. Can these different strands be woven together to create something powerful enough to tug

English men and women to the ballot box to vote for their own national interests?

Perhaps, but there is a lot of work to be done to transform this loose collection of grievances into a coherent political movement. There seems to be a profound contradiction at the heart of the CEP. Whilst its most powerful instincts stem from a dislike of bureaucracy and an instinctive feeling that English people shouldn't be dictated to by the State, its avowed intention is to create yet another national parliament which will inevitably be full of politicians with foolish, bossy ideas about what English people should do. Can this brand of populist anti-politics have a political future? And can the CEP, or another organisation, get electoral mileage out of the growing feeling of exclusion which English people are now starting to register?

The strangest feeling about sitting as the only Scot at a meeting of outraged English patriots came from the fact that 400 English people felt sufficiently exercised about such issues to give up their Saturday to discuss them at all.

During the 1980s and '90s it was commonly accepted by campaigners for a Scottish Parliament that one of the biggest obstacles they faced was the indifference of the English to any discussion about the nuances of national identity. Whereas Scots and Welsh opinion makers were hypersensitive to cultural difference, the English seemed complacently uninterested in the whole subject, and keener to get on with their private affairs than to engage in the sometimes tortuous debates on the subject which exercised their Celtic cousins.

In August 1993, the theatre critic and political activist Joyce McMillan, who was closely involved in the work of the Scottish Constitutional Convention, wrote an article in the *Scotland on Sunday* newspaper in which she said, 'Scottish identity requires constant assertion, whereas British identity is something taken for granted by every institution in which [the Scots] have to deal.' English silence was the enemy because English silence represented English power. The Scots might be voluble, exercised, edgy, even chippy about their place in the world and desperate to discuss it for hours in the opinion pages of their newspapers or even down the pub, but John Bull had other things on his mind.

226

Move on a decade and here in Holborn is an unfamiliar face of England: uncomfortable about Britishness, aggrieved at the results of constitutional change, feeling put upon and increasingly resentful. Yet, as if stealing the clothes of the very people who put them in this situation, the tone and tenor of their debates about Englishness are incredibly reminiscent of those long discussions about Scottishness and Britishness with which Scottish writers, academics and politicians tortured themselves, and each other, during the 1980s and '90s.

At that time it was a fashionable view in Scotland that Britishness was a kind of con perpetrated on the Scots by the English, and that whilst it was a national identity which made many Scots feel that they had bought into something bigger than themselves, it also kept them from realising that all the power in Great Britain plc was held in English hands.

Now, many in the CEP clearly believe that Britishness has been so culturally powerful in the UK that it has left England with little to call its own now that Scotland and Wales are showing signs of going their own way. 'We have a constant confusion between English and British which you in Scotland don't have,' admits one member. 'I don't know if the bulldog, the Tower of London, even Buckingham Palace, is British or if it's English. And I don't know if we've lost more than we've gained by believing in Britishness in the way we did.'

But while it was Scottish devolution that kick-started this anguished English soul-searching, it is Scottish devolution which could show a way out if it. Because the structural preparation which paved the way to the Scottish Parliament might provide an off-the-shelf model for English devolutionists to follow.

Scilla Cullen, who sits on the National Council, believes that the future for the English lies in the creation of an English Constitutional Convention, explicitly based on the Scottish one which was formed to articulate the case for self-government in the late 1980s. At the climax of her speech, she read from the Claim of Right for Scotland, substituting the word 'England' for 'Scotland'. 'When I first tried this in my bathroom at home,' she admitted bashfully, 'I feared that I would be branded a "Fascist English nationalist" or a "little Englander".'

As part of this new awareness of nationality, many of the

CEP seem to have a prickly attitude to the power of the Scots. Don Beadle speaks for many when he says that the Scots 'have done excellently' out of devolution. A reassessment of the funding mechanism of the Barnett Formula is high on the CEP's list of demands. And others deeply resent the votes Scottish MPs cast for foundation hospitals.

But despite all this, the meeting certainly didn't seem anti-Scottish. The mention of John Reid, the Scottish Secretary of State for Health, gathered some good-natured booing, but the root of his unpopularity was his position as Secretary of State for Health – imposing foundation hospitals on England while not representing an English seat. Scots were seen as the embodiments, and the beneficiaries, of a constitutional imbalance, not an alien race which should be disliked or despised. In the dark days of the 1980s and '90s, there were far more people in the campaign for a Scottish Parliament who were willing to attribute the success of Thatcherism south of the border to the implicit selfishness of the English; there were no similar slurs against the Scots being expressed at the Conway Hall.

Expressing a sense of resentment is fair enough, but where does the campaign go from here? At the moment, it seems to be long on grievance and short on any concrete plans for change. The Scottish Constitutional Convention was supported by the trade unions, the Churches, most of the political parties in Scotland, the regional councils, civic bodies and leading intellectuals, and also had the commitment of politicians like Sir David Steel and Donald Dewar. Even if the CEP were to form an English Constitutional Convention tomorrow, there would be no one to sit on it except itself. It may have a national network with branches the length and breadth of the country and may encourage its members to appear on television and radio to talk about the need for an English Parliament, but at the moment it is in the uncomfortable position of shouting its concerns into the void.

Simon Hughes came closest to suggesting a way forward: the campaign should argue that the House of Commons changes its procedures to ensure that only English MPs vote on English business.

Of all the options available, English votes for English MPs

seems to be the one with the greatest chance of success. Galvanised by the foundation hospital issue, it was taken up by serious politicians in the weeks following the conference. The former Conservative Secretary of State for Scotland Michael Forsyth spoke on the issue from the benches of the House of Lords, and also proposed that the Scottish Parliament be wound up. *The Times* reported the issue on its front page and an opinion poll commissioned by *The Herald* found that 50 per cent of Scots believed that English votes for English MPs was a sensible solution to the unbalanced nature of devolution.

But this is, of course, not devolution, just a self-denying ordinance on the part of Scottish MPs. The SNP has long held to the strategy of abstaining on English votes, except when there is a chance of forcing the government of the day into a no-confidence vote, and Peter Duncan, the sole Conservative MP to win back a seat in Scotland after they were wiped out in the general election of 2001, does the same.

On English devolution proper, the Opposition parties have been less vocal. In 1999, the then Tory leader William Hague spoke on the issue and dubbed the inequalities of devolution 'a ticking timebomb under the British constitution'. John Barnes wrote an article for the wet Conservative Bow Group questioning whether a 'Federal Britain [was] no longer Unthinkable?' Under Iain Duncan Smith's leadership, the party shied away from the debate, and Duncan Smith, who proudly boasted of his Scottish birth, at least when he was north of the border, seemed to take a more broadly Unionist line, though he noticeably chose a visit to Glasgow's Easterhouse, one of the most depressed housing schemes in Europe, to launch a commitment to his own brand of 'caring Conservatism'.

Federalism, which might seem to offer one solution to the problem, would actually create another set of dilemmas. Federal states tend to be composed of units of broadly similar sizes. A federated Britain would be a lopsided construction, with most of its population living in England. And in those federations where there is a vast disparity of populations, the smaller states tend to get preferential treatment. Few follow exactly the model of the United States, where the deserted state of Alaska elects exactly the same number of senators as populous Texas or California, but from Spain to Australia, federation boosts the power of minorities, which means that Scotland and Wales might end up electing proportionately more federal representatives to a reformed second chamber of the British Parliament than they do now, creating exactly the opposite effect of what the CEP intends.

As the meeting broke up with a commitment to keep talking, to continue agitating and to bring the issue to the attention of MPs, it seemed that a little anxiety had been aired, but there had been little political progress. So is the Conway Hall conference the beginning of a mass political movement or a blip that will disappear from the radar screen as suddenly as it flared up?

Geoffrey Wheatcroft, for one, doesn't think it will be the latter. The respected English commentator wrote a powerful piece in *The Guardian* in June 2003 arguing that England was 'Hammered by the Scots'.

'I think the current situation is so iniquitous that it will lead to a rise in English nationalism,' he says. 'I hate to say that because I hate nationalism in all its forms, but devolution forces me to be an English nationalist. If things continue as they are then it's inevitable that the general resentment of Scotland will increase.'

There is clearly a constitutional anomaly in the current organisation of the UK. And one reason for the anomaly is that the devolution settlement for Scotland, and to a lesser extent for Wales, was a response and an intended solution to the rising tide of Celtic nationalism. Up until now there has been no corresponding demand within England. If, in 1997, the Blair Government had attempted to give England devolution, they would have been faced with a chorus of complaint that there was no demand for such a thing. Now, a twenty-first-century version of Tam Dalyell's West Lothian Question is causing agitation in the CEP and other groups.

So should the CEP be taken seriously? Professor James Mitchell of the University of Strathclyde politics department has his doubts. 'They're not a serious bunch. They are a tiny minority without any strong issues to unify them. There is clearly an issue in the sense that devolution assumed that England's domestic politics would be catered for by the Westminster Parliament while Holyrood took on responsibility for Scotland's domestic agenda. But I can't see these guys going anywhere. There may be an English question, but I don't believe that they are the answer.'

Professor Robert Hazell of the Constitution Unit, which offered expert advice to the Scottish Office in the run-up to the devolution White Paper, has an interest in the CEP and what it represents, but he is also doubtful about whether it represents an inevitable uprising of English sentiment in the face of devolution. 'I think it's pretty clear that the English are quite slow to be roused on issues like this. It's taken 15 years for English resentment at the power of Brussels to rise to the level where the United Kingdom Independence Party is getting serious votes. It may take 20 years for English resentment to smoulder and then take political form if they feel that the Scots and the Welsh are being treated too favourably by the current devolution settlement.'

The other problem for the CEP is that the party which is most likely to champion the particular needs of England in a devolved United Kingdom, the Conservative Party, is also the party which is most reluctant to do it because it believes in the Union of Scotland, England, Wales and Northern Ireland. Teddy Taylor, the MP for Rochford and Southend East, who was a thorn in the side of the last Conservative Government as a veteran anti-common market campaigner but who served in Mrs Thatcher's Shadow Cabinet as Shadow Secretary of State for Scotland, doesn't believe that there is a case to be made: 'What you must realise, and I discovered this when I moved from Scotland to England, is that people in England just aren't interested in politics. Scotland, when I left it, was tearing itself apart over devolution, and it was a joy to get away from the nastiness of Scottish politics. Here it is just not an issue. I wish it were more of an issue because I believe that fundamental British rights are being eroded by Brussels and the growing European superstate, but it just isn't. Compared to the Scots, the English are almost entirely apolitical.'

Apolitical or not, just one week after 400 concerned English patriots met in the Conway Hall, the entire English nation was convulsed with patriotic fervour as their country won the Rugby World Cup in Australia. The pubs, and the media, exploded with excitement, plans for a victory parade were immediately unveiled and, writing in *The Observer* newspaper the following day, the commentator David Aaronovitch wrote a piece about English nationality which will have touched many people concerned about the country's place, not just in the world, but in the bewildering new United Kingdom. Lamenting England's traditional backwardness in coming forward in celebration of its way of life, Aaronovitch agreed with Orwell's assessment that English life was characterised by a complacent gentleness, but, using jargon which Orwell would never have employed, suggested that contemporary Englishness was characterised by a 'constant dialectic' between tradition and modernity. Where the rugby victory, beamed around the globe by satellites in geostationary orbit, but celebrated like a rerun of Agincourt, stood in the dialectic was unclear, but momentarily sport seemed to be able to unite England and to give it a modicum of national pride that politics could not.

Could this be the future of English national self-respect, an ideology of sporting victory on the rugby field, rather than a mass movement of political resistance, a brand of politics in which Jonny Wilkinson is more important than John Wilkes?

Perhaps, but as members of the Tartan Army who watched Scotland's self-respect go down the Argentinian plughole in the 1978 World Cup will testify, pinning national self-belief to the performance of fallible sportsmen is a risky bet.

Besides, the nature of sporting contests is that one side wins and the other loses, and English nationalism, if it is to have a future, needs to be based on something firmer than just 50–50 odds. The crowds who flooded into central London to cheer the returning rugby heroes a couple of weeks later may have felt that they were on the crest of a wave which last peaked in 1966, but for that national pride to become anything other than simple patriotism will require a lot of nifty political manoeuvring, and may also need a lot of time.

From the outside, what English nationalism might need is a firm external force to agitate against. Thatcherism did more to harden Scotland's home rule resolve than the nationalist activity which proved powerless to stop it. In the absence of a similarly powerful external force – a Scottish Thatcherism which imposes its views on England and gives every sign of not listening to, or caring, what it thinks – the CEP needs to tighten up what it stands for. The issue of foundation hospitals voted for by Scottish MPs may seem to be an obvious injustice, but a foundation hospital is not the poll tax, imposed earlier in one part of the country than the other and viewed as an iniquity forced on its citizens by their more powerful neighbour, so it is unlikely to have a similar effect on opinion south of the border.

In the conclusion to his book *The Day Britain Died*, Andrew Marr suggests that the empire-building ambitions of Brussels and the pressure of European integration may have a similar effect on English public opinion as Thatcherism did on Scotland. So far, that response has been confined to a hardening of anti-European sentiment in parts of the Conservative Party and the modest electoral success of the UK Independence Party. The CEP see the pressure on their brand of Englishness as coming from the internal anomalies of devolution, and, of course, a parliament for England does not in itself provide an answer to anyone's concerns about the pace of European integration. Indeed, an English parliament, which would likely be dominated by the Conservative Party, but have no control over the country's relationship with Europe, since that would remain in the hands of the British Government, might be a source of anti-European resentment with no place to go. As the impotence of the Scottish Parliament in the face of the 2003 war on Iraq shows, politics without influence is dangerous, increases the gulf between voters and professional politicians and may inflame support for radical parties of the left and right.

But the real importance of the CEP is that, small and apparently unimportant as they now are, they do represent the beginnings of an English attempt to grapple with the reality of modern Britain. Scotland's long and painful road to its own devolutionary settlement served as an incredible educational process and left many Scots with a sophisticated mental model of how Britain worked, a keen awareness of the difference between a state and a nation, and a feeling for the nuances of what was an acceptable model of national identity. The success of the campaign for the Scottish Parliament was to build on the ethos of Scotland's civic culture and to make it seem that there was a direct connection between the traditional Scottish way of doing things, and a new type of politics which could be embodied in the Scottish Parliament. Civic culture, with all its displays of what sociologists call 'banal nationalism' – flags, sports teams and the rest – became harnessed to a political movement for Scottish government.

It was a long, slow process. On the whole, England spent that debate on the touchlines. And now that the field of play has changed for good, the English team is scrambling around trying to learn the new rules for life in the United Kingdom. For once, in politics, if not in sport, the Scots are running rings around them.

Conclusion – Scots and 'Former' Scots

In November 1928, Lord Birkenhead, the Conservative statesman who had led his party's opposition to Irish Home Rule, stood in Aberdeen's Marischal College to address the newest graduates of the university. The end-of-term crowd was high-spirited and rowdy, and Birkenhead had to repeatedly interrupt his speech to quell enthusiastic barracking.

Graduation addresses always flatter their audience and look forward to the attractions of life outside the university's gates. But even by the standards of the genre, Birkenhead's speech was a slavish hymn of praise to Scotland and the Scots:

> Scotland is renowned as the home of the most ambitious race in the world. If you are respected for one quality more than any other, it is that you grimly persevere in your chosen callings until you excel, that you never rest content until you have surpassed your rivals by pertinacity and singleness of resolve . . . A dour ambition drove Thomas Carlyle from the village street of Ecclefechan to the triumphs of Cheyne Row.

The message was clear: London and the rest of the world awaited the contribution which ambitious and decisive Scots could make to British national life.

Eighty-four years later, and less than a quarter of mile away, just such an ambitious, decisive and successful Scot stood in the pulpit of the West Kirk of St Nicholas in Aberdeen to address the pupils of Robert Gordon's College. The occasion was

Founder's Day, the annual commemoration of Robert Gordon, the Aberdeen merchant who settled in Danzig in the late seventeenth century and made a fortune trading with the Baltic ports before returning to his hometown to found the school in 1730.

Founder's Day is an occasion for reflection and self-congratulation in which the college, one of Scotland's most respected independent schools, invites successful former pupils back to their alma mater and gives them a platform to share the insights they have gathered in the course of their careers. The speeches tend to be anodyne and rather predictable, a generally dull prelude to a half-day holiday.

The Founder's Day orator for 2002 was a model old boy. The businessman Don Cruickshank had achieved success on both sides of the border as the chairman of both the London Stock Exchange and the powerful Scottish Media Group, which controls Scottish Television and the north-east's Grampian TV.

Later, Cruickshank said that he had found writing the speech tough, and had decided to say something which would 'stick in a few pupils' minds'. He succeeded beyond his wildest dreams:

> I hear of anxieties about the forecast continuing decline of the population of Scotland. And I hear of the Scottish Executive's response to that, which is to plan to encourage more of Scotland's young people – you – to stay in Scotland . . . A better response might be the exact opposite. People leave Scotland in part because it's a somewhat self-centred, parochial place, where, if I may dare to say it here today, the school you went to still matters and forms the foundation of too many of Scotland's social networks. Maybe we'd flourish a bit better, both economically and culturally, if more of you gained more experience of the rest of the world. And I'm not, definitely not, talking about a gap year.
>
> I suspect that the accumulated wealth and experience which at least some of you would bring back to Scotland might bring an openness, vigour and freshness to Scottish life that would benefit everyone. We need a new Scottish Enlightenment to echo that which Robert Gordon experienced.

236

Normally, Founder's Day speeches merit a respectful mention in the inside pages of the Aberdeen *Press and Journal*. Cruickshank's comments made the national news.

'Quit Scotland to Get Ahead: Fury at TV Chief's Claim,' screamed the headline in the *Daily Record*. The leader column in the *Scottish Daily Express* informed its readers, more in sadness than in anger, that Mr Cruickshank may have been right 30 years before, but not now. 'And hasn't the south-east of England – which is obviously where Mr Cruickshank thinks Scots on the make should go – been very much more dependent on the old-boy network than anywhere else in Britain?'

On the BBC's *Today* programme, Jim Naughtie reverted to the language of his native Aberdeenshire and led a heated discussion on the 'stushie' which had unexpectedly fired up in a city which, oil industry stories aside, seldom made the front pages.

In the *News of the World*, the former, and future, SNP leader Alex Salmond joined the attack, dubbing Cruickshank:

> . . . a first-class berk who stunned pupils at Robert Gordon's College in Aberdeen on Friday by slagging off Scotland and telling them they'd have to leave if they wanted to be successful . . . just like him . . . All cringing Cruickshank has done is spend money on a plane ticket back to Scotland to slag off our country . . . The name 'Cruikshank' means bandy legged. I don't know what Don's pins are like. It's his thinking which is seriously twisted.

In reaction to this furore, Cruickshank sought to explain himself in the pages of the *Sunday Times*.

> Asked to react to press accounts of my speech, [Scottish First Minster] Jack McConnell was reported to have said 'For a growing economy we need a growing population . . . We must retain the talent we have, attract former Scots back home, and be open to welcome people from new cultures, nationalities and backgrounds.' I couldn't agree more. But I would ask: what's a 'former Scot'? Are we not Scots if we leave Scotland?

It was a good question, though it received little attention. There are always tensions between achieving Scots who prosper in London and the rest of Scottish society, but they are normally kept well hidden; Cruickshank's bluntly expressed views fired them up into open controversy.

To many Scots, Cruickshank fell into an obvious stereotype: the successful Scottish expatriate whose long absence from the country makes him believe that he can diagnose its ills more effectively than the Scots who had stayed at home. Such views always excite the Scottish press: in January 2004, the actor John Hannah's offhand remark that he wouldn't choose to bring up his children in the 'strange, little, wet, fried, angry place' that had sired him, gained blanket coverage in *Scotland on Sunday*. The paper was careful to describe Hannah's battle with depression; perhaps that was the explanation for his views.

But Jack McConnell's slip of the tongue had revealed an important truth about Scottish life: those who relocate elsewhere are often seen as having abandoned their birthright for private profit. Cruickshank's view was slightly different: he advocated that the pupils of his old school get out, gain experience and then come back to plough it into Scottish life. Though his views were more complex than the news coverage suggested, they nonetheless dug at an open wound in the Scottish psyche and exposed Scotland's profoundly conflicting views about emigration.

Emigration is, of course, real enough; the 2001 census showed Scotland's population at 5,062,011 souls, a 2 per cent fall on 1981. If the trend continues, some experts point out apocalyptically, Scotland will be entirely depopulated by 2041, which might make it even more attractive to tourists.

The debate about the effect which the Scots who go away have on the culture of the country they have left behind is one of the perennials of Scottish life, dating back to before the Union of the Parliaments. When someone leaves Scotland, the argument goes, they leave Scotland, depriving their homeland of the energy and drive which could have been harnessed to rejuvenate it.

Emigration 'implanted the idea that the one country in which Scots were not to employ their constructive abilities on a national scale was Scotland itself', William Power wrote in 1935, and ten years later in his maiden speech in Westminster Dr Robert McIntyre declared, 'We come with the intention of returning as soon as possible to our own country, where we may, under democratic government, achieve the long-needed reconstruction of Scotland.'

Minus one, plus one. The argument seems to have an impeccable logic. But for the country which sired Adam Smith, the man who anatomised the effects of the expanding market, it is reductive and rather restrictive. And besides, it hasn't always been seen that way.

Thomas Carlyle hymned the attractions of emigration to Canada and America. Victorian Scots saw the global reach of Scotland as a compliment to their homeland and their fellow countrymen. And in the modern world, other countries have formed a view of their emigrants which is expansive and understanding rather than regretful and bitter.

Ireland, that other great Celtic donor of population, has embraced the idea of a wider nation, encompassing those thousands of emigrants who were driven from their homeland by the potato famine and economic stagnation. Boston, Chicago and Brussels, the administrative centre of the European Union, are now important Irish cities too.

Some emigrants are so grateful for their Irish roots that they celebrate them, repackage them and send them back home. Michael Flatley's *Riverdance*, a glossy confection of Celtic hokum, has made millions of dollars around the world and played to capacity houses in Dublin. But Flatley, despite his strong imaginative connection to Ireland, is a Chicagoan, with tenuous genetic connections to his homeland. When Scots-Americans want to reinvent Scottishness, celebrating entirely fictional 'traditions' like the 'kirking of the tartan', they are treated as an embarrassment by Scottish historians. No wonder there isn't a Scottish *Riverdance*.

The reasons for Ireland's attitude may seem paradoxical. But unlike Ireland, most Scottish emigration was voluntary. The Highland Clearances loom large in the Scottish imagination, though, in fact, the clearances were the exception rather than the rule. Most Scottish emigration, as Marjory Harper has shown in her recent book *Adventurers and Exiles: The Great Scottish Exodus*, was based on a rational assessment of risk and opportunity, and supported by a thriving industry which celebrated the attractions of the new homeland awaiting them across the sea. Voluntary emigration, with its implication that the place where you are born is somehow insufficient for your needs, is a standing rebuke to those who stay. When the distance is so short and the destination is the capital of a country which itself arouses powerful and conflicting feelings, it's no wonder that the Scots who relocate to London have had such a mixed press.

But Scottish emigration shouldn't automatically be seen as a betrayal of Scotland. Many of Scotland's heroes would never have achieved the fame which affords their fellow countrymen such vicarious pleasure if they had stayed in Scotland. If Alex Ferguson had chosen to stay in Aberdeen after winning the European Cup-Winners' Cup in 1983, he would never have become the football manager who achieved far greater fame, and far greater rewards, with Manchester United. Gordon Ramsay would not be one of the most famous chefs in the country if he had stayed in Glasgow, and even the Scottish Nationalist Sean Connery needed to go to London to become 007.

Old feelings die hard in Scotland, though, and the creation of the Scottish Parliament has compounded the country's sense of its own significance. It is a profound irony that the Scots have achieved such conspicuous success in London just at the time when many of their countrymen are more suspicious about Britain than ever before.

But while many Scots at home are disenchanted with the attitudes and attributes of Britishness, it is a fact that any Scot who goes to London for professional reasons benefits from British stereotypes.

In Scotland, Scots wince at the Victorian era with its embarrassing tartanry and sense of Scottish pride; the Victorian Scot on the make still finds a ready audience down south. The views of Lord Birkenhead would strike a chord with many in England who still think of the Scots as hard working, career driven, ambitious and disproportionately successful: a perfectly reasonable description of the ones they see on their televisions and encounter in professional life. And being thought of as ambitious and driven is no bad thing for Scots in London, a city which rewards hard work and ambition.

Yet English people also see Scots on their television sets who argue passionately, and sometimes bitterly, that Scots are oppressed by Britain, and that its indigenous culture is 'colonised' by English people and English values. No wonder they find it hard to square the circle between the views of Scots at home and their views of the Scots in their home.

In the tensions between those two visions of Scots and of Scotland lie many of the misunderstandings about Scottishness which have at times in the last three decades made it seem that when the English talk about the Scots, and the Scots talk about themselves, they are describing two different kinds of people. Because in a sense they are.

But the reasons why Scots have done so well in the south isn't just down to the fact that they have a good image. In the early 1990s, the distinguished Scottish journalist George Rosie made a television programme which galvanised Scottish public opinion. *The Englishing of Scotland*, broadcast on Scottish Television, introduced a new phrase into the Scottish political lexicon and crystallised the impact which the Conservative Government (which had been in power for almost 15 years at that point) was having on Scotland.

Rosie, whose career had been made in newspapers north and south of the border, argued that Scotland was being colonised; so many key positions in Scotland were occupied by people who had been educated outside of the country that their distinctively Scottish ethos was in danger of being diluted or even eradicated.

The programme coincided with a debate about the enrolment policies of Edinburgh University, which had supposedly been infested by 'yahs', loud, wealthy English students who talked too much in tutorials and preferred the sound of their own voices to those of their professors. The conflict between these affluent, confident southerners and the apparently cowed Scots at one of Scotland's leading universities was taken to be a symptom of a more significant malaise.

Coincidentally another confident southerner, Timothy (now Sir Timothy) Clifford, had been appointed Director of the National Galleries of Scotland and had gathered some swingeing notices for his flamboyance. In the public imagination, these isolated examples were conflated with the number of English people who were relocating from the south of England to the Highlands and Islands. Notwithstanding the fact that many such incomers were refugees from the overheated economy of the south-east and showed an admirable sense of enterprise when they arrived in Scotland, often taking over failing hotels and businesses, they were the subject of suspicion and resentment, and were blamed for artificially inflating the cost of housing, making it unaffordable for local families.

Rosie and his colleague Les Wilson argued that the problem encapsulated Scotland's odd position within the Union. Incomers could quite legitimately claim that they were merely relocating from one end of Britain to the other, but the Scottish Establishment had been organised according to certain principles, and they were in danger of being swamped by outsiders.

The programme hit a nerve. Debates about the Englishing of Scotland ran in all the Sunday newspapers. The same papers also began to take an interest in fringe quasi-nationalist movements like Settler Watch, or Scotland Watch, whose avowed intention was to monitor the number of 'incomers' to Scotland, with the aim of encouraging them to leave. Scotland Watch produced a pamphlet called *The New Scottish Clearance*, which justified their stance:

> Scotland as a nation has 1.2 per cent of its population as non-white. The distribution of its non-white population is uniform with its white population except in the areas with high percentages of English-born peoples. In these English-born areas, non-whites are very few in number. This suggests a negative attitude towards racial integration by English-born settlers.
>
> Throughout history Scots have been the victims of English racism. In common with other nations subjected to English Colonialism, the Scots have been the victims of war crimes, genocide, ethnic cleansing and cultural persecution. Many peoples throughout the world have been on the receiving end of English imperialism and racism . . . Scottish Watch adopts a firm anti-racist stand.

It was ingenious: in order to keep Scotland non-racist it should kick out the English. Years later, the right-wing Dutch political leader Pim Fortuyn (who was assassinated in 2002) would argue a similar case in Holland, but nothing like this had been seen in Scotland before.

Rosie was uncomfortable about the views of these extreme groups, as were many Scots, but the feeling of being pressurised by outsiders was real enough. With the benefit of hindsight, and with one eye on the English experience, it actually seems remarkable that Scottish institutions have stayed as uniformly Scottish as they have.

The Faculty of Advocates reports no rise in the number of English applicants to the Scottish Bar during the Thatcher era, the Church of Scotland was not infiltrated by Anglicans, and the education system, certainly at school level, remained by and large a Scottish institution, in which Scots were educated by Scots. Edinburgh University, the subject of much controversy, was certainly less representative of that mix, and some departments, notably English literature, were disproportionately heavy with English students, but that had more to do with the policies followed by some English private schools during the late 1980s and early '90s than a conspiracy intended to take over and transform the ethos of the place. Other universities in the capital, and other departments within Edinburgh University, noticeably those devoted to science and technology, had a much larger percentage of Scottish students.

But the fact that Rosie's arguments carried such force seemed to suggest that Scots implicitly accepted the idea that Scottish institutions existed to employ Scots. If English people were employed in them then there must be something wrong. The fact that the Scottish Neil MacGregor did not cause a scandal in the London papers when he went to direct the National Gallery and the British Museum seems to say more about the different attitudes to national institutions north and south of the border than it does about the native tolerance of the English or the relative size of the two countries.

In England today, of course, the appointment of Scots to senior positions *is* likely to come under scrutiny, precisely because devolution has charged nationality with a political importance in England that it has not had since 1760. Whether devolution will make the number of successful Scots in London a political issue, seized upon by English nationalists as another sign that their country is being overridden by Scots, only time will tell.

A more pressing question is precisely why Scots in Scotland have been so reluctant to acknowledge that the number of their successful fellows in control of London institutions does impact on the perception and the reality of Scotland's role in the United Kingdom.

In Scotland, the current situation has been viewed as something between a joke and a short-lived anomaly. In a year or so, most Scots expect normal service to be resumed, with the Scots under the thumb of loud English outsiders.

To suggest that Scots now have an unprecedented place in the centre of the United Kingdom goes against the grain of Scottish politics. It falls right in the blind spot of most Scots because it runs contrary to the narrative of the Union that has been slowly put together since the Second World War. At the very time when Scottish people enjoy unparalleled power and influence in the south, Scottish domestic opinion is least amenable to recognising that fact as significant, or even at all.

Scottish radicals used to sneer at those who ambitiously climbed the greasy pole of British politics. The aim, they claimed, was not to gain the glittering personal prize of a glorious career at the centre of British power, but to engage with the restructuring of Scottish society at home. Now Scots have achieved both: they hold power at the centre of Britain and at the periphery. Devolution, the ideology which was intended to loosen the control of Westminster on Scotland, has ironically contributed to the grip of Scots on Westminster.

But the real irony for modern Scots is that they have achieved a dominance in British life which their Victorian forbears could only dream of, but none of their public figures want to celebrate it. The Labour Party is anxious not to champion its Scottish success for fear of provoking an English backlash and the SNP is discomfited by it, sniffing that it has nothing to do with the real needs of Scotland.

In the past, when Britishness was a vibrant political and economic reality, and a source of pride to many Scottish people, ambitious Scots who aspired to the highest offices in the land and achieved them were a source of quiet national pride. The fact that Scots held senior positions in the British army and navy, in the dominions and the centres of Empire, was looked on as a sign that Scotland was a remarkable country, which produced remarkable people and contributed to the well-being of the world through the mechanism of the British State.

If our current situation, with Scots dominating the British political class, and holding influential positions in the worlds of media, commerce and entertainment had occurred in the Victorian era, it would have served to emphasise the value of the status quo. But in this more complicated age, the tie lines between Scots at home and Scots in London have become frayed and in some cases have snapped entirely.

Now, with Britishness utterly transformed, the success of Scots down south is greeted with an embarrassing silence or a blank look back home and with growing restiveness in an England which feels edged out of the heart of the United Kingdom.

Soon the argument will be put to the test. When Tony Blair leaves office, if Gordon Brown succeeds in his lifelong ambition to be prime minister, it is almost certain that the ideology, as well as the staff, of the British Government will take on an increasingly Scottish hue.

Writing in *The Spectator* in October 2003, in a piece which cast an ironic look forward to the first Brown premiership, Simon Heffer argued that Brown's values are rooted in his Scottish upbringing, but, 'In these days of devolution, and Scottish distance from England, will the English accept a Scottish prime minister whose "values" are so alien to most of them?'

Brown's beliefs – in the value of work as the wellspring of social independence and self-respect, in the value of community and public service – are certainly profoundly Scottish. Are they so alien to modern English life that they will be rejected by English voters? 'English people know that Gordon Brown is a socialist, and the English people are not socialist,' Simon Heffer told me.

Brown is an unmistakably Scottish politician, and one whose premiership would almost certainly serve to galvanise further anti-Scottish feeling in England. And yet if the Granita pact is a reality and not a myth, Brown may become prime minister without fighting a general election, leaving him a clear four years to put his case to the people of Britain.

Could a Brown premiership see the Scottishing of England, the transformation of Britain in the image of Scotland, with parts of the English population reduced to resentful witnesses to changes in a society which they once felt they owned?

In September 2004, the forces of English reaction within the Labour Party asserted themselves as Tony Blair brought Alan Milburn back into the Cabinet and punished Brown by dispatching some of his most loyal supporters, notably Douglas Alexander MP, who was stripped of his honorary title of Chancellor of the Duchy of Lancaster, and, more importantly, removed from his key role in election planning.

After the election, Blair may use his renewed authority to remove Brown from the Treasury, ending one of the longest and most successful chancellorships of modern times. The scenario proposed by keen Blairites is that Brown will be moved to the Foreign Office, ensuring that Blair will end his time in 10 Downing Street as he began it, with a Scottish Foreign Secretary. But even this is unlikely to clip Brown's wings. As the success of his trip to Africa in January 2005 shows, Brown is able to wield considerable influence on the world stage. And in the nineteenth century, the Foreign Office was considered a natural stepping stone to the premiership.

Milburn, the most visible of a group of north-east of England MPs who have bridled at the Scottish dominance of their party, is at the moment the most likely 'stop Brown' candidate for leader of the party when Blair finally decides to go. Thanks to Robert Peston's book, *Brown's Britain*, which sent shock waves through the government when it was serialised in the *Sunday Telegraph* in January 2005, at least a little of Brown's proposed legislative programme as Prime Minister is in the public domain. Amongst the headline-grabbing proposals, like those intended to end the internal market in public services, another passed with little attention: Brown would seem to favour a written constitution for the increasingly complex state which he would lead. Whether Brown's proposals could tackle head-on the need for a legislative voice for England, articulated by the Campaign for an English Parliament, amongst others, only time will tell. What is certain is that a Labour Party led by Brown would provide a new justification for English anxiety that the largest country in these islands has relinquished its role as natural leader. Could a more concerted, and bitter, English backlash be on the cards?

Perhaps. But even if Brown fails to take control of the British centre, the grip which senior Scottish political figures have on the ranks of New Labour will not lessen; many of the Scottish-born MPs representing English constituencies will hold them even when the tide of Blairism retreats, and the Scots in the media, entertainment, commerce and the rest will not go away. Scots at home may not have woken up to the fact that they have taken over the south, but Londoners have. The Scot on the make is here to stay.

Select Bibliography

Ackroyd, Peter, *London: The Biography* (Chatto and Windus, London, 2000)

Anderson, Benedict, *Imagined Communities: Reflections on the Origin and Spread of Nationalism* (Verso, London, 1991)

Ascherson, Neal, *Games with Shadows* (Radius, London, 1988)

Ascherson, Neal, *Stone Voices: The Search for Scotland* (Granta, London, 2003)

Barrie, J.M., *The Admirable Crichton* (Hodder and Stoughton, London, 1918)

Barrie, J.M., *Auld Licht Idylls* (Hodder and Stoughton, London, 1888)

Barrie, J.M., *Better Dead* (Hodder and Stoughton, London, 1888)

Barrie, J.M., *Peter and Wendy* (Hodder and Stoughton, London, 1911)

Barrow, G.W.S., *Robert Bruce and the Community of the Realm of Scotland* (Edinburgh University Press, 1988)

Brown, Gordon (ed.), *The Red Paper on Scotland* (Edinburgh University Student Publications Board, 1975)

Brown, Gordon, *James Maxton* (Mainstream, Edinburgh, 1986)

Bruce, Duncan A., *The Mark of the Scots: Their Astonishing Contributions to History, Science, Democracy, Literature and the Arts* (Birch Lane Press, New York, 1999)

Buchan, John, *Memory Hold-the-Door* (Hodder and Stoughton, London, 1940)

Buchan, John, *Sick Heart River* (Hodder and Stoughton, London, 1941)

Buchan, John, *The Thirty-Nine Steps* (Oxford University Press, 1993)

Buchan, John, *Witch Wood* (Oxford University Press, 1993)

Cameron, George, *The Scots Kirk in London* (Becket Publications, Oxford, 1979)

Cameron, James, *Point of Departure: Experiment in Biography* (A. Barker, London, 1967)

Campaign for an English Parliament, *Think of England* (campaign newsletter), Issue 19, November 2003

Campbell, Ian, *Kailyard* (Ramsay Head, Edinburgh, 1981)

Colley, Linda, *Britons – Forging the Nation 1707–1837* (Vintage, London, 1996)

Cooper, Charles A., *An Editor's Retrospect: Fifty Years of Newspaper Work* (MacMillan, London, 1896)

Craig, Cairns (gen. ed.), *A History of Scottish Literature*, 4 vols, (Aberdeen University Press, 1987–8)

Craig, David, *Scottish Literature and the Scottish People: 1680–1830* (Chatto and Windus, London, 1961)

Crosland T.W.H., *The Unspeakable Scot* (Grant Richards, London, 1902)

Devine, T.M., *The Scottish Nation 1700–2000* (Penguin, London, 1999)

Devine, T.M., *Scotland's Empire and the Shaping of the Americas 1600–1815* (Allen Lane, London, 2003)

Donaldson, William, *Popular Literature in Victorian Scotland* (Aberdeen University Press, 1986)

Doyle, Sir Arthur Conan, *The Adventures of Sherlock Holmes* (G. Newnes Ltd, London, 1892)

Duffy, Maureen, *England: The Making of the Myth: From Stonehenge to Albert Square* (Fourth Estate, London, 2001)

Ferguson, William, *Scotland's Relations with England – A Survey to 1707* (Saltire, Edinburgh, 1994)

Fleming, Ian, *Casino Royale* (Jonathan Cape, London, 1953)

Fry, Michael, *The Scottish Empire* (Tuckwell Press, East Linton, 2001)

Galt, John, *Autobiography* (Cochrane and M'Crone, London, 1833)

Galt, John, *The Ayrshire Legatees* (Blackwoods, Edinburgh, 1823)

Galt, John, *The Last of the Lairds; or The Life and Opinions of Malachi Mailings, Esq. Of Auldbiggins* (Blackwoods, Edinburgh, 1826)

Galt, John, *The Member: An Autobiography* (Oliver and Boyd, Edinburgh, 1832)

Galt, John, *Sir Andrew Wylie of that Ilk* (Blackwoods, Edinburgh, 1822)

Gibbon, Lewis Grassic (Leslie Mitchell), *A Scots Quair* (Jarrolds, London, 1946)

Gray, Alasdair, *Lanark: A Life in Four Books* (Canongate, Edinburgh, 1981)

Gray, Alasdair, *The Fall of Kelvin Walker: A Fable of the Sixties* (Canongate, Edinburgh, 1985)

Greenslade, Roy, *Press Gang: How Newspapers Make Profits from Propaganda* (Macmillan, London, 2003)

Harvie, Christopher, *Cultural Weapons – Scotland and Survival in a New Europe* (Polygon, Edinburgh, 1992)

Harvie, Christopher, *Fool's Gold: The Story of North Sea Oil* (Hamish Hamilton, London, 1994)

Harvie, Christopher, *No Gods and Precious Few Heroes: Scotland Since 1914*, 3rd edn., (Edinburgh University Press, 1991)

Harvie, Christopher, *Scotland and Nationalism: Scottish Society and Politics 1707–1997*, 3rd edn. (Allen and Unwin, London, 1998)

Hay, Ian (John Hay Beith), *The Oppressed English* (Doubleday, Page and Co., New York, 1917)

Heffer, Simon, *Moral Desperado: A Life of Thomas Carlyle* (Weidenfeld and Nicolson, London, 1995)

Heffer, Simon, *Nor Shall My Sword: The Reinvention of England* (Weidenfeld and Nicolson, London, 1999)

Herman, Arthur, *The Scottish Enlightenment: The Scots' Invention of the Modern World* (Fourth Estate, London, 2001)

Heward, Edmund, *Lord Mansfield* (Barry Rose, Chichester, 1979)

Hitchens, Peter, *The Abolition of Britain* (Quartet, London, 2000)

Junor, John, *Listening for a Midnight Tram* (Chapmans, London, 1990)

Junor, Penny, *Home Truths: A Life Around My Father* (HarperCollins, London, 2002)

Kampfner, John, *Robin Cook: The Biography* (Phoenix, London, 1998)

Kelman, James, *The Busconductor Hines* (Polygon, Edinburgh, 1984)

Knight, Charles (ed.), *London* (6 vols) (C. Knight and Co., London 1841–44)

Lownie, Andrew, *John Buchan: The Presbyterian Cavalier* (Pimlico, London, 2002)

Lynch, Michael, *A History of Scotland* (Century, London, 1991)

Lynch, Michael (ed.), *Image and Identity: The Making and Re-making of Scotland throughout the Ages* (John Donald, Edinburgh, 1998)

McCrone, David, *Understanding Scotland: The Sociology of a Stateless Nation* (Routledge, London, 1992)

MacDiarmid, Hugh, *Selected Prose* (edited by Alan Riach) (Carcanet Press, Manchester, 1992)

McIntyre, Ian, *The Expense of Glory: A Life of John Reith*

(HarperCollins, London, 1993)

Martin, Peter, *A Life of James Boswell* (Weidenfeld and Nicolson, London, 1999)

Milne, Alasdair D.G., *The Memoirs of a British Broadcaster* (Coronet, Sevenoaks, 1988)

Miller, Karl, *Boswell and Hyde* (Syrens, London, 1995)

Miller, Karl, *Doubles* (Oxford University Press, 1985)

Miller, Karl, *Rebecca's Vest* (Hamish Hamilton, London, 1993)

Morris, Frank, *The First 100: A History of the London Scottish Football Club* (Richmond, London, 1977)

Morton, Graeme, *Unionist Nationalism: Governing Urban Scotland, 1830–1860* (Tuckwell Press, East Linton, 1999)

Morton, H.V., *In Search of Scotland* (Methuen, London, 1929)

Mudie, Robert, *Babylon the Great: A Dissection and Demonstration of Men and Things in the British Capital* (Charles Knight and Co., London, 1828)

Mudie, Robert, *Glenfergus, A Novel* (Oliver and Boyd, Edinburgh, 1820)

Mudie, Robert, *The Modern Athens: A Dissection and Demonstration of Men and Things in the Scotch Capital* (Charles Knight and Co., London, 1825)

Nairn, Tom, *After Britain: New Labour and the Return of Scotland* (Granta, London, 2000)

Nairn, Tom, *The Break Up of Britain: Crisis and Neonationalism* (NLB, London, 1981)

Naughtie, James, *The Rivals* (Fourth Estate, London, 2001)

O'Hagan, Andrew, *The Missing* (Picador, London, 1995)

Paterson, Lindsay, *The Autonomy of Modern Scotland* (Edinburgh University Press, 1995)

Pittock, Murray G.H., *Inventing and Resisting Britain: Cultural Identities in Britain and Ireland, 1685–1789* (Macmillan Press, Basingstoke, 1997)

Pittock, Murray G.H., *A New History of Scotland* (Sutton Publishing, Gloucestershire, 2003)

Pittock, Murray G.H., *Scottish Nationality* (Palgrave Macmillan, Basingstoke, 2001)

Rawnsley, Andrew, *Servants of the People: The Inside Story of New Labour* (Hamish Hamilton, London, 2000)

Scott, Paul H. (ed.), *Scotland: A Concise Cultural History* (Mainstream, Edinburgh, 1993)

Scott, Paul H., *Scotland Resurgent* (Saltire Society, Edinburgh, 2003)

Scruton, Roger, *England: An Elegy* (Chatto and Windus, London, 2000)

Sharp, Alan, *A Green Tree in Gedde* (Joseph, London, 1965)

Sillars, Jim, *Scotland: The Case for Optimism* (Polygon, Edinburgh, 1986)

Sisman, Adam, *Boswell's Presumptuous Task: The Making of the Life of Dr Johnson* (Hamish Hamilton, London, 2000)

Smout, T.C., *A Century of the Scottish People, 1830–1950* (Collins, London, 1986)

Smout, T.C., *A History of the Scottish People, 1560–1830* (Collins, London, 1970)

Spark, Muriel, *The Ballad of Peckham Rye* (Macmillan, London, 1960)

Spark, Muriel, *Curriculum Vitae* (Constable, London, 1992)

Spark, Muriel, *The Girls of Slender Means* (Macmillan, London, 1963)

Spark, Muriel, *The Prime of Miss Jean Brodie* (Macmillan, London, 1961)

Taylor, Justine, *A Cup of Kindness: The History of the Royal Scottish Corporation, a London Charity 1603–2003* (Tuckwell Press, East Lothian, 2004)

Thomson, G.M., *Caledonia or the Future of the Scots* (Kegan Paul, Trench, Trubner and Co. Ltd, London, 1927)

Weight, Richard, *Patriots: National Identity in Britain, 1940–2000* (Macmillan, London, 2002)

White, Jerry, *London in the Twentieth Century: A City and Its People* (Penguin Viking, London, 2001)

Williams, Gordon M., *From Scenes Like These* (Secker and Warburg, London, 1968)

Yeoman, Louise, *Reportage Scotland: History in the Making* (Luath Press, Edinburgh, 2000)

Index

Aaronovitch, David 232
Adam brothers 11
Adelphi buildings 11
Adventurers and Exiles: The Great Scottish Exodus 239
Adventures of Roderick Random, The 203
Aitken, Max *see* Beaverbrook, Lord
Alexander, Douglas 27, 41, 43, 106, 109, 246
Alexander, Wendy 43
Allerton, Mark 64
Ancram, Michael 40, 48
Anderson, Benedict 127
Anderson, Moira 77
Arbuthnot, James 48
Archer, William 59
armed forces 16, 128, 136, 139, 157, 216, 244–5
Armour, George Denholm 215
Armstrong, Neil 15
Army and Navy Club 157
Arnott, Robert 130
Arrol, Sir William 12
Ascherson, Neal 66–9
Asquith, Herbert 26
Autonomy of Modern Scotland, The 21
Ayrshire Legatees, The 169

Babylon the Great 164–5
Baird, Euan 18
Baker, Norman 49
Balfour, Arthur James 25–6
Balfour, Lord 124–5, 178
Ballard, Jackie 49
Barnett Formula 56, 222, 224, 228
Barrie, J.M. 9, 107, 171–4, 176, 182, 184, 280

Barrow, Geoffrey 153
BBC 14, 44, 63, 69, 70–80, 81, 185, 194, 224, 237
Beadle, Don 222, 228
Bean, Sawney 198, 204
Beatty, Admiral 216
Beaverbrook, Lord 60–1, 64
Begg, Professor David 46
Beith, Major John Hay 215–17
Benn, William Wedgewood 53
Better Dead 172
Beveridge, Craig 20
Birkenhead, Lord 235, 240
Bishop of London's Fund 108
Blackfriars Bridge 11–12
Blackie, Professor 115, 217
Blair, Tony 14, 26–8, 33, 38–42, 44–5, 47, 49, 67, 82, 183, 225, 245–6
    see also Brown, Gordon; Labour
Blind Harry 149–50, 152
Blyth of Rowington, Lord 18
Bolland, Mike 78
Borderline 140–2
Boswell, James 18, 162–4, 201
Bottomley, Virginia 49, 52
Bowman, Edith 18
Boyd, Alexander Stuart 215
Boyd, William 182
Boyle, Manus 'Jock' 88–9
Braveheart 55, 148–9, 152, 153, 159
British Museum 243
British National Party (BNP) 223
Briton, The 203–4
Britons 199
Broadcasting in Scotland 76

Brown, Sir George Washington 12
Brown, Gordon 8, 26, 29–45, 49, 57, 106, 155, 215, 245–7
see also Blair, Tony; Labour
Brown, John 128
Brown's Britain 246
Bruce, Duncan 14–15
Bruce, Malcolm 51
Buchan, John 106, 177–82
Burchill, Robert 75
Burnett, Alastair 78
Burnett-Stuart, Maj. Gen. Sir J. 16
Bute, Lord 124, 202–4, 206
Byng, Jamie 189

Cairns, Lord 82
Caledonian Asylum 136, 138, 208
Caledonian Club 17, 113, 120, 122, 135, 157
Caledonian Games 131
Caledonian Society 16, 117
Calvinism 105, 186, 189
Cameron, Maj. Gen. Sir A.R. 16
Cameron, James 63–5, 80
Cameron, Rhona 18
Cameron, William Ernest 63
Campaign for an English Parliament *see* CEP
Campbell, Earl 82
Campbell, Alastair 42, 81
Campbell, Bobby 66
Campbell, Lt. Gen. Sir David 16
Campbell, John McLeod 100, 102
Campbell, Mary 100
Campbell, Menzies 34, 57
Campbell, Nicky 18, 79

Campbell-Bannerman, Sir Henry 25–6
Campbell Tait, Archibald 107–8
Canada Company 168
Canada, Governor General of 177, 181–2
Cant, Bob 145
Canterbury, Archbishop of 107–9
Carlyle, Alexander 202
Carlyle, Robert 18
Carlyle, Thomas 12, 59, 99, 170–1, 235, 239
cartoon images 198, 200–1, 204, 211, 215
Caskie, Donald 98
Catholic Apostolic Church 102–3
Century of the Scottish People 1830–1950 178
CEP (Campaign for an English Parliament) 220–33
Chalmers, Thomas 99–101
Chambers, Sir William 11
Channel 4 78, 194
Church of England 102, 104–9
Church of Scotland 50, 70, 71, 95–9, 102–4, 106, 108–9, 121, 133, 135, 136, 243
churches in London, Scottish 95–109
Churchill, Winston 53
Clark, David 49
Clifford, Sir Timothy 241
Cochrane, James 170
Coffey, Ann 49
Colley, Linda 52, 199
Colquhoun, Patrick 89–92
Colquhoun, Robert 143
Coltrane, Robbie 18, 78

Companion to Scottish Culture 20
Connery, Sean 183, 199, 240
Conroy, Harry 66
Conservative Party 30, 44, 47,
    49, 55–7, 231, 233
    see also Thatcherism
Constable, Archibald 170
Constable, Christine 224
Cook, Robin 27–9, 32–5, 37–8,
    189
Cooper, Lord 84–5
Cooper, Charles 60
Cooper, Yvette 49, 52
Cowie, Gordon 93
Craig, David 170
Cran, James 49
Cripps, Sir Stafford 73
Crockett, S.R. 174, 176
Crosbie, Annette 215
Crosland, T.W.H. 9, 25–6, 57,
    197, 209–11, 217
Cross Street Chapel 99
Crowley, Aleister 209–10
Crown Court Church of
    Scotland 97, 106
Cruickshank, Don 236–8
Cullen, Scilla 227
cultural activities 113–32, 133
Cunningham, Alan 170
Cunningham, Jim 49
Currie, Colin 38

Dad's Army 215
Daily Express 61
Daily Mail 21, 62, 195
Daily Record 89, 237
Daily Telegraph 28, 69, 173
Dalrymple, William 184
Dalyell, Tam 27, 30–1, 56, 230
    see also West Lothian
    Question

Darling, Alistair 27, 38, 46, 51,
    189
Davidson, Thomas 107
Davie, George 170–1
de Quincey, Thomas 115
Defoe, Daniel 200, 203
Devine, Tom 14
devolution, Scottish 15, 21,
    28–31, 37, 40, 42, 44, 45,
    46–8, 55–6, 66, 68–9, 220,
    225, 227–31, 233, 243–6
    English reaction to 13, 189,
    214, 230
    and Westminster MPs 27, 30,
    56
Dewar, Donald 29, 34, 38, 42,
    228
Dobbin, Jim 49
Docherty, Willie 134–5
Donoghue, Denis 75–6
Douglas, Lord Alfred 209–10
Douglas Brown, George 175–6
Douglas-Home, Alec 26
Doyle, Sir Arthur Conan 125,
    176–7
Dunbar, William 161–2
Duncan, Peter 30, 229
Duncan, Maj. Gen. Sir Robert
    16
Duncan Smith, Iain 26, 33, 49,
    229
Dundas, Henry 209
Dunnett, Sir Alastair 196–7
Dunsmore, Reverend Barry
    96–8

East India Company 209
Eclipse of Scottish Culture, The 20
Economist, The 44, 59, 78

Edinburgh 14, 26, 27, 29, 32–4, 36, 38, 40, 41, 45, 46, 48, 49, 50, 51–4, 57, 58, 59, 66, 68, 80, 87, 95, 99, 103, 104, 106–8, 119, 129, 134, 138, 140, 144, 153, 156, 157, 159, 162, 163, 166, 176, 177, 183, 186, 189, 190, 200, 202, 207, 215
    University 14, 33, 34, 36, 41, 48, 85, 115, 176, 182, 183, 186, 188, 189, 241, 243
Edinburgh Evening Dispatch 173
Edinburgh Evening News 33
Edward, Alfred S. 127
Edwards, Owen Dudley 35, 37
Elder, Murray 39
Elizabeth II as Queen of Scotland 84
Elizabeth, Queen, the Queen Mother 129
Emigrant's Pocket Companion, The 167
English Democrats 224
English nationalism 43, 52, 55, 57, 195, 223, 225, 230, 232
Englishing of Scotland, The 20, 241
Episcopal Church 107
Esler, Gavin 18, 80
Evening Standard 213
Ewing, Winifred 88, 212
Expositor, The 173

Faintheart 195
Fairbairn, Sir Nicky 88
Falconer, Lord 27, 82
Fall of Kelvin Walker, The 184–5
Fallon, Alexander 138
Fallon, Michael 49
Fanon, Franz 20

Farage, Nigel 222, 224
federalism 229
Ferguson, Alex 240
Ferguson, Euan 69
financial expectations 133–46
Financial Times 44, 68
Findlay, Lord 216
Findlay, Donald 88
Fitzpatrick, Jim 49
Fleming, Archibald 95–7
Fleming, Ian 182–4
Fleming, Peter 182
Forbes, John 205
Forsyth, Michael 49, 153, 229
Forth, Eric 49
Foulkes, George 51
foundation hospitals 30, 224, 228–9, 232–3
Fowlis of Colinton, James 83
Fox, Liam 49

Gaelic Society of London 117–18
Galbraith, Sam 46
Galloway, Janice 185, 188
Galt, John 136, 168–70
Gardiner, Barry 49
gay community 143–5
Gibbon, Lewis Grassic 176
Gibson, D. Begbie 130
Gibson, Ian 50
Gibson, J.R. 126
Gill, A.A. 193–4, 197
Gilroy, Linda 50
Glasgow 32, 40, 45, 46, 49, 50, 51, 54, 58, 62, 69, 70, 76, 77, 79, 89, 93, 99, 106, 119, 126, 140, 143, 144, 149, 150, 160, 170, 182, 184, 185, 186, 215, 229, 240

University 14, 33–4, 39, 50, 121, 178
Glasgow Evening Citizen 64
Glasgow Herald see *Herald, The*
Glenfergus 165
Goodman, Norman 51
Gordon, George 171
Gordon, Robert 235–7
Gorrie, Donald 52
Gove, Michael 18, 52, 69
Graham, Robert Cunninghame 115
Graham, W.S. 143
Gramsci, Antonio 36, 48
Grant, George 130
Gray, Alasdair 160, 184–5, 188
Gray, James 50
Gray, Muriel 78
Green, John 152, 156
Green Tree in Gedde, A 188
Griffiths, Nigel 27, 38
Grimond, Jo 78
Guardian, The 68–9, 151, 194, 230
Guinness, Alec 215

Haig, Sir Douglas 216
Hamilton, Ian 84–5
Hamilton, Sir James 83
Hannah, John 238
Hardie, Keir 48, 54, 67, 219
Hardy, Bert 64
Hardy, Thomas 209
Harper, Marjory 239
Harvie, Christopher 217
Hay, Ian 77, 215
Hazell, Professor Robert 231
Heathcoat-Amory, Edward 28
Heffer, Simon 29, 43, 195, 197, 214, 245
Henderson, Doug 50

Henderson, Hamish 36
Henderson, Bishop Jock 107
Henley, W.E. 173
Herald, The 28, 76, 196, 229
Herman, Arthur 15
Herron, Neil 224–5
Highland Clearances 239
Highland Games 15, 128, 131
Hirst, Michael 46
Hogg, James 170
homelessness 138–46
Hong Kong police 94
Hood, Stuart 77
Hood, Thomas 170
House with Green Shutters, The 175–6
Hughes, Simon 222, 228
Hunter, Anji 39
Hurd, Douglas 212
Hutton Inquiry 81

Idea Juris Scotici 83
Independent on Sunday 66
Independent, The 44, 57
Indian police 94
Innes, James 83
Ireland 29, 35, 58, 85, 120, 127, 131, 219, 231, 239
    Irishophobia 194, 196–8, 213
Ironside, Maj. Gen. Sir Edmund 16
Irvine, Derry 27, 39, 40, 88
Irving, Edward 99–103
Isaacs, Jeremy 78

Jackson, Gordon 208
James VI and I 12, 19, 49, 83, 98, 133, 198
Jaspan, Andrew 69
Jenkin, Bernard 50

Jenkin, Patrick 50
Jennings, Charles 195
Johnson, Dr 60, 164, 184, 193
Johnson, Boris 193, 211
Johnson Smith, Geoffrey 51
Jones, Right Reverend James
    109
Jowell, Tessa 50
Junor, Sir John 61–3, 65–6, 175,
    213
Junor, Penny 61

Kailyard writing 63, 105, 174–5,
    210
Kelly, Lorraine 18
Kelman, James 185, 188
Kennedy, A.L. 185, 188
Kennedy, Charles 26, 34, 57
Kennedy, Helena 78, 88
Kennedy, Sir James 83
Kennedy, Ludovic 78
Kerr, Morag 154, 156
Kerr, Philip 183
King, Andy 50
King, Tom 50, 52
King's Cross fire 138
Kingsley, Charles 198
Kingston Synagogue 106
Kinnock, Neil 45, 46, 196
Knowles, Mike 220–3

Labour Party 34, 35, 40, 42, 54,
    67, 88, 106, 244, 246
    in Scotland 37–9, 41, 45, 214
    see also Blair, Tony; Brown,
    Gordon; devolution; New
    Labour
Laing, Eleanor 50
Lait, Jacqui 50
Lamont, Norman 54–5

Lanark 160, 185, 188–9
Lancaster, Duchy of 109, 246
Lang, Cosmo Gordon 107–8
Lang, Ian 30
Lauder, Sir Harry 18
Lawrence, Stephen 81
Lee, Joseph 215
legal system 18, 27, 81–94, 193,
    243
Lennox, Duke of 83
Liberal Democrats 26, 34, 49,
    51, 78, 213, 222
Liddell, Alvar 74–5
Liddell, Eric 106
Liddell, Helen 37
Lindsay, Isobel 214
Little, Allan 63, 80
Liverpool, Archbishop of 109
Liverpool Caledonian Society
    123
Livingstone, Ken 53, 158, 194,
    213, 214, 221
Lloyd, John 44, 68
Lockhart, John Gibson 59
Logan, James 118
London 207
London Banffshire Society 17
London Dumfries-shire
    Association 117
London Evening News 215
London Highland Athletic Club
    117
London Highland Society 113
London Labour and the London Poor
    of 1851–66 139
London Scotsman 114–17, 120,
    125, 127
London Scottish rugby 130
London street names, Scottish
    12

Lothbury Scotch Church 98
Love, Andrew 50
Lownie, Andrew 177
Lynch, Michael 119

McAdam, John Loudon 11
MacBride, Robert 143
McCabe, Stephen 50
McCall Smith, Alexander 188–9
McCartney, Ian 50
McConnell, Jack 42–3, 237–8
MacCormick, John 84–5, 158
MacCormick, Neil 85
MacDiarmid, Hugh 9, 125,
    154–5
MacDonald, Gus 27, 40
MacDonald, Ian 87
MacDonald, Ramsay 26
Macdonald, Sheena 79
MacGlashan, Neil 130
McGrath, John 35
McGregor, Ewan 18, 199
MacGregor, Neil 243
McIntosh, Anne 50
McIntyre, Ian 71–2
McIntyre, Dr Robert 88, 239
McIsaac, Shona 50
Mackay of Clashfern, Lord 82
MacKay, Fulton 215
McKay, John 34
McKay, Peter 62
McKee, Andrew 69
MacKellar, Alexander 93
McKellar, Kenneth 77
Mackenzie, Compton 154
McKillop, Sir Tom 18
Maclagan, W.E. 130
MacLagan, William Dalrymple
    107
McLaren, Ian 123, 174

McLean, Alan 81
Maclean, David 50, 57
MacLean, Duncan 188
McLeish, Henry 42–3, 214
McLeod, Catherine 28
MacLeod, Donnie B. 78
McMaster, Gordon 43
Macmillan, Daniel 170
Macmillan, Harold 26
MacMillan, James 105, 189
McMillan, Joyce 226
MacMurray, John 39
McNee, Sir David 94
McNeill, Angus 211
    see also Crosland, T.W.H.
Macpherson of Cluny, Sir
    William 82
MacShane, Denis 51
MacTaggart, Fiona 51
M'Turk, James 207–8
McWilliam, John 51
Macklin, Charles 200
Mair, Eddie 18, 79
Man of the World, The 200
Mansfield, Lord 86–7
Mark of the Scots, The 14
Marr, Andrew 44, 70, 233
Marshall, Dr William 128
Martin, Paul 156
Mason, Rabbi David 106
Masonic lodges 17, 122
Massie, Allan 21
Mathers, MacGregor 100
Mayhew, Henry 139, 166
Mayor of Casterbridge, The 209
media 58–80
Metric Martyrs 224–5
Metropolitan Police 82, 89,
    91–3, 194
Milburn, Alan 246

Miller, Karl 189
Milne, Alasdair 77–8
Milne, Gen. Sir George 16
Mitchell, Sir Andrew 203
Mitchell, Professor James 230
Mitchell, Leslie 176
Modern Athens, The 166
Morning Chronicle 166
Morton, H.V. 58–9
Mudie, George 51
Mudie, Robert 60, 164–7
Muir, Edwin 105
Muir, Kate 69
Munn, David 156
Munro, James 91
Murray, Lord 201
Murray, John 170
Murray, William, Lord
    Mansfield
    see Lord Mansfield
Mylne, Robert 11

Nairn, Tom 35, 105
National Front 223
National Gallery 243
Naughtie, Jim 18, 44, 80, 97, 237
Naysmith, Doug 51
Neil, Alex 66
Neil, Andrew 18, 21, 63, 66
Nerberg, Fiona 156
New Labour 28–30, 33, 36,
    38–9, 41–2, 44, 46–7, 67, 109,
    195, 214, 224, 247
    see also Blair, Tony; Brown,
    Gordon; devolution; Labour
    Party
New London Bridge 12
New Scottish Clearance, The 242
New Statesman 68, 194
News Chronicle 65

News of the World 237
Newsnight 14, 69–70, 77, 79
Nicoll, William Robertson
    173–5
Nilsen, Dennis 144–5
Noble, Sir William 70
North Briton, The 204–5
North London Scottish Society
    128

O'Brian, Patrick 209–10
O'Hagan, Andrew 69, 105, 189
Observer, The 66, 69, 231
One Foot in the Grave 215
Oppressed English, The 77, 216
Orr, Deborah 69
Osborne, Francis 198
Oscar of Sweden, Prince 119
Osmond, Andrew 212

Paris, Scots Kirk in 98
Paterson, Lindsay 21
Paton, Sir Joseph Noel 153
Paxman, Jeremy 14, 43
Pearson, John 183
Pebble Mill 78
Peston, Robert 246
Picture Post 64
PM 79
police *see* Metropolitan Police
political world 25–57, 79, 214
poll tax 56, 223, 233
Porridge 215
Portland Place 11
Power, William 238–9
Prentice, Bridget 51, 53–4
Prentice, Gordon 51
publishers 14, 18, 21, 63, 66,
    167, 170, 188–9
Punch 214, 215

Purdie, Bob 154, 158
Pym, Hugh 97

Quarterly Review 59
Queen's Chapel of the Savoy
    106, 109

Raban, Jonathan 160
Ramsay, Gordon 240
Rankin, Ian 189
Ratcliffe, Don 93
Red Paper on Scotland, The 35
Regent's Square National
    Scottish Church 99–101
Reid, Dr James 128
Reid, John 27, 228
Reid, Sir Robert 122
Reith, John 70–8, 80
religious institutions 95–109
relocation, English 242
Rennie, John 12
Riach, Alexander 173
Rifkind, Malcolm 33, 52, 57
Rimington, Dame Stella 183
Rivals, The 44
Robertson, Fyffe 78
Robertson, George 29
Robertson, Robin 21, 188
Robertson, Sir William 216
Rosebery, Earl of 25, 129
Rosie, George 20, 241–3
Ross, Willie 34, 36
Rowling, J.K. 190
Roxburgh, Angus 80
Royal Scottish Corporation 117,
    120–1, 133, 135
rugby 129–31, 154, 232
Rugby School 107

St Andrew's National Church,
    Stepney 99
St Andrew's Society 113
St Columba's, Pont Street 70,
    95–7, 104
St James's Gazette 171–3
St James's Scotch Church 96
St Paul's Bridge 12
Salmond, Alex 55, 152, 155–6,
    237
    see also SNP
Savidge, Malcolm 51
Schweitzer, Albert 65
Scotch on the Rocks 212–13
Scotland and Nationalism 217
Scotland on Sunday 69, 226, 238
Scotland Watch 242
Scotophobia 193–218, 241
Scotsman, The 42, 44, 66, 76, 108
    editors 60, 66, 196
Scott, Father Bill 106–7, 109
Scott, Paul H. 20
Scott, Walter 85, 171, 177–8,
Scottish Associations of London
    117
Scottish Clerks' Association 123
Scottish Constitutional
    Convention 226, 228
Scottish Daily Express 60, 237
Scottish Enlightenment, The 15
Scottish Home Rule bill 216–17
Scottish Labour Party (SLP) 41,
    66–7, 115
Scottish Nation, The 14
Scottish National Party *see* SNP
Scottish Parliament *see*
    devolution
Scottish Six, The 77
Scottish Television *see* STV
Scottish Tourist Board 113

Selkirk, Alexander 200
Serle, Fraser 144
servants 128, 208
Settler Watch 242
Sharp, Alan 188
Shepherd, Richard 51
Showalter, Elaine 177
Sillars, Jim 66–7, 152
Sinclair, Sir John 118–19
Sir Andrew Wylie 169
Skeen, Maj. Gen. Sir Andrew 16
Skene, Sir John 83
Smith, Adam 239
Smith, Chris 27, 97
Smith, John 33–4, 39–40, 43–5
Smith, W.C. 77
Smollett, Tobias 202–4
Smout, T.C. 178
SNP (Scottish National Party) 17, 21, 41, 76–7, 84–5, 88, 106, 152–3, 155–8, 197, 212–13, 223, 237, 240, 244
   criticism of 55, 212–14, 229
   Labour attitude to 36–7, 47–8, 53
   see also devolution; Salmond, Alex
Somerset House 11
Somerville, Jimmy 143
South Sea Bubble 87
Southwark Bridge 12
Souttar, Robinson 122
Spark, Muriel 186–7
Spectator, The 59, 211, 221, 245
spiritualism 100–2, 125
Spiteri, Sharleen 18
sport 130–2, 197, 215, 232
Stair, James Viscount 86
Star Trek 215
Steel, Sir David 106, 228

Stewart, Ian 51
Stewart, Sir Robert 83
Stone Voices 67, 69
street performers 134, 139
Stuart, Sir John *see* Bute, Lord
STV (Scottish Television) 40, 60, 77, 79, 236, 241
Sunday Express 61–2
Sunday Herald 195
Sunday Telegraph 246
Sunday Times 60, 63, 66, 167, 183, 193, 237
Sunset Song 176
Swaggerers 198

Tartan Army 197, 232
Taylor, Ann 51
Taylor, Teddy 51, 231
Thatcherism 20, 41, 75, 223, 228, 232–3
   see also Conservative Party
Thomson, E.P. 223
Thomson, James 103, 138, 162, 203
Thomson, James B.V. 162
Thomson, Roy 60
Times, The 18, 66, 69, 119, 125, 131, 229
Timothy, Andrew 75
Today 44, 80, 237
tongues, speaking in 100–2
Toolis, Kevin 68
Tower Bridge 12
Tranter, Nigel 103
Traquair, Phoebe Anna 103
Trefgarne, George 28
tuition fees 30, 56, 223
Tullibardine, Marquis of 120
Tunes of Glory 215
Turnbull, Ronald 20

Turner, George 51
Tweedsmuir, Lord *see* Buchan, John
Two of a Kind 63

UK Independence Party 222, 233
Union, Act of 13, 52, 84, 202
Unspeakable Scot, The 9, 25, 197, 209, 217
Upstairs Downstairs 208

Victoria, Queen 95, 124, 128–9, 131, 153

Wallace, William 148–54, 158–9
Ward, Eileen 140–1
Wark, Kirsty 18, 69–70, 79
Waterloo Bridge 12
Watson, Reverend John 123, 174
Weldon, Sir Anthony 199
Welshophobia 193–6

Wemyss of Gala, Jock 131
West Lothian Question 27, 30, 56, 230
Westminster
    English holding Scottish seats in 51–2
    Scots holding English seats in 48–51
Wheatcroft, Geoffrey 230
Whigman, Gen. Sir Robert 16
Wilkes, John 86, 87, 204–6, 232
Wilkie, David 170
Williams, Gordon 187
Wilson, Brian 27
Wilson, Charles 66
Wilson, J.M. 131
Wilson, Les 242
Wood, Wendy 212
Worthington, Tony 51–2
writers 160–90

Young, Kirsty 79